Praise for
HANDBOOK FOR AN UNPREDICTABLE LIFE

"I read Rosie Perez's magnificent, very real, and heart-wrenching book with equal parts joy and horror—horror that the world can and routinely does inflict its terrors on its children, and joy that Rosie made it out to become not only the superior, iconographic artist she is, but the magnificent woman this book reveals her to be. Her voice is the captivating instrument here: forthright, funny, and utterly her own."

—HILTON ALS, *THE NEW YORKER*

"Rosie Perez's *Handbook for an Unpredictable Life* is a shockingly brave, honest book filled with so much grace, forgiveness, and humor that you feel invigorated reading it. A deeply moving story, told with unapologetic courage and heart."

—GEORGE C. WOLFE, AMERICAN PLAYWRIGHT, DIRECTOR OF THEATER AND FILM, AND PRODUCER

"With refreshing candor and sass, Perez transforms the painful details of her life into an inspiring reminder that even the most unforgiving of personal circumstances can be overcome. A spunky and heartfelt memoir."

—*KIRKUS REVIEWS*

"Utterly revealing."

—*NEW YORK DAILY NEWS*

"Breezy and sassy."

—*NEW YORK POST*

"Rosie Perez has written a brave, hysterical, wise, and compulsively readable chronicle of growing up and surviving the dual challenges of a crazy family and crazy life in Hollywood. Like *Running with Scissors* before it, *Handbook for an Unpredictable Life* is ultimately a story of survival and will inspire us all."

—LIZ GARBUS, DIRECTOR OF *LOVE, MARILYN*

"An easy and enjoyable read, thanks to Perez's colorful, conversational writing style and a cracking pace."

—BROOKLYN PAPER

"Moving."

—BUFFALO NEWS

HANDBOOK FOR AN
UNPREDICTABLE LIFE

*How I Survived Sister Renata
and My Crazy Mother, and Still Came Out Smiling
(with Great Hair)*

ROSIE PEREZ

THREE RIVERS PRESS
NEW YORK

Originally published in hardcover in slightly different form in the United States
by Crown Archetype, an imprint of the Crown Publishing Group, a division of
Random House LLC, New York, in 2014.

Library of Congress Cataloging-in-Publication Data
Perez, Rosie.
    Handbook for an unpredictable life : how I survived Sister Renata and my
crazy mother, and still came out smiling (with great hair) / Rosie Perez. —First
edition.
    1. Perez, Rosie, 2. Actors—United States—Biography. 3. Choreographers—United
States—Biography. I. Title.

PN2287.P387A3 2013
791.4302'8092—dc23

                                    2013033958

ISBN 978-0-307-95240-0
eBook ISBN 978-0-307-95241-7

PRINTED IN THE UNITED STATES OF AMERICA

Cover design by Tal Goretsky
Cover photograph by Eric Johnson

10 9 8 7 6 5 4 3 2 1

First Paperback Edition

Dedicated to

Tia
Dad
All the kids from the Home

And . . . My Mother

AUTHOR'S NOTE

This book is based on my recollection of what went down and what was told to me by friends and family. Some names, characters, and situations have been changed to protect the innocent and the guilty. I hope you enjoy . . .

PREFACE

"The artist is born in the suffering child."

I SAW Israel Horovitz, the playwright, say this in the documentary *I Knew It Was You: Rediscovering John Cazale*, a celebration of the short career of the actor who played Fredo in *The Godfather*. I was moved by this comment, but angered too, because more often than not that cliché is all too true, and one thing I will not be defined by is a cliché.

I didn't really want to write about this story of mine. Yet I felt like I was supposed to write it, like it was a responsibility that I couldn't avoid. It's so hard to go there, you know? And I was always concerned that if and when I did tell my story, I would have to constantly defend my recollection of my truth. Unfortunately, I have family relations and folks who "knew me when" who, solely out of motives of fame, greed, or both, have jumped out of the woodwork to contest my truth and would do it again, which would only waste time and miss the point. And more important, I was concerned that people would pity me, and I don't want anyone's pity. That is not the point either. The point is to get it out, to validate my feelings, to communicate how good it feels to no longer live in fear of what others may think, and to share my journey and move on. I have more than survived. And in writing my experiences I know that however sad it was, it is more or less the same story shared by a lot of people who are messed up as a result of a difficult childhood.

The abuse and neglect from my mother and the time I was forced to spend in Saint Joseph's Catholic Home for Children, aka "the Home," have affected a big part of my life. And I've hated that fact. I'm a forward-moving and positive-thinking person, and it was hard to have that albatross hanging around my neck. I've hated my past so much that I've spent countless hours downplaying or even hiding bits of the truth of my childhood in an attempt to make it seem less severe, less hurtful, less shameful, than it felt.

I hated the fact that my mother was crazy. I wanted her to be normal. Even when she acted normal—something that many mentally ill people can do, despite what you see in the movies—I was always walking on eggshells, waiting for the insanity to hit. And when it hit, it hit hard and fast—leaving deep emotional and physical scars.

People who are "normal" as a result of good parenting—even just decent parenting—are very lucky. Yeah, I know, everyone's hell is relative, and blah, blah, blah, but those people are very fortunate. Am I bitter? No, not at all. Every child should have a loving and stable upbringing. There would be less violence and hate, for sure. But most of us didn't, and regardless of what the experts say, trying to get past your past sucks. Most of us would rather just ignore it or numb it with any or all types of drugs, legal or illegal. Those of us who are a bit stronger—and I say that without judgment—try to avoid those options and deal with our past legitimately: through psychoanalysis, psychiatry, medications, spirituality, whatever. Truth be told, even when you work every day to do so, it's hard to not lose it, or give up, or worse, fall into a depression.

That's the worst—depression. I'm a relatively happy person who also happened to be clinically depressed for years (sorry, that just cracks me up). I know that it's probably hard for most people, especially those who know and love me, to fathom that, because I'm a person who's usually in a good mood, cracking jokes or telling funny stories. And the good moods are absolutely, 100 percent authentic. It's just that there was this underlying feeling of blah, or sadness, or even fright, which at times I was aware of and at other times I was not. I refused to let this hold me down. I wanted to move on. I wanted to fully enjoy the wonderful life I've worked so hard to obtain.

I finally resorted to seeking professional help, the one thing I had resisted for years. When my shrink diagnosed me with dysthymia—a sneaky, chronic type of depression—I was actually relieved. God bless America two times for that, as my Tia Ana would say. It's most common with people who suffer from post-traumatic stress disorder (PTSD). Yeah, I had that one too. Still do. But now at least I had a starting place and could take some kind of ownership of the healing process.

After a couple of years of therapy, and I don't know exactly when or how it happened, I noticed that my depression wasn't there and the PTSD subsided considerably. I felt joyful, secure, and empowered. My inner strength and sense of self had never been stronger. I guess I allowed time to play its role, and I did my part by working hard on myself to grow past the pain. Gosh, I sound so full of shit there. Let me be more honest: I grew past most of the pain and continue to do the work. Every day gets better. xo

—Rosie Perez

June 2013

HANDBOOK FOR AN UNPREDICTABLE LIFE

CHAPTER 1

THEY MET in Williamsburg, Brooklyn.

Although Ismael was married to his wife, Angel (pronounced Halo), at the time, he was on his way to his sister's, my Tia Ana's house, to meet her girlfriend for a date. Yes, folks, a date. And my aunt cosigned. He was the quintessential Latin male when it came to women and romance, minus the machismo. It wasn't clear if the date knew that Ismael was married or not. He never really kept it a secret, but then again, he wasn't the first to volunteer that information either—you know what I'm saying? It probably didn't matter—the man had mad game. Ismael wasn't gorgeous, but he was what people would call brutally sexy, meaning not conventionally good-looking, but extremely attractive and charismatic. He could be very suave too, in an intentionally goofy way. He had this undeniable, unassuming, yet aggressive charm that would knock the most beautiful women off their feet.

Ismael had been a merchant marine during World War II, and in the Korean War after that, though he never wanted to talk about it. He hated war, but loved America, and he loved to wear his army jacket whenever he was not on a date. He always dressed sharp for his dates—he had mad style. After the wars were over, he spent half of his time out at sea, the other half in Puerto Rico with his wife, and whatever free time he had left in New York visiting Tia, but mainly living the life of a playboy.

Tia's full name was Ana Dominga Otero Serrano-Roque, God rest her soul. Her friends called her Minguita, which came from her middle name, Dominga. Her style was simple and pragmatic, but not in an old maid type of way. And she *always* wore dresses. I saw her in a pair of pants for the first time when I was in my twenties, and I was shocked. She'd gotten fat after having four kids—three girls and one boy—all of whom she had to give to the oldest of her two brothers, Monserrate, to raise because she had a nervous breakdown and was sent to "the Loony Bin" (that's where they sent women back then when they got hysterical) when she caught her husband in bed with her girlfriend—scandalous! When she got out of the "hospital," her brother, Tio Monserrate, only gave her the girls back. He kept the boy—we'll get into that later. This left a pain in her heart that never healed.

Tia lived on the corner of Wallabout and Lee Avenue in a shotgun-railroad apartment in a broken-down tenement building. It was at the edge of the Hasidic Jewish neighborhood of South Williamsburg, an area that looked as if time had stopped in the 1940s. The Hasidic Jews walked around dressed in the style of that period, all year round. To this day, the neighborhood is still 90 percent Hasidic and retains the same vibe. Tia lived there with her three daughters, Titi (whose real name was Carmen), Millie, and Cookie (whose real name was Lourdes, pronounced Lou-day); little Lorraine would come later. Across the hall were her friends, also all Puerto Rican. When I was little, I used to think the whole building was Puerto Rican, but in fact it was just those two apartments.

The place was sparsely decorated, but it featured a few of the stereotypical tacky Puerto Rican items: a plastic-covered sofa; fake eighteenth-century porcelain figurines that sat on a wooden television/bookshelf, and lastly, the staple of all Nuyorican interiors, an oil rug painting of The Last Supper hanging over the plastic-encased sofa. The French doors that led into her bedroom, just off the living room, were my favorite feature of Tia's house. The rest of the place was furnished with eclectic stuff that people left out on the curbside for the garbage trucks in expensive neighborhoods.

. . .

The air was brisk that December afternoon. As usual, Ismael was dressed sharp for his date and had the look of a well-manicured man: suit and tie, of course, with a gray overcoat and scarf, and a fly hat to finish it off. He loved hats. He liked his women to dress up as well. If a chick wasn't that pretty—though he usually only hooked up with the fine-looking ones—but she knew how to dress and carry herself, he was there, on the hunt.

Tia's girlfriend, the one she was setting her brother up with, was fairly attractive and well groomed, despite her lack of money. (It can happen, folks—there are poor people who can pull it together. We don't all look busted like they show us in the movies.) She waited anxiously for her date to arrive, pacing back and forth for an hour, constantly looking out the window to see if he was coming down the block.

Before he arrived, this girl's sister, Lydia, stopped by, along with a couple of other young ladies, to sneak a peek at this man her older sister had bragged about for a week. Lydia, in her early twenties at the time, had been married since the age of fourteen and had five children. She was also stunningly beautiful, eclipsing all of her sisters by a mile. She was a sexy siren, cunning, self-centered, condescending, mean at times, and extremely intelligent. She was a cross between the movie stars Ava Gardner and Miriam Colon, with a petite, apple-shaped face and a wry smirk.

Lydia had been a singer in Puerto Rico until her husband, ten years her senior, made her quit, crushed all her dreams, and moved her to New York City in the fifties. Although she was madly in love with her husband, she feared him. He used to beat the shit out of her because of her mouth. Her tongue was cutting—sharp and deadly. She would never back down from a confrontation. And since she was mentally ill, she never stopped mouthing off, so he never stopped beating her.

Lydia felt trapped as a poor housewife and young mother of five. Her spirit was way too free and wild for that kind of life. She hated her husband's control over her, but was torn between feelings of resentment and intense love, a powerful combination, especially for someone suffering from an undiagnosed psychological disorder. So she did what most paranoid schizophrenics would do with that kind of anger: beat the shit out of her kids. (I know—horrible, but sadly all too true.)

So, as Ismael strolled down Wallabout Street, Lydia's older sister stuck her head out the window, then quickly tucked it back inside, screaming with glee. While she was fretting about fixing her makeup, Lydia quietly went over to the window to see him for herself.

Just at that moment, my father looked up and took in Lydia's mesmerizing beauty—that's how he described it to me anyway—and stopped dead in his tracks. Lydia gave him one of her infamous smirks and casually popped her head back inside. With a nonchalant shrug of her shoulders, she turned to her sister and said, "He's all right looking—a little ugly. Ay, fo, the garbage is so stinky. I'm going to take it out for you, Minguita. I'll be right back."

She grabbed her coat and quickly ran down the staircase. Ismael ran up just as fast. When she saw him come into view, she slowed down to a sultry strut, step by step.

"When I saw your mother, I almost had a heart attack right there on the stairs," my father told me years later. "I had to grab my heart. I couldn't breathe." (I know, Puerto Ricans, melodrama—gotta love it.)

They met halfway on the staircase, stopped, and just stared at each other without saying a word.

"You are the most beautiful thing I've ever seen in my life. Would you do me the honor and join me for a cup of coffee?" he said, with a tip of his hat and a flirtatious smile.

She took his arm. Just like that, without a word to anyone, they took off. I don't know what my Tia Ana or Lydia's sister, the abandoned date, thought happened, but I know her sister was pissed when she eventually figured shit out.

Both of my parents were very sexual, so I'm sure they didn't waste any time and probably had sex right away. That's so embarrassing to say, on one level, and incredibly cool on another. It had to be pure lust, with a touch of whimsical romance—at least for my father it was like that. (With that scene on the staircase? Come on!)

I know it's weird, but I've always wondered how it went down. Where did they go to do it? How did the room look? Was the bedding nice? Was it cold inside or was the radiator steaming heat? I imagine that everything was white—the walls, the sheets, and the curtains billowing from the slight crack of the window to let some air in because everything was crazy. (I was going to say "hot and heavy" but didn't want you to think I'm a pervert.)

What about her, what about my mother? Was it romantic, or just an escape for her, or both? What was she wearing? My father never told me that. I even wonder if she had nice underwear on. I'm such a Virgo that I wonder if she looked put together, if she'd planned a nice bra-and-panties combination.

More important, I always wondered how she felt. Was she scared, even just a bit? I wonder if she thought of her husband as she and Ismael kissed, if she thought of her five kids as she started to undress. Did she give a shit about the consequences? Did she think, *What the hell am I doing?* Probably not. With the whole mental thing, and her self-centeredness, I'm sure she was just living in the moment. She sure didn't give two shits about her sister whose date she stole.

Or perhaps she was just so disappointed in her life that she saw in Ismael a shot at escape—maybe for a moment, or maybe permanently. And she took it, regardless of who got hurt along the way. I do know this about my mother: she always wanted more than she had. And not just with money, but with life. It's kind of sad, it really is.

. . .

Within months of their meeting, she got pregnant with me, left her husband when she started to show, took her five kids, and moved into an apartment in Bushwick, Brooklyn, that my father set up for her. He then left his wife and moved in with them—real classy move on both parts, right? He took her on hook, line, and sinker. It was a scandal of large proportions.

It was great the first few months. My half-siblings loved my father. He was a captain's chef on the ships and could cook his ass off; he helped with the cleaning and played and talked with them like they mattered. They thought they had a new beginning, had seen the light at the end of the tunnel. Then the shit hit the fan. As the months passed and my mother's pregnancy progressed, Ismael slowly started to see her mental malady. He didn't understand at first—the unprovoked violent outbursts, the combativeness that would drag on for hours. He was at a loss. He tried to please her, but nothing worked. By the eighth month of her pregnancy, she was going at him full tilt—rages, paranoia. The arguing was constant, and the suspicion was at an all-time high. About that, I can't blame my mother. With his reputation as a womanizer, and considering the way they started off, well, it's understandable that anyone, even a crazy person, would assume the worst.

What's sad, and ironic, is that my father told me he was being faithful. Lydia was his world, and he loved her children. But Mom couldn't buy it. That paranoia was too strong.

One day he came home and she started in.

"Where the fuck was you? Out fucking some fucking slut?" my mother screamed. She had a mouth like a truck driver. (Explains a lot, right?)

He pleaded and pleaded until he finally snapped and started to scream back, told her he was sick of her craziness, that he was leaving her. So, of course, she got her pistol. (Yes, Mom carried a pistol.)

"You gonna leave me? Me? You motherfucker!" she yelled.

Bang! Bang! Bang!

She started shooting. My father jumped out the window, climbed down the fire escape—while she was still shooting—and ran for his life. He never went back.

This was my father's recollection of events.

Now, in fairness to Mom, her version of this story is that they'd had an argument over his cheating—at least they agreed on that—and that he started screaming, she started screaming back, and then he packed his things and left her, eight months pregnant with me, and her five kids. However, according to her, there was no gun, no shots fired. I tend to believe Pops, since other people who lived on their block confirmed his story to me over the years. Plus, Mom did carry a pistol and was quick to pull it out. She would frequently bring it along with her, in a plastic bag for "protection," just to go to the corner store that was half a block away—true story. Either way, it must have been tough to be left eight months pregnant.

Lydia, heartbroken, had no other recourse than to go back to her husband, Ventura, who everyone called Durin, with her tail between her legs. Ventura was a tall, dark, extremely handsome, smoldering-with-sex-appeal grump who had his moments of kindness. He was also a man of very few words. (I think I heard him speak maybe a total of three sentences the entire time I knew him—no kidding.) He took her back, but wasn't happy about her being pregnant with another man's baby, even though he claimed me as his and gave me his last name—all to preserve *his* and *Lydia's* honor, of course. When she gave birth to me at Greenpoint Hospital, in September, there was a rumor that Ventura put a hit out on my father if he dared to show his face there.

Tia told me she stayed all day and through the night, standing guard, gazing at me through the maternity ward's viewing window, falling deeply in love with me. A few mutual friends of Tia's and my mother's walked up, stood beside her, scanning the rows of newborns, searching for the scandalous love child.

"*Hola*, Minguita, which one is Lydia's baby?" they asked.

"That one," she replied, pointing to me.

"Which one?" they'd ask again, feigning confusion.

"That one, the tiny blonde, *jellow* one," Tia answered again.

Shock crossed their faces. They were giddy and gasping.

"Oh!" one of them stated with an affected melodramatic pause. "Are you sure?"

"You know, Minguita," another friend chimed in, "that baby kind of looks like . . . you . . . and your brother."

Tia coyly shrugged her shoulders, trying hard to play along, concealing her pride in order to save the family's face. She knew that they knew I was her brother's notorious newborn, but she didn't dare let on.

It didn't matter. The streets of Bushwick and Williamsburg were filled with even more *bochinche* (gossip) after that! All of Lydia's other children were strapping like their father, had dark hair like their father, and had a reddish-olive complexion to boot. There I was, yellow, with sandy blonde hair and tiny as shit. I looked just like my father. There was no doubt that I was his.

Ismael snuck into the hospital late that night. When Tia saw him, she was pissed. She had told him that there was a hit out on him. But he said he didn't care. Actually, he did. He just cared about me more. He told me later that he was scared as shit as he crept through the hospital's hallways. He went up to the window, looked, knew who I was immediately, and cried, just cried. Then he ran out, without a word to his sister or anyone else. There was no shooting—just sad, pathetic drama.

. . .

Just a week after my birth Lydia decided to pay Tia a visit so she could see the baby. My mother arrived with me all bundled up.

"Hi, how are you? I brought the baby so you could see her," my mom said in a panicked huff. "Listen, I have to go to the bodega. I'll be right back."

She handed me to Tia, left, and didn't come back for three years. She never came to check on me. She never called. . . . And Tia never called her either. I guess the situation was understood and that was that.

CHAPTER 2

TIA SPOILED the shit out of me by smothering me with love and attention. Her three daughters—Titi, the oldest; Millie, the next oldest; then Cookie—were all instructed to take extra good care of me. When I was a baby, I thought they were all my sisters rather than my cousins, and they treated me in kind.

Everyone, all the neighbors also, treated me special, like a "miracle" baby. Some new friends thought that having another baby at Tia's age was beyond incredible. Yes, a lot of people thought I was her daughter—to this day many are surprised to learn I'm not. Her dear friends knew the truth but never spoke on it. Tia never officially stated that I was not her daughter, but she didn't explain the situation either. That was private family business. That's why, when I was a baby, I knew her as my mother and referred to her as "Mommie" instead of "Tia."

I was a good baby, happy, sweet, polite, and a ham, except when I had one of my crying fits. Apparently I'd have these screaming spells all through the night, and my cousin-sisters would take turns holding me and stroking me back to sleep so Tia could have her rest. I was probably screaming for my mother. By the time I was crawling, I'd sporadically start crying and banging my head repeatedly on the floor for no reason. Weird thing, I remember that. My cousin Millie later told me that every time I did that it would bring her to tears.

I remember a lot, as far back as one or two years old, mostly it comes to me in just bits and pieces, and flashes of images. Fortunately, I don't just remember the bad things; I remember the good things too—especially the hammy parts! I loved television—from day one! And loved music even more. When I told Tia one day that I remembered dancing in my crib, her mouth dropped slightly and she said, "*Ay*, my goodness. You were less than one when you started doing that."

The memory of dancing on my bed was really, like I said, just a flash of a moment. My cousin Millie filled in the rest. She said like clockwork, every day at three-thirty in the afternoon, I'd stand up in my crib, which was in Tia's room, looking through the French doors into the living room, waiting for my cousins to come home from school. As soon as they came into view, I'd start gleefully jumping and screaming for them to put my favorite song, "I'm a Soul Man" by Sam and Dave, on the record player in the living room. And I wouldn't stop screaming until they did.

As soon as the needle dropped, I'd hold on to the rail with one hand and do the "hitchhiker," with my thumb sticking out, with my other hand. When I got tired, I'd suck on that thumb until I caught my breath and start hitching all over again—my cousins would die with laughter. Millie said that as soon as the record ended, I'd start screaming and they'd have to play it over and over until I was too exhausted to stand. She said at times I'd lie down in my crib from exhaustion, with my eyes closed, still dancing in my slumber.

What can I say, I was a cute kid, especially with my sandy blonde, curly, cotton-candy hair to boot . . . except for one major thing: I had the biggest forehead in all of Brooklyn. It was a monstrosity. Everyone would always tease me about it too. Everyone—except for Tia, of course—would call it a "big mofo," which was short for "big motherfucking forehead." What's worse, when Tia would have a house party, she sometimes pulled all of my hair tightly back, up into a big moño (bun), leaving the rest of my hair to stick out like a wilted Afro puff on the top of my head—not a good look, people.

The house was always filled—with family, or neighbors, or just friends. It was like a revolving door. Tia was very social and generous. Parties were a constant: Spanish, soul, and pop music playing; people dancing; the smell of rice and beans and roasted pork—heaven. I remember it as a sea of legs and shoes. That's probably where my foot fetish started.

My cousins would put me in the middle of the floor to show off my dancing skills. I was too shy to do it if there were too many people. It would scare me, and I would stay close to Tia. But if it was just a few friends, or people I was familiar with, the ham and cheese would come out and I'd take center stage, doing my little ditty.

By the age of two, I was starting to complete full sentences (most two-year-olds only use two- to three-word sentences, thank you very much!) and pointing to words and saying them out loud while the very few children's books Tia had around—like *Fun with Dick and Jane*—were read to me and to the new baby Lorraine by my cousins and our babysitter—a Jewish woman and friend of Tia's named, of all things, Rosie. And when Tia watched *telenovelas*, I'd walk up to the television and point to the familiar Spanish soap opera characters, saying their names too.

I loved watching movies with Tia. She loved classic American film noir and Westerns. She told me that when I was two and three I also loved musicals and comedies. She would lie on her side, rubbing her feet together, with me lying next to her—or, my favorite position, on top of her—watching Shirley Temple or Bob Hope. I loved Bob Hope. Singing was another favorite thing we'd do together, especially the Beatles and Shirley Temple tunes ("Animal crackers in my soup, Monkeys and rabbits loop the loop . . ."). Tia had a horrible singing voice, but I thought she sang like a bird.

The best memory I have from that period is when I was three. It's in bits and pieces, but Tia later filled in the parts I couldn't remember. It was a hot Sunday in summertime, and all of the girls were out, hanging on the block with the other Puerto Rican and Hasidic kids. Tia was in the kitchen, making the early Sunday dinner, which was usually served at four o'clock. The house smelled like *pollo guisado* (a Puerto Rican criolla-style chicken stew made from a saucy red *sofrito*, a liquid blend of green peppers, garlic, onions, cilantro, *culantro*, and tomatoes), and it was so hot from all the pots boiling on the stove that the walls started to sweat. All the windows were open. Tia's permed hair started to kink up. I was lying on the kitchen floor with just my diaper on, not making a peep. My behavior was disturbing her: I wasn't sucking my thumb, like usual, and I was being strangely quiet.

Tia picked me up, took off my diaper, and washed me down in the kitchen sink with her hands. My eyes started to close from the relief of the cold water. She toweled me off and carried me into her bedroom to put on a new diaper. She went back into the kitchen, leaving the French doors open so she could still see me.

I slipped off the bed, wanting to follow her, but the room was so cool from the breeze crossing through the rooms. I stayed standing next to the edge of the bed with my head lying on top, sucking my thumb and rubbing my fingers on the little peach balls on her bedspread. My head was turned in a way so that I could still see her, over the stove, cooking. She turned to me and smiled. I was in heaven. I felt loved, safe, cool, and clean.

I felt like that most of the time in Tia's house. Outside of my screaming fits, the only time that I had conflicted memories was when Tio Ismael would come around.

Tio Ismael, as I knew him when I was a baby, would visit the house often. Well, often enough for me to remember him. He was always in a suit and tie, or in his army jacket—always clean. He was so curious to me. I was attracted to him as if a magnet was pulling my attention toward him. I always had this urge to touch his big, brutal Taino nose, his coarse, curly hair, or his bottom lip that teardropped down whenever he smiled. And he smelled good, but different. There weren't a lot of men around our house, so the male scent was perplexing and titillating.

Tio Ismael was always happy to see me, but would cry whenever he'd pick me up, which would then make me cry. Tia was always right there to scoop me up in her arms if I began to get upset by him. After a while, I became afraid of him. He was so jumpy and stared at me all the time. When he'd come into a room, I'd run on my tiny feet to Tia, quietly grabbing at her big, cottage-cheesy thighs, screaming, "Mommie! He scares me," with my eyes still glued to his.

. . .

Three years had passed. I was happy and loved. Then my mother reappeared, out of nowhere. Millie, who was about twelve years old at the time, answered the door. Her mouth fell to the floor.

"Doña Lydia!" she gasped. "Mommie!" she screamed as she bolted down the hallway.

She ran to Tia. The house went quiet. Tia nervously picked me up and walked over to the door.

"Hola, Lydia. Como tu tas?" Tia nervously asked with a forced, polite smile.

Tia told me that when I turned and saw my mother's face, I immediately reached for her. Unbeknownst to me, this broke Tia's heart, but she concealed her pain. Lydia grabbed me up in her arms.

"I came for the baby," she said nonchalantly, with a casual smile. "Thank you for taking care of her, Minguita. I must go. I have a lot of things to do. Wave good-bye, say, 'Bye, bye, Tia.'"

"Tia"? Who's Tia? I immediately knew something was wrong. I

saw Tia's tears roll down from her eyes, and then she screamed a scream that jolted me to my core. I started screaming too. I reached back out to Tia. Tia reached for me.

"Let's go, Rosamarie," my mom said as she snatched me away from Tia's reach. "Come with Mommie."

Mommie? She's not my mommie—Mommie's my mommie. Confusion flooded my head and frightened my heart. Lydia rushed with me down the hallway, while Tia and my cousins followed right behind her. At the door, my aunt fell to her knees, grasped her hands together, and pleaded.

"*Ay, por favor,* Lydia! Don't take her. I beg you. *Yo te'dinero!* [I'll give you money]. *Algo! Algo!* [Anything! Anything!] *Por favor!* Please! *Don't take my baby!*"

"*My baby!*" That was the wrong thing to say to a crazy person. Lydia's face contorted with hate, resentment, pain, guilt, and revenge. She quickly turned and was out the door, slamming it behind her. Tia screamed a scream that was heard throughout the building. She grabbed her heart, fell to her knees, and went into cardiac arrest—literally. My cousin Titi rushed to the neighbors', banging and screaming on the door, pleading for someone to call an ambulance.

CHAPTER 3

SAINT JOSEPH'S Catholic Home for Children in Peekskill, New York, was fifty miles north of the city. "The Home" was situated on the edge of the Hudson, along the Metro-North train tracks, right up the hill from the train station. The campuslike compound, consisting partly of medieval-looking stone buildings and partly of plain cement buildings, sat on eight sparsely green, hilly acres.

I don't remember the ride up to the Home. I don't remember how many days had gone by since Lydia took me from Tia. I don't even remember if I went to Lydia's house or if she took me straight up to the Home. I just remember finding myself sitting in the "Baby Girls" playroom, seated on Lydia's lap across from an old lady with a funny scarf on her head. She looked like those church ladies in the old black-and-white movies Tia and I used to watch. Lydia was talking to the old lady—in a calm way, negotiating a deal, but also like a victim, acting as if she didn't want it to happen.

I started to get scared. I was fidgeting, looking around at this unfamiliar place. There were other ladies with the same thing on their heads, along with some young women dressed in regular clothes, leading other tiny kids around who were formed into lines. Some stole glances at me. A couple of men with dark robes on came in. They made me more scared than I already was. I didn't want to be there. Lydia kept bouncing me up and down on her legs, trying to calm me. I tried to wiggle out of her arms. Then she shook me, hard, and I went still. I had never been spanked, punished physically, ever. That was the first time I began to fear her wrath.

All of a sudden, we were walking into another room, with an open door that led outside. *Oh*, I thought, *it's all going to be over*. Next thing I knew I was being handed over to the old lady with the scarf on her head as Lydia continued out the open door, waving good-bye to me, with tears streaming from her eyes. Were the tears sincere? Who knows? I started to scream, reaching my arms out to her, pleading for her to take me with her.

"Don't you worry, Mrs. Perez, we will take good care of her. Say good-bye to your mother, Rosemary," Sister Mary-Domenica cheerfully said.

Mother? Who is this lady? And why is everyone calling her that? She's not mother. Mommie's my mother. What's going on? My heart started racing. The door shut behind Lydia, and she was gone. In that moment, I became a ward of the state of New York and the "property" of the Catholic Church.

. . .

"Shh! Now stop that crying. It's all right," Sister Mary-Domenica said as she was trying to wipe my tears away. "I said now stop that. You don't want to get a spanking, young lady, now do you?" Her tone was seemingly nice yet I detected a tinge of meanness. I stopped crying—sort of, sniffling up my snot, still looking toward that door. The younger ladies with the scarves on their heads watched what was happening with reluctant pity.

One of them reached out and took me in her arms and said, "I'll take her, sister." "Thank you, Sister Ann-Marie," replied Sister Mary-Domenica.

Sister? Why are they calling each other "sister"?

"Come on, Rosemary. Let me take you to your bed," Sister

Ann-Marie said to me as she set me down on the floor. "Would you like to see where you're going to sleep?"

Rosemary? Why was she calling me that?

Sister Ann-Marie was petite, with a hint of blond hair peeking out from her habit. Her voice was soft and high-pitched. She led me up three steps into a dormitory filled with small bunk beds, all in a row. The room was painted a kind of baby blue and was dark, as if the lights were dimmed, even though it was still midday afternoon. There were other girls in the dormitory, ranging from infants to five-year-olds. Some heads turned to take a look at the new kid. Others ignored me, as if the arrival of a new kid was routine.

Sister Ann-Marie pointed to the upper bunk. "This is going to be your new bed, Rosemary," she explained. "Let's get your sheets." She led me to a large closet where all the linens and clothes were set up in bins with each of the girls' names on them. "Do you know how to make your bed yet?" she asked. *Do I know how to make my bed? I'm three, lady!* "I'm going to show you the first time; next time you're going to do it all by yourself."

She showed me how to make a bed, military style, with the bottom sheet tight as hell and the top sheet folded in neat, tight, perfect angles at the corners. Are you kidding me? I have to do it the exact same way? Did you get that fact that I'm still just three years old? Haven't aged yet the whole two hours I've been here.

I guess my feelings showed on my face because I caught this girl sitting on top of her bunk directly next to mine, snickering. I was in too much of a state of shock to snicker back.

"Cindy!" Sister Ann-Marie snapped. "Stop that right now or you will get a spanking, or be put on punishment again, right away!"

"Yes, Sister Ann. I mean, Marie, I mean, Ann-Marie, I mean—"

Sister Ann-Marie cut her off and snapped again. "Stop it, Cindy!"

She turned her attention back toward me. "Dinner will be in a few minutes. I'll see you later," she said quickly, and she was gone.

I climbed up on the bunk and just sat there, numb, shocked, eyes and nose swollen from crying. I couldn't even suck my thumb. I didn't know what was going on! I wanted Tia. I wanted Millie. I wanted Cookie and Lorraine and Titi. I wanted to lay my head on Tia's peach bedspread with the little peach balls. Then I looked over at the other little girls, and for some reason I knew that I was here to stay. Maybe it was the way they looked back at me with such somber eyes. That's when my heart really started to break.

"Hi! I'm Cindy. What's your name?" the weirdo girl asked. She talked so fast too.

"Wosie," I quietly replied. (I had a speech impediment, and that's how I pronounced my name—cute for a while, not so cute past the age of six. And yes, for the record, it lasted to some extent until I was ten!)

"I'm four and a half. How old are you?" she asked.

I shrugged, looking down at my hands. "I'm three. Nice to meet you, Cindy."

She cracked up in my face. I didn't understand why she was laughing at the time. Tia always taught us proper manners. I later came to understand that proper etiquette was only used around the nuns and priests. Kids interacted on a more casual level.

Cindy was strange, seemed mature for her age, but I liked her instantly. I couldn't express it because I was too paralyzed with fear and confusion. Her kinky light brown hair was crazy, uncombed, and sticking up like a mad scientist's. She was skinny as a bone, with knobby knees and a dirty face that could have been mistaken for a boy's.

Two younger ladies came in. They both wore conservative knee-length dresses with conservative low-heeled shoes.

"Dinnertime! Line up!" one of the ladies announced loudly.

"Come on, Rosie, we gotta get in line or the nuns will spank the bejesus outta you," Cindy said, in a happy panic.

Nuns? Is that what they are? Cindy grabbed my hand, pulling me off the bunk. I fell and hit my head. Cindy started cracking up again. "Oh my God, you hit your big forehead. You okay? Come on. Hurry!"

All the little girls quickly formed a straight line. "All right, girls, let's go!" said the nicely dressed lady who looked much younger than the older nun. We started to march down the small steps, past the room where my mother had been with me, through a different door, into a dark, small hallway, through another door, down a long corridor, into a cafeteria filled with a bunch of round tables with tablecloths and place settings on each of them. We were led to two sets of tables. Cindy motioned for me to sit next to her. I did so. I was still stunned, not uttering a word. A bunch of ladies, some with white scarves on their heads, some without, placed plates of food at each setting.

I looked back toward the entrance as many other girls, ranging from toddlers to eighteen-year-olds, formed another line, waiting at an open counter for their turn to grab a plate of food. Most of them were black or Latino. Some were white. No Jews, I thought, since none of them were dressed like the Hasids in Williamsburg. Their chatter was deafening.

"Hi, Amelia!" waved Cindy to an older girl.

The girl paid her no mind.

"That's Amelia," Cindy remarked as she turned back to me. "She's my friend; she's in Group One. You have to be five to be in Group One. Groups Two and Three are for the big girls. You can't go yet, 'cause you're only three. That's why you're in Baby Girls, like me."

A really old nun, dressed with a bigger, longer, and more ridiculous black scarf on her head, stood in front of all of us, flanked by two other nuns, almost as old as she was. She clapped her hands three times, and all the girls stood up and began to sing:

Oh, the Lord is good to me. And so I thank the Lord. For giving me the things
I need, the sun and the rain and the apple trees. The Lord is good to me. I
thank the Lord!

At the end part ("I thank the Lord!"), everyone clapped four times on each of the last words. Then they all sat.

The head nun began another prayer as everyone followed along with their heads bowed and hands pressed together in prayer.

Dear Lord Jesus. Please bless this food we are about to receive and make it
nutritious to our bodies, in your precious name. We thank you Lord. Amen.

Wow. They pray a lot here. I don't recall if we prayed at Tia's, but it probably wasn't as much as they did here.

Everyone dug in, and the loud-ass chatter began again. The food looked foreign and bland. The vegetables were overcooked, and the fish smelled funny. Where were the rice and beans?

"You're not gonna eat your food?" asked Cindy.

I shook my head no.

"Can I eat it?" she asked. "If you don't eat it, you're gonna get in trouble. . . . Can I eat it?"

"Leave her alone, Cindy. Let her eat her food," said this chubby, reddish-olive-skinned Spanish girl with big hazel eyes.

I looked up at her.

"That's Puerto Rican–Jew Evita Feinstein. She's in Group One."

"Shut up, Crazy Cindy Berrios."

They both cracked up.

"What's your name?" asked Puerto Rican–Jew Evita Feinstein.

"Wosie."

"The nuns call her Rosemary," replied Crazy Cindy.

"They do that shit to everybody," Evita chimed in. "Except me, 'cause I'm a half-Jew."

Again laughter, from both of them.

I couldn't believe Puerto Rican–Jew Evita Feinstein was Jewish. Well, half Jewish. She looked like us, and she didn't wear those funny dresses with the dark stockings. And she cursed! Jewish girls never cursed, even if they were only half. Only the Italians, Polish, Irish, and Puerto Ricans cursed, like my cousins—not in front of Tia, of course. A slight smile emerged from the corner of my mouth. I liked these cuckoo girls. Still, I couldn't eat.

Afterwards, we went back to the Baby Girls' dormitory, and the young ladies who dressed in street clothes were there. These were our counselors, and each girls' dormitory was assigned two. One of them showed me how to fold my clothes and put them in the bin assigned to me. We went back into the playroom, and she showed me around—the toy box, the bookshelf, and the play table. I grabbed one of the books.

"*Puedale lee este a mi, por favor* [Can you read this one to me, please]?" I asked one of the ladies.

"We do not speak Spanish here. We speak English, okay?"

"Why?"

"Because those are the rules, and we are here to teach you and help you."

"Why?"

"Because you're one of God's children . . ."

What the hell did that mean? God isn't bilingual?

"I'll ask Sister Mary-Domenica if she will read it during reading time tonight. Let me show you the courtyard where you can run and play," she answered.

"No, thank you," I replied. "I want to read the book, please."

"I'm sorry. It's time to go outside," she stated firmly. "Let's go."

"Can I take my book, *por favor*?" I pleaded politely.

She paused, trying to hold back a smile, and then said, "Sure."

I excitedly opened it.

"Ooh! *Lookit!* She has the ball. Ball!" I said, pointing to the word.

"You know what that word is, Rosemary?"

"Yes! It says, 'ball'! She likes to play with it, right?"

"Yes. Please take it outside."

She left quickly.

I took the book and sat close to the door, watching the other kids romp and play with each other. I tried to read the book, but was distracted by my misery and by the girls playing as if nothing was wrong. They all seemed okay with being here.

Before bedtime, all the little girls in Baby Girls lined up again in the bathroom, each of us in a nightgown, a bathrobe, and slippers, holding a toothbrush. There were three or four sinks, a couple of bathroom stalls, and one humongous shower. Three by three, the girls walked up to the sinks, washed their hands and faces, and brushed their teeth.

I was standing behind Crazy Cindy, who couldn't stop talking and making jokes and acting silly. I was still quiet. I was uncomfortable. I'd never worn a bathrobe. I only saw people wear them on television, like Shirley Temple in *The Little Princess*. I wasn't sure if I liked wearing one or not. I wanted Tia so bad. I wanted to suck my thumb so bad. I wanted to cry and run out, but I didn't dare. I just moved along the line with the rest of them, inching closer and closer to the sink.

It was our turn. I turned on the faucet. The light of the moon, peering from a small window above, glistened on the running water. My eyes were transfixed by the dancing sparkles of light. I slowly began to wash my hands, and I started singing, "A tea for two, a two for tea. . . ." I didn't even realize I was singing until I heard laughter. I turned around and the girls were all pointing and laughing at me. I flushed with embarrassment.

"That's enough, girls!" commanded Sister Mary-Domenica as she stood at the doorway of the bathroom. "And you! What is your name again?"

I was terrified.

"Wosie," I answered.

"Her Christian name is Rosemary, sister," said Sister Ann-Marie.

"Hurry up and brush your teeth," she snapped. "We don't have all night here."

I looked at Sister Mary-Domenica towering over us, with a paddle in her hand. Her mouth was tight and stern. The bathroom fell silent. I grabbed the toothbrush and started brushing. I don't remember if I even knew how to properly brush by then. I wanted to vomit. I swallowed the feeling instead.

"Everyone over here. Reading time," Sister Ann-Marie commanded politely.

We all formed a semicircle around Sister Mary-Domenica, who was sitting in a rocking chair, holding the same book I'd been reading earlier. I looked up to Sister Ann-Marie; she smiled and winked at me. I smiled and winked back. A lot of the girls couldn't sit still during the reading, but I did.

Sister Mary-Domenica closed the book and shouted, "Get ready for bed, girls!"

I walked over to my bunk and began to climb up. Crazy Cindy pulled me down. "No. You have to wait to say prayers." She pulled me next to her, told me to kneel, and indicated with her hands for me to put mine together in prayer.

"Our Father who art in heaven, hallowed be thy name. Thy Kingdom come, thy will be done, on earth as it is in heaven. Give us this day our daily bread. And forgive us our trespasses, as we forgive those who trespass against us. And lead us not into temptation, but deliver us from evil. For thine is the kingdom and the power and the glory, forever and ever. Amen."

Everyone quickly jumped up into bed. No one tucked us in. No one kissed us good-night. No one told us they loved us and they'd see us in the morning. Sister Mary-Domenica shut off the lights and left. I started to cry.

"Psst. Psst. Rosie. Where you from?" whispered Crazy Cindy. She was leaning over her top bunk toward mine.

"From my mommie's house," I whispered back through a few snotty tears.

"But where, stupid?"

"Why did you call me stupid? That's not very nice," I replied, hurt.

She tried to smother her laughter.

"I didn't mean it like that, stupid. Where's her house? Is she from the city?"

I shrugged. I didn't know. I just knew it was in a neighborhood with a lot of Puerto Ricans and Jews.

"Where are we?" I asked.

"Saint Joe's. I've been here since I was one. I'm four and a half."

"I wanna go home." I whispered back, tearing up.

"You can't. You have to wait for your mother to come back and ask permission."

My mother? Oh no! Which one, my real mommie or that other pretty, mean lady who brought me here? I lay back on my pillow and cried, quietly. I finally put my thumb in my mouth, trying to soothe myself to sleep.

"Rosie. Rosie," Crazy Cindy continued to yell in a loud whisper.

"Who's talking?" screamed Sister Mary-Domenica as she came marching back into the dorm wearing a granny nightgown and a cotton nightcap on her head!

Crazy Cindy quickly pretended to be asleep. I sat up.

"*Perdoname*," I squeaked.

"English!" she snapped.

"I wanna go home," I said, softly crying.

"This is your home now," Sister Mary-Domenica again snapped. "Go to sleep. And stop that crying."

With that, she left again. This time I began to cry out hysterically, tears pouring out of my eyes with fear, pain, and anger. This just can't be. Why is this happening to me? I want to go home! I want to go home!

"I said stop that crying!" screamed Sister Mary-Domenica as she came rushing back in. Crazy Cindy, in a loud whisper, told me to lie down and be quiet before I got hit. I tried my hardest to quiet myself. I pulled the covers over my head, stuck my thumb in my mouth, and tried to control my breathing, which was coming out in big gulps of pain.

. . .

It was 6:00 AM the next morning. The old bag, Sister Mary-Domenica, came out clapping her hands together to wake us up. *Clap, clap, clap!* "Let's go. Time to get up. Line up for showers," she barked. I woke up, drained and exhausted. Everyone jumped out of their bunks, took off their nightgowns, put on their bathrobes and slippers, and headed to the bathroom.

One girl—skinny, Latina, looked around my age—wouldn't get out of her bunk. She sat there, crying. Sister Mary-Domenica went over to her bed.

"Get off, now," she said through her clenched teeth. "You know better than to wet your bed. Get your sheets and bring them to the laundry chute!" The young girl pulled her sheets off, crying the whole time, and put them down the chute. She returned to get her bathrobe and slippers.

"Lift up your nightie!" ordered Sister Mary-Domenica.

The girl did so and bent over with her hands on her knees. Sister Mary-Domenica pulled out a paddle from under her robe. *Whack! Whack! Whack!* Right across her bare bottom. Fear and astonishment went straight through my body. The girl was crying even harder now. Everyone else stood quiet, watching. I started to shake.

"Stop crying or I'll give you something to really cry about. Get in line!"

Inside the bathroom, everyone took off their bathrobes and placed them on hooks against the wall. Sister Ann-Marie was waiting inside. I didn't understand what was going on. I felt funny and numb, but I continued to follow along. Then they all formed a line in front of the big shower. There were four showerheads turned on. In groups of five or six, or however many of us could fit inside the shower at a time, the girls went inside and started to wash themselves. I got nervous. I felt weird standing there naked with strangers. Plus, I never washed myself before. I watched to see how they were doing it. They were quick and thorough about it. There was no horseplay or enjoyment involved.

It was my turn. I followed behind Crazy Cindy. Seeing how sad and uncomfortable I was, Crazy Cindy splashed water in my face to try to make me laugh. I didn't. She then stood directly under one of the four showerheads with her mouth open, took a bar of soap, stuck it in and out of her mouth, swishing the mixture around to create bubbles. All of a sudden she sneezed and bubbles shot out of her nostrils. I started to laugh. I couldn't help it. She started laughing too.

Sister Ann-Marie screamed, "Both of you, out!" We quickly got out and stood in front of her, naked, shaking from the cold, Cindy with soap bubbles still foaming from her mouth.

"Who started it?" she asked.

We said nothing.

"Cindy? No one wants to say anything? Okay, both of you are on punishment."

"It was me, Sister Ann-Marie." said Crazy Cindy.

I looked at Cindy. I couldn't believe she went to bat for me.

"You're on punishment, Cindy. Sister Mary-Domenica will deal with you later. Go get dressed."

Crazy Cindy began to head out, then sneezed—snot and bubbles splattered all over Sister Ann-Marie's clothes. Silence! A beat passed, then Crazy Cindy couldn't help herself and started laughing. Sister Ann-Marie was not amused.

I went over to Sister Ann-Marie and tugged at her robe.

"*Perdoname*, Doña Sister Lady," I pleaded. "Please don't be mad at Crazy Cindy. I laughed too. I'm sorry."

"Oh, Rosemary. Thank you very much for apologizing. That was very honest and charitable of you. And please remember to speak in English."

"What's 'chaweeable'?"

Sister Ann-Marie turned to the other young nun, Sister Elizabeth-Claire, a stout, round thing, clasping her mouth with her hand, trying to suppress a smile.

Sister Elizabeth-Claire bent down to my height. "It's pronounced 'char-i-ta-ble.' It means that you weren't thinking of yourself, you were thinking of your friend, Cindy. It means that God came into your heart." "Huh?" "God is our heavenly father who protects us and guides us," she answered.

Father. Hmm.

"Why?" I asked.

"Because he loves us. He loves all of his children."

"How many children does he have?"

"We are all his children. You and me and everyone in the whole wide world."

"Wow. He has a lot of children, right?"

They laughed. I smiled.

"I made you laugh?" I clapped my hands together, applauding myself. "Yay!"

They giggled.

"Want me to do it again?" I asked. (Disgustingly shameless! Begging for applause already, at the tender age of three.) I kept going. "You look like these ladies that were in a movie I saw with my mommie. And I loved it very much," I added. "And it's called *Bell of Mawees,* and the man in the movie sings a lot of songs, all the time, and in all his movies. His name is Bing Cwossie. I like him. I wish he was my friend, and I wish he could come to my house and sing with me and Mommie and my sisters. 'I'm dreaming of a white Christmas, Like the ones I use to snow. . . . ' "

They cut me off with their giggling.

"When can I go back to my mommie's house?"

They looked at each other again, this time with pity in their eyes. That look of pity made me so angry inside that I wanted to scream, but after just a day at the Home, I knew better.

CHAPTER 4

SEVERAL WEEKS in the Home went by, maybe even months—who the hell knows, I was in a time warp—with the same routine every day. With everything, we were told what to do, when to do it, and how to do it: when to wake up, when to shower, how to shower, when and how to clean up, when to eat, how to pray, when to play, when to fucking pee and poop, and how to wipe our ass. And I knew I'd better follow the rules. A lot of brutal spankings were doled out, and I wanted to be sure not to get one. And the amount of praying was staggering! I hated praying. I quickly learned how to fake it and to daydream instead about blueberry and apple pie. Since snacking and second helpings were not allowed, and withholding food was also used as a punishment, I daydreamed a lot about scrumptious delights.

I remember becoming more and more withdrawn. At meals I ate silently, without joining the girls' chatter. I made my bed, neatly and thoroughly, and did my chores, which consisted of picking up a handful of toys and books and folding the few clothing items I had into my bin without any horseplay. At playtime I sat to the side while the other kids played, daydreaming while I drew in the dirt, making pictures of blueberry pies, wishing they were real, writing out letters of the alphabet. At times I'd play with Crazy Cindy, but mostly, I'd wander back into the playroom and grab a book, read to myself, and daydream some more—about Tia and Titi and Millie and Cookie and Lorraine. For some reason, their faces were getting harder to remember.

One of my few enjoyments was when I'd sing to myself or when Sister Ann-Marie and the counselors sang along with me. Some of the other girls would make fun of me when I sang. I'd blush with embarrassment, go quiet, and start sucking my thumb. But my favorite thing was when we got to watch TV—oh the sweet, sweet joy of joys—for an hour in the afternoon, an hour or two at night, and a lot more on the weekends! The TV room was in the back of the first floor. I loved it. I was in there every chance I got. I'd sit there, sucking my thumb, in a trance, escaping into the world of Bugs Bunny, Casper the Friendly Ghost, The Jetsons. I remember hating Captain Kangaroo—that old man creeped me out. One of my favorites was The Little Rascals, and I loved pretending I was one of them. Once in a while they would let us stay up late and watch The Flying Nun, I Dream of Jeannie, etc. My favorite was The Jackie Gleason Show, and I loved imitating Jackie Gleason for the nuns. I'd really ham it up, and it would kill, every time—holla!

One day Sister Ann-Marie came over to me as I was coming back from breakfast.

"Rosemary, come with me. You're not going outside today to play," she explained. "We would like you to play a couple of games with us, okay?"

I nodded as I followed her into the playroom. I got a little nervous, but remained quiet.

"Rosemary, this is Miss Beth. She is one of our nursery-school teachers."

"Hello, Rosemary. It's very nice to meet you."

"It's very nice to meet you too. My name's not Wosemary, it's Wosie."

"Oh, okay, 'Rosie.' Sister Ann-Marie tells me that you like books."

"Yes I do," I replied, softly. "I like to read. I like to sing songs too, but some of the other girls laugh at me."

"May I see you read a book, please?" she asked.

She handed me a picture book with the name of each picture written in big bold letters beneath it.

"When can I go home?" I asked.

Miss Beth looked uncomfortably at Sister Ann-Marie.

"This is your home now," Sister Ann-Marie told me. "And you know that we call all the girls and boys here by their Christian name, okay?"

I said nothing in response. There was a moment of awkwardness in the room.

Miss Beth tried to change the mood. In a perky voice, she asked, "Would you like to read the book to me, Rosie?" I nodded yes slowly, opened the book, pointed to the first picture, and said, "Apple," then the next, "Ball," and so on. "Do you know what the words under the picture say, or do you just know the name of each picture?" This made me nervous, so I just shrugged. "It's okay, Rosie, if you know it or not."

"Sometimes I know them, but sometimes I don't."

She pointed to a word. "Do you know what this word means?"

"Yes, 'ball.' You play with it and have fun."

"How about this one?"

" 'Cat.' It's a cat, and the cat says, 'Meow.' "

"This one?" she asked as she giggled.

I shook my head no.

" 'Boat,' " Miss Beth explained. "It spells 'boat,' b-o-a-t, boat."

I pointed to the picture and repeated her words. "Boat. B-o-a-t. Boat!"

"Very good, Rosie."

I applauded myself with my little hands: "Yay!" (What can I say?) Both of the ladies laughed and clapped with me.

Miss Beth took out a more advanced book. It was one from the classic "Dick and Jane" series. She smiled at me and asked, "Can you read this one for me?" I froze up again, I think because I recognized it and it probably brought up a bunch of memories of my nice, safe, and loving home with Tia.

"Do you know what it says?" she asked as she pointed to the word "look."

I nodded yes, then no.

"That's okay. It says, 'Look.' Do you know what the little girl is doing in the picture?"

"Yes," I answered. "She's putting on big shoes."

"Did your mother teach you how to read?" asked Miss Beth.

"Yes. My mommie reads to me sometimes when she's not tired, and Millie and Cookie, and Miss Wosie. Miss Wosie reads to me all the time. She plays with me all day till Mommie comes home. I miss my mommie."

I bit my bottom lip, trying not to cry.

Sister Ann-Marie turned to Miss Beth and said, "She means her aunt and her cousins. Her aunt helped her mother raise her before her mother came and brought her here." (Okay, sidebar here: "helped my mother raise me"? That was a good one.)

"What else did your aunt teach you?"

"Who?" I asked Miss Beth.

"Who's who? Your aunt?" she replied.

I nodded yes.

Sister Ann-Marie interjected, "Ana Dominga's your aunt, Rosemary. The lady you came here with is your mother. Do you understand?"

I sat silent, confused. Miss Beth put her hand on my shoulder. "Would you take a look at these flash cards for me?" she asked. I didn't want to. I shook my head no. Things were starting to come together, but at the same time I felt more confused than ever. I couldn't handle responding to Miss Beth.

They continued anyway and put me through a series of IQ and other tests. After a while, I forgot about my mommie/aunt and started to get into it. My enthusiasm began to pop like fireworks. Every time I got something right, my smile grew and I'd applaud myself. By the end of the test, I was elated.

"You can go outside and play with the other girls now," Miss Beth finally said.

"Can I stay inside with you?"

I wanted her to be my friend and hold my hand and play with me.

"Well, I have a lot of work to do, and Sister Ann-Marie is going outside to play with you and all the other girls."

I didn't want to cry in front of Miss Beth, but the tears still came. Sister Ann-Marie took me by the arm and led me outside. I kept looking back at Miss Beth, wishing that she was my friend and that she'd save me from this place.

. . .

That night I had a nightmare. I don't remember what it was about, but I remember waking up in the middle of the night, feeling soaking wet. I sat up. I had peed the bed. I don't think I'd ever peed the bed before. I was so scared. That old, ugly, mean nun was going to beat me like she did all the other girls who peed their beds.

I looked around. Everyone was fast asleep. I took off the bottom sheet and climbed down my bunk, being very cautious not to wake the other girls. I tiptoed to the laundry chute. I was too short to reach it. I panicked! What to do? I went into the linen and clothes closet and stuffed the sheet into one of the bins. I grabbed a clean one. The other sheets on top of it came tumbling down on my head. I tried to stuff them back, tried to make them look like they did before I messed them up. I tiptoed quickly back to my bed, climbed up, and put the sheet on. I sat there looking around to make sure that no one saw me.

"You peed the bed?"

My head snapped to the right, and I saw Crazy Cindy sitting up looking at me.

"No," I answered.

Look at that! The nuns already had me lying—probably for the first time too, I might add.

"Don't worry. I won't tell."

She lay back down. I did the same. I couldn't go back to sleep right away. All the possible scenarios of getting caught and being beaten were running rapidly through my head.

Morning. *Clap! Clap! Clap!* The old bag came in, and everyone jumped into the regular routine. As I was climbing down my bunk, Sister Elizabeth-Claire, the short, stout, round thing, came over to me.

"Come with me," she said with a serious, solemn face.

My heart started to pound. I looked at Crazy Cindy. She was shaking her head at me behind Sister Elizabeth-Claire, as if to say, *Don't say anything!* I followed her down the hallway of the dormitory. She went straight to the closet, opened it, and pointed to the smelly, yellow-stained bedsheet.

"Did you do that?" she asked.

How the hell she knew I was the one who did the crime is still a mystery. I couldn't answer. Tears ran down my face. She lifted my nightgown and smacked me so freaking hard across my bottom. The shock from the instant pain and sting stopped my tears. I'd never been hit. I couldn't believe this was happening. I tried to use my hand to block the blows. She grabbed it, holding my arm straight up in the air, and resumed the spanking. I used my other hand to block her again. Then she grabbed both arms, holding them up in the air with one of her hands, and went at it again with the other. I don't know what came over me, but I started to kick her with my tiny foot.

A crowd of little girls formed around us. Crazy Cindy was crazed with excitement, cheering me on. I wanted her to stop. She was only making it worse. The old bag came in with Sister Ann-Marie running behind her. All the girls, scared of punishment for being nosy, ran into the bathroom—all except for Cindy.

"What is going on here?" demanded Sister Mary-Domenica.

Sister Elizabeth-Claire, flustered and red-faced, turned to her and said, "She peed the bed and stuffed the sheet in here, and when I spanked her for it, she started kicking me."

"We do not hit, kick, or do anything to the nuns here, young lady. Do you understand me? Do you?!" the old bag screamed.

I stared at her with fear and contempt. The decrepit hag grabbed me by my wrist and proceeded to pull me down to the end of the hall. I was now screaming at the top of my lungs in full rebellion. Where the hell did all this come from? All the angst, fear, confusion, terror, and anger wailed out of me, all the way down that hallway.

Some of the girls came out of the bathroom and timidly followed behind. Crazy Cindy was right there too. Sister Mary-Domenica sat on a chair, grabbed her spanking paddle with one hand, and pulled me over her lap with the other. She then lifted up my nightgown, exposing my bare bottom, and beat the shit out of me until my bottom cracked with a slight hint of blood. She pushed me off of her.

"Get that sheet," she ordered. "Put it in the laundry chute and go back to your bed and don't move until I say you can. There will be no breakfast for you, missy. And let that be a lesson to all of you. You will respect each and every nun here. Is that understood? Is it, Rosemary?!"

"Yes."

"Yes, sister!" she corrected.

"Yes, sister," I answered, filled with crazy emotions.

I walked back down the hallway, past the glares and stares. I can't tell you the humiliation I felt. I kept looking straight ahead. I went over to the closet, got the sheet, and tried my best to stuff it up in the laundry chute, but still couldn't reach it. Crazy Cindy rushed over to help me. Sister Ann-Marie came over and put her hand on Cindy's shoulder, moving her out of the way. She lifted me up, and I pushed the sheet down the chute. She set me back down.

"Why don't you take a shower?" she said softly. I looked at her, my face drained, turned away, and headed for my bunk instead.

CHAPTER 5

THE NEW school year had begun. They told me my birthday, September 4, was coming up too. I was about to turn four years old, and I was filled with double the excitement. I don't remember a birthday party, but I'm sure there was one. They always remembered your birthday and cut a cake for you, though they'd deny you a celebration if you'd been bad.

Most of the girls went to school in the Baby Girls' playroom, but I was sent to a separate nursery school on the same floor as the Baby Girls' dormitory across the hall. They had handpicked me and one other girl because of our test results. They gave me a nice, simple dress to wear, with lace bobby socks and practical Mary Jane shoes. Sister Ann-Marie did my hair into two ponytails. The other girl was wearing a dress too, but it was plainer than mine. I felt bad about that. Sister Mary-Domenica and Sister Ann-Marie came into the playroom where we were waiting for them with another pretty lady with a television frosted hairstyle.

"Girls, this is Mrs. Connie Burton," said Sister Ann-Marie. "She is going to be your volunteer [nowadays referred to as a Big Sister]. She's going to be your friend and your guide, okay?"

I nodded and looked at this beautiful, full-figured, dyed-blond woman. She got giddy and remarked how tiny and cute I was—holla!

"Hi, girls. I hope we can be friends," this extraordinary-looking woman said. "Would you like to come with me to class?"

Miss Connie held out her hand toward me, and I took it. I was drawn to her instantly. She had a warm and sincere quality. As we started walking down to the nursery school, I began to feel bad as I looked back at the other little girl trailing behind. I wanted to reach out for her hand, but I was too afraid that I'd get in trouble, so I motioned with my hand for her to follow us. She ran up to us and we walked on, side by side.

The room was medium-sized and colorful. In the far back were paint easels, toys, books, and the usual nursery-school parapher-nalia. My eyes widened with excitement at first. The Baby Girls' dorm didn't look as wonderful as this room did. I started to rush in, but then hesitated. The room was filled with little kids I hadn't seen before, all white except for one black boy. They were dressed really nice too. I looked down at my dress and lacy socks, and then back at the other girls in perfectly ironed baby doll dresses or two-piece flowered coordinates. The boys wore V-neck sweaters, collared shirts, and blazers. Suddenly my new outfit no longer felt so special.

These were the "outside" kids. They weren't part of the Home; they had their own homes and parents who paid extra for a Catho-lic school education and who tucked them in at night. I was intimi-dated by their casualness, a casualness that I recognized, but that had been erased from me in less than a few months. I wanted them to be my friends, but I knew that wouldn't happen.

Despite this, school became another escape. I enjoyed it, ran in cheerfully each morning. I absorbed everything like a sponge. I felt I was in my own magical learning world, that I wasn't in the Home, and that I was just like the other kids who had parents and slept in their own bedrooms and woke up to a breakfast of pan-cakes with gobs of maple syrup. Miss Connie helped to make me feel special too every time the outside kids' parents would come for some event—she would be with me as if she were a relative of mine.

At first the kids liked me, sort of. Their parents already had a prejudice against us because we were from the Home. There was this one irritating boy, with light blond hair and blue eyes, who dressed as if he was attending Oxford. He was a condescending little snot; he'd go out of his way to make me feel like I was stupid and less than. I couldn't figure out for the life of me why he'd engage in conversations with me just to eventually put me down. "This is a crayon," the snot would say to me. "Do you know crayons have lots and lots and lots of colors?" I would answer, "Yes," my mouth tight with anger. "That's very good," he'd condescendingly add. I remember embarrassing him later when Miss Beth asked the class what color does red and yellow make. He raised his hand up and shouted, "Brown!" Miss Beth told him he was incorrect. "Anyone else know the right answer?" I raised my hand and answered, "Orange." I turned to him and smiled, hoping for a smile back. He gave me the nastiest look instead—fucking little snot.

At the end of a nursery-school day, I'd run to the window to watch the outside kids leave and get picked up by their parents. There was a street that ran through the grounds of the Home and divided the girls' dormitory from the boys', and parents would ride up or walk up to get their children, ruffle their hair, kiss them on their cheeks, and squat down with their arms wide open to receive them. I wanted that; it weirdly excited me. Their parents didn't abandon them. Their parents weren't so poor that they were forced to give them to the Church. Their parents weren't mentally ill or dead or just didn't give a fuck and left them there to grow up all emotionally damaged. Although I felt a bit jealous, it brought me hope. Maybe one day that would happen to me and I'd be just like them—casual, at ease. I'd wish that their parents would be my parents and ruffle my hair and squat down with their arms wide open. I'd just stand there trying my best to act as if my conflicting emotions didn't bother me, as if nothing special was happening. As the months went by I began to hate watching, but I couldn't stop.

. . .

Every Sunday was visiting day. All the boys' and girls' parents, grandparents, what have you, would come up on the train from the city—a few by car—to visit their children. I never got a visitor, and neither did Crazy Cindy. It would hurt. Cindy acted as if it didn't bother her in the least. I kept wondering why nothing affected this girl. Was it because she was a little kooky? Or was it because she was stronger than me, since I was a crybaby, like all the other girls accused me of being?

But all was not lost. Oh no. There were some benefits to having no visitors. The first was that most of the nuns were busy making sure that everyone who had visitors was on their best behavior and looked their best, and I mean *everyone*. Most of them supervised the visits as well—which took place either in the cafeteria, the canteen, or on the various playgrounds—weather permitting—which meant that those with no visitors were pretty much forgotten about. Yay! Second, we had the place more or less to ourselves. I was definitely a loner, but not when it came to one-on-one time with Crazy Cindy! She was my best friend. On visiting day, we would hang out together and play, or explore the nooks and crannies of the Home, sometimes with Puerto Rican–Jew Evita Feinstein, although her mother would usually come every Sunday. Evita would always share the candy that her mother brought her with us too. We looked up to her, and her generosity meant a lot.

I liked playing in the bathroom the most because there was an extra radio high up on the shelf. We would crank up the volume on Cousin Brucie's show on WABC, which was never allowed any other time, and when Cindy and I sang it would sound really cool, the echo bouncing off the tiles with just the two of us in there. Sometimes we'd go into the bin closet—a radio was usually always on in there too. We'd act like the groups we were listening to, fighting over who would be Diana Ross in the Supremes or dancing like we were the Temptations—snapping our fingers with the steps, singing our hearts out. Fun! Fun! Fun!

I loved all of Motown and Stax. I liked the Beatles too. Actually, I loved the Beatles. Man, did I get shit for that. Puerto Ricans and blacks weren't supposed to like the Beatles. That meant you were trying to be white. But I didn't care. Plus, I was in love with John Lennon too. And I loved corny songs as well, like Neil Diamond's "Sweet Caroline"—ba, ba, ba—or "Love (Can Make You Happy)" by Mercy. But the first time I heard the Rolling Stones' "Satisfaction" I stopped dead in my tracks. I loved it! I bounced up and down to Keith Richards's guitar riff like a bunny rabbit. Cindy died laughing at me.

We loved to play hide-and-seek too. Well, Crazy Cindy loved to play hide-and-seek. I was afraid of hiding in dark places and was even more afraid of getting caught by the nuns and getting spanked. Although I did my best to avoid spankings, they still happened. So I became even more of a Goody Two-shoes, and my best defense was my sense of humor.

. . .

It was Sunday again, visitors' day, months into my time at Saint Joseph's. Crazy Cindy and I began to discuss what adventures we were going to get into while the other kids spent time with their loved ones. Sister Mary-Domenica came into the dormitory and walked over to my bunk with a nice off-white dress and a pair of brown Mary Jane shoes. She told me to put them on. I had no idea why, but I did.

"You have a visitor today," she said. "Your aunt, Ana, has come to see you."

I stared at her blankly.

"Are you not excited?" she asked.

I couldn't say anything. I was confused. I didn't know I had an aunt. Or at least, I had forgotten. It was probably my mind and soul's attempt to protect me from being hurt any further. It was weird because I could count up to twenty-five by now, knew all of my ABCs and all of the primary colors, but couldn't remember a thing about Tia.

"Do you not remember her? Do you not remember your Aunt Ana?"

I shook my head no.

"Well, of course you do."

I looked back at Crazy Cindy and asked, "She can come too?"

"No. This is your visit, not hers," she replied.

Cindy shrugged and said, "So? I don't care."

"Watch that tone, young lady. Get me the brush so I can brush this bush of hers," Sister Mary-Domenica commanded Cindy.

As Cindy ran off to get the brush, I looked up at the old bag with a deep sigh. I hated getting my hair combed by her. She was so harsh about it, not like the counselors and Sister Ann-Marie. I was what they would call "tender-headed," meaning my head was extremely sensitive, and you had to go very slowly when pulling at my cotton-candy, curly bush. Cindy came back, dragging her feet, handed Sister Mary-Domenica the brush, and leaned against the bunk post. I took a deep breath and squeezed my eyes tightly shut, anticipating the pain. And boy, did it come. With every stroke of the brush, I winced and jerked away, only to have her pull me back. "Keep still, Rosemary!" she barked. Man, oh man, the witch was killing me. It felt like she had pure hate for my frizz, like she was pulling all the Caribbean out of each strand.

"Ouch! It hurts," I whined.

"Of course it hurts," she sternly replied. "With this kind of hair, what do you expect?"

I left with Sister Mary-Domenica, looking back at Crazy Cindy. She looked so sad, so abandoned. I felt like I was betraying her, betraying our little "outsiders" pack. For the first time, I saw Cindy cry.

Sister Mary-Domenica brought me out to one of the smaller courtyards and told me to wait there. It was early fall. The leaves had just started to turn colors. I climbed up on a white iron bench. No one else was there. I turned around to see where Sister Mary-Domenica had gone. She was talking to this light-skinned, plump woman who was holding a large brown paper shopping bag, pointing at me. The woman slowly walked over to me.

"Hello, Rosie. I mean, Rosemary. Do you remember me?"

I shook my head no. I really didn't, but then again she kind of looked familiar. For some reason, I felt threatened. My breathing began to quicken, and I pressed my lips together, trying to prevent them from quivering. I hated being a crybaby, especially in front of this woman, who was looking more and more familiar, but I couldn't put my finger on it.

"May I sit down with you?" she asked softly. I didn't answer her. I couldn't answer her.

She sat down next to me anyway. I inched away.

"You don't remember me?" she asked again. Again, I didn't reply. I shook my head no.

Who was this woman?

"I'm your Tia. Oh, sorry, I mean your aunt, Ana. De nuns told me not to speak Spanish to you. They say you get confused. I brought you some food, your favorite, *arroz y gandules*. Oh, sorry. I mean rice with pigeon peas. And a little birthday cake." She pulled out a small, hard plastic bowl covered with aluminum foil. "I'm sorry I couldn't come for your birthday. I was very sick." She then took out the tiny round cake and began to put four candles in it. "Would you like some?" Again, no response from me. "How about some chocolate? I brought you a 100 Grand candy bar."

She held it out for a minute. I didn't take it. Boy, she was making me pissed and confused. *This woman is my aunt? I don't want her to be my aunt. I can't stand this woman.* She set the candy bar next to me anyway. I wanted it so bad. The only time I had candy was when Puerto Rican–Jew Evita Feinstein shared hers or when Crazy Cindy would give me any leftovers she got after she begged the other girls for candy at the end of visiting day, since I was too proud to beg. But I wanted to get away from this lady. Where were the nuns, who were always up your ass, when you needed them? I held my ground and replied, "No thank you, ma'am. May I go now?" Her eyes flooded with water. With a sad smile, she simply replied, "If you like."

I didn't move. I couldn't move. There was an awkward pause. I wanted to go, but I didn't want to leave either. I didn't want to hurt this nice, plump lady who I hated for no reason.

I looked down at my shoes and started swinging my feet back and forth. "Do you like your shoes?" she asked, looking down at them as well. "I picked them out myself. Your cousin Millie helped pick out de color." This got my attention.

She looked back at me, hopefully, and said, "I sent you de dress you're wearing too. *Espero que te guste. Espero que te guste a todos los robes que si.* [I hope you like it. I hope you like all the dresses I sent you.] You look very pretty in it."

Tears started to roll down my face. She touched my hand—I pulled it back. I felt bad for doing that. I knew I was hurting her, but I couldn't stop myself. She began to cry too, but she never stopped smiling. I looked at her. I saw those big sad eyes, the full lips, and the high cheekbones. I thought to myself, *I know this lady. But who is she?* Why did I recognize her voice when she spoke Spanish?

"I brought you some more birthday presents. This one is one of your favorites," she said with a light smile.

She pulled out a Shirley Temple coloring book and some crayons. Shirley Temple? How did she know I liked Shirley Temple? My heart was exploding; it felt like it was too big for my chest.

"Do you remember Shirley Temple?"

I nodded yes.

"Do you remember when we used to watch her movies together?"

I couldn't move. I did, kind of. I wasn't sure. But I *was* sure. Was this why I hated her? Could she be the one who allowed that lady everyone was calling my mother to take me away? Was she the one who didn't come and save me from this awful place?

We sat there for a while not saying anything to each other. I looked up at the puffy clouds, then at the leaves turning brown on the trees. I watched a leaf fall off its branch and twirl down to the ground. The tension slowly started to erode. I looked back down at my feet. She handed me a box of animal crackers. I took the box and said in a whisper, *"Gracias." Gracias?* Why am I speaking Spanish?

I took out an elephant cracker and bit into it. It was so good. I missed eating animal crackers. I remember eating them at Mommie's house. Wait! Mommie's house? Oh my goodness! Who is she? There was a lump in my throat that felt like a big rock.

Tia started to sing softly, "Animal crackers in my soup. Monkeys and rabbits loop *de* loop. . . ."

I looked up at her. I do remember her! I remember her, and watching Shirley Temple with her. I wanted to tell her that I did, but I was so confused. She looked like my mommie, but she was calling herself Tia, and telling me that she was my aunt.

She continued to sing. Her soothing, out-of-tune voice danced in my head and through the early fall air. My foot started swinging back and forth, this time without tension, but in time with the rhythm of the lyrics. My fear began to subside. I looked back into the box of cookies and pulled out a lion. I quietly joined in between bites.

Animal crackers in my soup. Monkeys and rabbits loop de loop. . . .

Tia laughed with so much joy, with that great cackle. I looked up and smiled. She smiled back and softly said, "I love you, Rosie. You know that? *Te quiero mucho.* I love you very much." I got quiet. I hadn't heard those words—"I love you"—said to me or to anyone at this place since I'd arrived. I looked at the coloring book, then back at her, waiting for an okay. "Sure. It is yours," she replied. I opened the book, grabbed the crayons, and started coloring.

As the days went by I started to put the pieces together. Mommie was Tia, and Lydia was Mommie. Got it. Sort of. Oh my goodness, why? Why did Mommie have to be my aunt, and why did that beautiful, mean lady have to be my mother? Although I kind of wanted her to be my mommie. Or maybe I just wanted to be able to say I had a mommie. Confused? Think how I felt.

The days following the visit were spent vacillating between hating my aunt for not being my mother and missing her and wishing she was my mother and would take me out of this place. I also started fantasizing about the beautiful lady everyone called my mother, wishing she liked me.

The most painful thought that permeated my brain and heart was why neither of them came to get me out of the Home, or at the very least, why neither of them had come to see me sooner on a visiting day. That one visit from Tia made the following Sunday, when she didn't come back, so much harder. I tried to learn from Crazy Cindy how to be nonchalant about it, but it was difficult. Being silly was definitely an option, like having farting contests with Cindy. It sure beat being so depressed and withdrawn.

But eventually Tia did come back. And started to come at least twice, sometimes three times a month. Cousin Millie told me that whether it was raining or sunny, even when there was four feet of snow on the ground, Tia would get up in the wee early hours of the morning while it was still dark out, take the subway to Grand Central Station, and get on the Metro-North train for an hourlong ride to Peekskill. The whole trip took about two and a half hours. My cousins would watch her leave from the window, worried out of their minds. She'd be the first to arrive, she'd stay with me for most of the day, and then she'd get on the six o'clock train back into the city and do it all over again a week or two later.

I'd wait anxiously for Tia in the front office, watching the other kids greet their mother or father with a kiss. I wanted parents to do that with me too. By the time Tia would arrive, I would be sullen and quiet. "Hi, Rosemary. How are you?" Tia would shyly say as she timidly walked over to me. I'd look down at my shoes and say hi. "Why don't you give your Aunt Ana a kiss, Rosemary?" the nuns would always say to me. Tia would tell them it was okay if I didn't want to.

Tia never pressured me to do anything she felt I wasn't comfortable with. She would, however, hold out her hand to me, every visit. At first I wouldn't take it. I'd just follow closely behind or hold on to the side of her dress.

After a while I got used to seeing her, and some of the time I did take her hand. It felt good. We'd sit for the whole visit talking up a storm as I told her silly jokes or about a favorite book I had read. I loved it most when she'd tell me stories of my cousins and our neighbors in Williamsburg. I even got to introduce her to Crazy Cindy. She was doing her usual sneaking around and found me and shyly came over. Tia loved her! That made me feel so good inside. I was falling in love, all over again, with my mom. I mean my aunt.

CHAPTER 6

THANKSGIVING WAS around the corner. I started to get bored in nursery school. It was beginning to get harder for me to remain focused. I'd daydream about Tia, about Marlo Thomas or Elizabeth Montgomery or the Little Rascals, about Williamsburg, hoping to see it again. At naptime I couldn't keep still, and I'd wander off by myself and pick up a book or I'd color or whatever. Miss Connie would take me for walks or just chat with me during class, trying to discover why I was so distracted. Sometimes I would open up to her, but most of the time I didn't. I was wary of her telling on me and the possibility I'd get a spanking from Sister Mary-Domenica.

It was visitors' day again. Tia made sure that I knew she wasn't coming so I wouldn't be too disappointed. I was watching TV with a couple of the girls, sucking my thumb. Sister Ann-Marie came in and excitedly told me to change my clothes, that I had a special visitor. A special visitor? "Who is it?" I asked. She said that my mother was coming to visit me, along with my other brothers and sisters.

Say what? What other brothers and sisters? Did she mean Titi, Millie, Cookie, and Lorraine? And who were the brothers—maybe Tia's cousin Rachel's sons Sixto, who everyone called Junior, or Edgar? And wait a minute, which mother? Was it the woman who everyone told me was my mother? It had to be her. The nuns went out of their way to make sure I knew she was my mother, especially after my first visit with Tia. I wanted to throw up.

I immediately went looking for Crazy Cindy. I found her out in the Group One playground, playing in the mud.

"Cindy!" I screamed. "I got a visit, from my mommie!"

"You lie."

"No, I'm not. Sister Ann-Marie told me. Dag, I wish you could go with me!"

"I'll go!" she answered excitedly.

"No, you'll get in trouble for sure!"

"So I'll sneak in and meet you outside of the main office!"

"Okay!"

Of course I wanted her to go with me. She was my bestest friend, and I was too scared to go it alone. We both rushed into the dormitory and over to my bunk. Sister Mary-Domenica—aka Sister Evilene, as I referred to her in my mind—was waiting impatiently for me. We both stopped dead in our tracks! Her hands went up on her hips when she saw the two of us staring at her like two deer in headlights.

"What's the matter with you two? I know something's up. And where do you think you're going, young lady?"

"I was gonna help Rosie get dressed, sister," Crazy Cindy answered in her beguiling way.

"Yeah, right, missy! Hurry up and get me the hairbrush so I can brush this bush. Then you can help me clean the closet bin instead of wasting your entire Sunday doing only God knows what! How's that for ya, little Miss Smarty Pants!" she barked.

As I started to dress myself I watched Cindy slowly and dejectedly walk away to get the brush. Why were they so cruel? Yes, Crazy Cindy was a fuckup, but innocently and hilariously so. We were freakin' little kids—come on!

Sister Mary-Domenica walked me into the main office and instructed me to wait. I climbed up and sat on one of the chairs, my feet dangling. Another even older-looking nun brought in two girls. I'd seen them around, I thought, in the cafeteria and on the playgrounds. One was skinny and tall, with a dark olive complexion, dark, long, and wavy hair, pretty, and she wore Coke-bottle glasses. The other one was very short with the same kind of hair, just slightly less wavy, and the same skin tone. She looked older than the first one, even though she was shorter and even prettier. And everyone knew her, she was very popular because she was so pretty and funny. "Rosemary, I'd like for you to meet your sisters, Betsy and Terry," said the archaic nun. "Betsy and Terry, this is your youngest sister, Rosemary. They're both in Group One."

My sisters? Wait! Why didn't they tell me that I had siblings here? I thought that was so weird. Imagine how shocked I was to learn that they had been in the Home before me. How long, I really don't know. Gosh, I thought, they are so pretty, and look at all their long, soft, beautiful hair. I betcha they're not tender-headed. Gosh, these are my sisters? They had that Ava Gardner essence. I looked down at my little chubby stomach and put my arms around it in an effort to hide it. They, however, looked, with surprise and envy, at the still fairly new-looking shoes Tia had given me, as if to say, *Who the hell are you and why do you get to wear new shoes?*

"Hi!" I said, like a stupid, overly excited cornball. Ooh, I hope they like me, I hope, I hope, I hope!

Another older girl, who looked around sixteen—tall, same coloring and hair—came in. "Rosemary, this is your other sister, Amy. She's in Group Three," explained the nun. I'd seen her around as well. She was one of the popular girls too. And oh boy, she also was a stunner. With the utmost sincere sweetness, Amy bent down to me and said, "Hi, Rosemary. Nice to meet you." Ooh, I hope, I hope, I hope she likes me too! Then two boys came in, sixteen and fourteen. They looked like the rest of the tribe as well. Man, how many kids did this woman have?

"Mommie!" the three girls screamed out. I turned and saw that pretty, mean lady who'd brought me here. Gosh, she was prettier than all of them. She was so petite too. They greeted her with a kiss, and she returned their kisses with kisses and hugs of her own. Ooh, I hope, I hope, I hope!

"Hello, Rosa," she said, as if she were saying hello to the postman. She held out her cheek toward me. I kissed it. She didn't kiss me back—no hug either. She seemed uncomfortable around me. Oh great, what a great start. Not only were my "sisters" and "brothers" beautiful, but this even more beautiful lady was not excited about seeing me like I'd fantasized she'd be. Really, I had scripted the whole thing in my head as Sister Mary-Domenica walked me to the main office. In my mind, it would be a total Shirley Temple scenario with the happy ending to boot—so much for that. I looked up at the big handsome man standing next to her. Man, he was really handsome. I was told that this was my "stepfather." He gave me a nod and motioned with his head for all of us to head out. Things weren't looking too good. I suppose we went over to the playground or the visitors' room or something. I don't remember. It must not have been good because I blocked it out.

One thing I do remember is that after that Sunday, whenever my mother visited—which was very rarely—with her handsome husband, Ventura, I was ostracized from the family group, and it wasn't just my imagination. I was literally set apart. When we would go to the benches to eat the delicious Puerto Rican food that my mother made, my siblings would all get served, but not me—no lie. I would have to wait for Ventura to nudge Lydia the "okay"—then and only then would she make me a plate. In hindsight, I'm sure that in her crazy head she did that because of the whole "love child" thing—she didn't want him to think that she favored me or showed special treatment to another man's child. But at that time, it made me feel like she had stomped on my face while trying to step over me. I did my best to play it off.

My siblings rarely interacted with me even after the introduction. It was in part because we were separated by dorms. I barely saw the boys. When I'd see the girls—I mean my sisters, not my cousins who used to be my sisters—I couldn't stop staring at them. Betsy would roll her eyes at me each time she caught me staring, then would make fun of my hair or my potbelly or whatever she could pick at. Why? I didn't understand. And Amy, well, I didn't see her much either. She was always sweet, yet distant. Terry had warmed up to me too, kind of. Since we both were natural comedians and loved to act silly, we had a few moments. But I never felt connected to them the way I wanted to be. It was all very detached.

I told Crazy Cindy they were my sisters and made her promise not to tell anyone because I thought my sisters might become angry with me. I don't know why I felt that way, maybe an instinct. She, of course, told Puerto Rican–Jew Evita Feinstein, who told everyone on the goddamn planet. Man, that did not go over well. And I was right, sort of. For some reason, not all of my sisters liked me claiming them as my blood. The word that got back to me was that Betsy was telling everyone I wasn't their "real sister," I was only their "half-sister." Half? Yeah, I understand, now, the biology behind that statement, but how does the heart and soul divide that up when you're under the age of five? Do you half-love them? It hurt like hell, but I began to learn how to suppress those types of feelings, so it was okay—or at least that's what I told myself. Okay, it wasn't okay, and it hurt like a biatch!

CHAPTER 7

IT WAS the first week of December. The leaves had all fallen, and the cold air was brisk. I loved the cold. Everything seemed clean, ready for something new. Each group had its own Christmas tree, and the nuns and counselors let us put tinsel and one ornament each on our tree. I loved it. Thank goodness I was able to enjoy the festivities because I wasn't going on a holiday home visit like some of the other girls or like . . . wait for it . . . my siblings! Yes, they all left to spend the holidays with my "mother." Tia had already warned me that she wasn't going to be able to send for me because my "mother" didn't allow it. I loved Christmas too much, though, for all of that nonsense to bum me out.

One night a couple of weeks before the holiday we all gathered around the TV with Sister Mary-Domenica and Sister Ann-Marie, in our bathrobes and slippers, and watched *A Charlie Brown Christmas*. I loved the Charlie Brown Christmas special. I identified most with Charlie and Linus and was surprised that many saw me as Lucy. The fireplace was glowing; snow was falling outside. We were given cookies with warm milk. I think that was the first time I was somewhat happy at the Home—at least for that moment. It felt like Christmas in a Shirley Temple or Bing Crosby movie.

On the day before Christmas, to my utter surprise, I was told that I was going on a five-day home visit for the holidays. "A home visit! To my mommie's?" Nope. It was to Tia's house. My heart dropped just for a second. Despite the rejection, a kid still wants her mother to want her, you know? But I was excited to go. I still don't know what changed, but I was going!

Tia and her best friend, Doña Ida, came to pick me up. As we rode the Metro-North down to the city, even though I was so happy to be with Tia, I kept wondering if our mother Lydia picked up my "half-siblings" or whether they went it alone, like most of the kids did. I kept wondering what her house looked like. I wondered if she would ever come to like me one day.

Tia, Doña Ida, and I entered into the main hall of Grand Central Station. Wow! The place seemed so big and scary and beautiful. My head was spinning—from the ride, the masses of people, and the architectural grandeur. I don't remember arriving at Tia's. But I do remember that her apartment smelled of yummy food!

At first everything looked and felt foreign to me. I felt lost going from one room to another. Little things would make me close up, especially when I saw the French doors to Tia's bedroom. I just froze and went silent. Tia tried not to freak out over my reactions, acting as if they weren't a big deal, as if I'd never left, as if the fact that I was ripped away from her and sent to a home never happened. She played it as if I had just been away for a brief moment and now I was back. But it didn't work. Her anxiety was too close to the surface.

Like when Millie first saw me, she cried and cried and picked me up, twirling me around. I went silent again. It was too overwhelming. Tia, with a controlled yet panicked command, told Millie to put me down: "No! Don't! De nuns say she don't like to be touched!" Or when my cousins would ask, "Rosie, you wanna play with . . ." "No!" Tia would yell in a whisper. "You have to call her Rosemary now. That's what de nuns say."

What the hell was up with that name? I stomped my foot on that one, demanding they all call me Rosie. It drove me crazy, like Rosie was dead and this "Rosemary" had taken her place. Their whispering about me when they thought I wasn't listening drove me bonkers as well. They would lean into each other and say things like, "I feel so sorry for her," "She looks so sad," "I can't believe Lydia didn't want her to stay at her house for the holidays," etc. Their intention was wonderful but misguided: the "handle with care" treatment came off more like "handle with anxiety." It made me self-conscious and even more aware of the fact that I lived at the Home.

The medium-sized Christmas tree in the living room paled in comparison to the one at the Home and was decorated in the weirdest way. It just had Christmas balls on it—all the same color— and a string of lights. That was it. Tia wasn't big on decor.

Titi and Millie put on "Soul Man." "Come on, Rosie, dance, dance." The pout on my face from my little fit over them calling me "Rosemary" quickly disappeared. Millie grabbed my hands and swayed me to the beat while everyone else formed a little circle, clapping their hands, encouraging me to dance. The ham in me couldn't resist. How could I let a captive audience down? The beat took over my tiny body, and I was gone. I bounced, twirled, bobbed my head, and jumped up and down. My goodness, I was in heaven. What made that day even better was that night Tia had made *arroz y gandules* and *pasteles* (similar to a tamale, made of green plantains instead of cornmeal, and stewed meat, pork, chicken, or seafood in the middle, wrapped in banana leaves): heaven all over. I stuffed my face like a fat little pig until my potbelly swelled even bigger.

Tia took me into the bathroom to bathe me. I immediately tensed up. For the past six months I'd been showering with twelve strangers, feeling humiliated each time. Tia's bathroom was really narrow, making me feel claustrophobic. She began to take off my clothes while I stood next to the porcelain tub. "No!" I said with a paranoid pout.

"What's the matter, *mija*?" Tia asked confusedly.

"I wanna do it . . . please," I replied with my eyes cast down toward the cheap linoleum floor. I felt so bad being so curt and mean to her.

"Okay," she softly said with a warm smile.

She let me undress myself, and I slowly got in the old-fashioned bear-claw tub. Tia sat on the toilet seat. Cookie came in shouting, "Mommie, me and Millie are going to the park. See you later, Rosemary!" I tensed up again. "Don't come back too late!" Tia shouted back as they left. She looked at me and started laughing. "Ay, you look so mad again. No worry. I'll tell them to call you Rosita, 'kay?"

I exhaled a sigh of relief. Tia looked at me, smiled, and said with her thick Spanish accent, "God bless America two times that they left. They drive me crazy." Then she made a silly face. I cracked up. She cracked up with me, both of us cackling in unison. She took the big white bar of soap and gently washed me. It felt good, soothing. I started to play with the soap, letting it slip in and out of my hands.

Tia picked me up out of the bath, wrapped me in a towel, and carried me into her bedroom. Gosh, that felt so good, to be held like that. Nuns never held us, not ever. When I saw the French doors again, a smile began to form at the corner of my mouth. I looked down at the peach bedspread with the little puffy balls as she set me on it. I laid my head down, ran my hands over it, stuck my thumb in my mouth, and drifted off to sleep. I was home, even if I didn't know it. I was home.

. . .

After the third day or so, things started to become more familiar, and I was happy to be there. I still couldn't shake the feeling of being left out, of not being with my mother and my new siblings. But since I had learned to keep my feelings to myself at the Home, I tried not to let on how it was affecting me.

On Saturday my cousins and I gathered around the TV set and watched Stevie Wonder or someone like that lip-synch on *American Bandstand* while Tia went to work, under the table, for the Jews, selling the irregulars from the dress factory door to door throughout the neighborhood. I think she got 20 percent of each sale.

Titi, Millie, and Cookie, with their hair all in big-ass rollers wrapped in a fake silk scarf, got up and tried out the new dances the *Bandstand* dancers were doing. All of them knew how to dance, and they'd criticize all the white people for dancing so corny and would show off how they knew how to do the dances correctly. "Nah, nah, you doin' it wrong. That's not how it goes," Titi, who was the coolest chick on the block, said to Millie. "Lemme show youse. It goes like this," and she would do the steps. "*Perate! Perate!* [Wait! Wait!] *Mira.* [Look.] Ahhh!" answered Millie, who was the jokester, trying to outshine her older sister. "Both of ya'll look stupid," interjected Cookie—who had the best wit—as she did her thing, killing them both. I sat there with a smile on my face watching my sister-cousins dazzle and shine.

Saturday was housecleaning day. A holiday party was happening that night so the house had to be extra clean, which meant it was going to take all day. Since Tia was always working and too tired to tidy up and my cousins were lazy—except Cookie, who was a neat freak—by Friday the house was a cluttered mess. There were always dishes piled up and clothes thrown all over the beds. That was shocking for me to see since the Nazi nuns kept everything spotless and in its place at the Home. Tia and all her kids except Cookie, of course, would take off their street clothes as soon as they came in the door—including Tia's "American Express" (her girdle: she never left home without it . . . get it? I know, corny, but true)—fling them on their beds, and put on a *bata*, also referred to as a *bata de casa*, which literally means "housedress." All *batas* looked pretty much alike—a sleeveless, semi-baby-doll-looking, plain dress, often with a paisley print, that hit at the knee. There was no zipper, but the head opening was large enough that you could just whip it on. Every Latin female has or has had a relative who's worn one.

So, after *Bandstand*, the cleanup started, and it seemed like nothing had changed in the six months that I'd been away. On Saturdays Cookie was always the anal housecleaning sergeant, ordering everyone around with a broom in her hand, a joint—yes, folks, a joint—dangling from her lip, wearing a *bata* or shorts and a tank, with her fake silk scarf wrapped around her big pink-and-blue hair rollers that she wore from when she got up until she went to hang at night. The record player or radio was always blaring, and it had to be her choice of music. If anyone dared to change it, she'd scream at the top of her lungs in her husky, low-octave voice, "Leave iiiittttt!" And it would take her hours to clean because if one of her favorite songs was playing, like "Grazing in the Grass" by the Friends of Distinction, she'd start singing, then dancing, then the other girls would join in, and then she'd take me by the hand and dance with me too. By the time dinnertime came and went, the house would start to be messy again from all the company—the neighbors, friends, family—who'd stop by.

But I digress.

Tia loved company. She loved parties even more, although she'd get stressed out over them. Mostly she hated the cleanup afterwards, but she also hated the preparation, except for the hair and makeup part. For most Nuyoricans, getting ready for a party is just as big of an event as the party itself. I loved watching the girls put on their makeup. Titi used the most, at least twenty or so strokes of mascara—no lie. The amount of mascara and black eye liner that was used in just our house was not to be believed. However, being Puerto Rican, the hair took precedence—it was all about the hair, first and foremost. Right after breakfast everyone started the ritual of shampooing, conditioning, and roller-setting.

Everyone would wash their hair with either Lustre Cream or

Prell shampoo. I forget what kind of conditioner we used, but we used *a lot*. Since we were so freaking poor, we used Vaseline Intensive Care Lotion as a leave-in. (Yes, we were ahead of our time with the leave-in shit.) Miss Cool setting lotion was applied afterwards, and then the hair was rolled up real tight with those big-ass plastic hair rollers and bobby pins. It was a hilarious sight, the three girls and Tia, all in big-ass hair rollers, cleaning and cooking up a storm. My hair was done last just in case I messed it up before the company came. Millie usually did my hair. Dippity-Do was gently applied to my cotton candy and produced two pigtails with the smoothest looped curls.

Sorry, digressed again—conversations over hair will do that to me.

That night the house was packed. Everyone was dressed up. I had on a blue velvet dress with a white ribbon wrapped around it, just below my chest, white laced bobby socks, and black patent leather Mary Janes. The salsa music was flowing. Boogaloo was still in fashion, but the latest sound was jazz salsa; Willie Colón, Héctor Lavoe, Eddie Palmieri, and all the new Fania All-Stars took precedence. Tia loved to dance salsa. She was so cute when she did. I loved it when she'd take my two hands and partner with me. The best part was when we'd break and do our little solos. I tried my very best to do it just like her.

While I was enjoying the party, dancing in my little frock, I felt a tug at my blue velvet dress with the white ribbon wrapped around it. I turned and saw Tio Ismael clapping and smiling with a glassy look in his eyes. I recognized him instantly! I remember that he had on such a nice suit too. He was sitting in Tia's blue wingback sofa chair with a glass of Harvey's Bristol Cream on the rocks. "Psst. Psst. Rosamarie. Come over here," he said in a drunken whisper. "Please. Come here. One minute." I slowly and cautiously walked toward him. *Oh God,* I thought. *I hope and pray this man doesn't start crying again.*

He grabbed me close. "Rosa. I mean, Rosemary. Rosemary, right?" he clumsily slurred. "I'm your daddy."

There was an awkward pause. My face tensed up into a stern frown. "I'm your daddy. Me. Tio Ismael. Okay? I daddy. Okay. Me. I'm your daddy," he kept saying over and over. I shook my head no. I couldn't stop. I kept shaking it no over and over again each time he repeated those words. I couldn't speak. This man isn't my father. I hate him. I hate him so much.

"It's true, Rosie. I am."

No! No, you're not. Oh no. I knew it to be true. Why? I don't know. I just knew it to be true. I didn't want it to be true. Why? I didn't know. I don't know!

"No! I hate you!" I finally shouted and ran to Tia, crying, burying my face into her dress.

"*¿Pero que paso?* [But what happened?]" she asked me.

"*Yo le dije, yo le dije* [I told her, I told her]," my uncle-father loudly declared. "*Es verdad.* [It's the truth.] *Tu ya sabes.* [You know it.] *Todo el mundo sabe!* [Everyone knows!]"

A few of the party guests who were dancing nearby stopped.

"*Callate, studipo* [Shut up, stupid]. *Por que esta haciendo esto?* [Why are you doing this?]" Tia said. "You're drunk." She turned to everyone. "He's drunk. Pay him no mind. Don't cry, *mija* [my daughter]. He's stupid. It's not true. He's so stupid. Tell her, Ismael! Tell her, please!"

My father looked dead at me and smiled. "I'm your daddy." Tia ran over and started to hit him.

"Okay. Okay. I'm sorry. I was kidding. I'm Tio. Okay. Sorry."

Tia's friends pulled her back. She scooped me up in her arms and carried me into her bedroom through the French doors. As she was carrying me, I turned my head back and looked at him, giving him an angry, pissed-off look. He looked up at me, smiled through his drunken tears, and mouthed, *I'm your daddy. I love you.*

. . .

Millie told me that after that first Christmas back home, Tia went on a mission to try to get custody of me. But Child Welfare Services told her that the "mother" or "father" (meaning my mother's husband—my dad was not recognized on the birth certificate), along with the Catholic Church and the state of New York, were the only ones who had any say over me.

Tia was friends with Lydia's older sister—the one Lydia stole her date from, but didn't know Lydia as well. (She did however know of my mother's infamous temper.) Tia began to make an effort to become friends with her. She felt if my mother liked and trusted her, she would have a better chance at getting custody of me. So, after that Christmas, Tia would often take my cousins over to my mother's house for a Saturday afternoon visit and make small talk over coffee while her kids played with my half-siblings—yes, they were there on many a visit without me.

After several Saturday social calls, Tia told me that she waited awhile, after she and Lydia had drunk their Café Bustelo, then casually brought me up.

". . . And she was acting out all the commercials in *de* television. Ga, ga, ga, ga, gaaaa! She was so funny. She was—"

Tia stopped in the middle of her story. The look my mother had on her face as she slowly nodded her head up and down made Tia very uncomfortable. She knew that look. It was suspicious in nature. It was hard to pull anything over Lydia.

"So, anyway, thank you so much for letting me take Rosie . . . to my house, I mean."

Awkward pause.

"*Tu sabes, yo puedo ayudar si lo desea.* She can stay at my house instead of the Home. . . . So you don't have to worry about Durin [Ventura, Lydia's husband]. And you can see her anytime you like, and I can bring her here anytime you like or whatever you want. So it could help to make it easier for you and Rosie."

Lydia slightly cocked her head back with an indignant, per-plexed look on her face.

" 'Anytime I like'?"

"Yes, of course, Lydia."

"Oh! So . . . you are telling me what I can do? Because you said, 'Anytime "you" like,' as if you were giving me permission to de-cide what I can do with my daughter."

"No, no, no. Please. Lydia. I didn't—"

"Because it just sounded like you were giving me permission."

"No. I would never. Please forgive me. You are her mother and I am not."

"I know I am her mother. You don't have to tell me that," Lydia austerely stated.

"Yes, you are. You are right, Lydia."

"I know I am right. Why would you assume that I wouldn't know that I'm right? You think I'm stupid, ignorant? You think I don't know I am her mother?"

"No, Lydia. Please, I am *de* ignorant one. Please. *Lo siento.* [I'm sorry.]"

After an even longer, excruciating, awkward-ass pause, my aunt got up to leave.

"*Ay, me voy.* I have to go. Please tell my girls to come home before dinner."

My mother walked Tia to the door.

"Minguita, let me ask you a question. So . . . you think Rosie doesn't belong in the Home, but my other kids do?"

"Whaa? Oh no, I didn't mean it like that. I—"

"Oh, okay. You didn't mean it like that. I see. (*pause*) Because it sounded like you wanted me to leave all of my other kids there and just let Rosie go. So it could be 'easier' for her."

"No, I—"

"You think that's fair?"

"No, I—"

"Then why did you say it?"

"I didn't, I—"

"Ah, but you did. You said—"

"Lydia, please."

"YES! You said you wanted me to leave all of them there and let Rosie go! Because *you* said that it would make it 'easier for Rosie.' Did you not say that?!"

Tia knew that when Lydia started repeating herself it was time to go. My mother could be like Robert De Niro's portrayal of Jake LaMotta in *Raging Bull*, with his neurotic, ranting fits of jealousy. I think the paranoia hit hard because of the guilt Lydia felt over placing all of her kids in the Home. Why did she do so? Well, the social workers told us she was too poor to have all of us. And that's why she kept having more kids, of course—right. I know, horrible for me to say, but true.

The whole walk home, Tia worked hard to shake off the oppressive sense of intimidation that Lydia had pressed upon her. She knew she had to find another way to get me out.

CHAPTER 8

IT WAS a new spring. I was five now and still in Baby Girls. Diana Ross and the Supremes' hit "Love Child" and the Rolling Stones' "Honky Tonk Woman"—which we were not allowed to sing (in front of the nuns)—sang through the crisp, sunshiny air. And my disposition was just as sunshiny . . . and very complicated. I was known to be the first to greet you with morning cheer, and yet I had my moody moments for sure. I was beginning to develop a short temper as well as greater shyness.

I began to fall into the routine of the Home and started to like it. "Like"? I don't know if that's the correct word. Perhaps it's more accurate to say I became "habituated" to it. The strict structure and repetitive routine offered a strange, if false, sense of security: it gave me less free time to think about my reality. Get up, line up, shower up, line up, pray, eat, line up, do chores, pray, eat lunch, line up, go to school, line up, eat a snack, line up, play, line up, clean up, line up, pray, eat, line up, shower . . . and then . . . *TV time!*

> *Oh, TV time!*
> *La, la, la, la, la, la, la,*
> *TV time!*

Yes, I made up my own "TV Time" theme song (sounding suspiciously like the song "Hooray for Hollywood"). And there was a little jig to go along with it, of course. We saw so many movies too—classic Hollywood love stories, dramas like *It's a Wonderful Life,* sometimes film noirs that had a moral ending (duh), comedies, and musicals. Oh, how warm and fuzzy TV time seemed: the lights dimmed, all us little girls in our bathrobes and slippers gathered around the wood-encased television set while the nuns sat in their rocking chairs knitting or reading their Bibles. I'd always be wishing this magical time could be played out in a real home instead of "the Home."

I loved being silly, especially with our group's counselors. I felt more comfortable with a few grown-ups as opposed to a group of kids. We were always in a damn group, and I needed something different. One counselor taught me how to flare my nostrils in and out and curl my tongue. It brought me hours of joy. I would go up to an adult or a nun and flex my nose back and forth continuously.

"What are you doing, Rosemary?"

"Nothing, Sister Mary-Domenica" (nostril flare, nostril flare). Why are you asking?"

I would teach all that I had learned to Crazy Cindy whenever I saw her. She had already moved up to Group One, so I didn't get to spend as much time with her as I used to. I missed her a great deal, too. I especially missed how we would talk to each other in hushed whispers after lights out until one of us fell asleep. At least I got to see her outside on the playgrounds, even though she had a new group of friends from her new dorm. Sure, we were still friends and played together whenever I saw her, but now I didn't have her undivided attention. That was okay, sort of.

We didn't have Hot Wheels or Barbies (I never got into dolls anyway), but we had an Olympic-sized pool and a few toys, chalk for a homemade skelly court, jump ropes, old cans for Kick the Can, Spaldeens for handball, a basketball, and my favorite, baseball—with a real baseball field on the grounds! I don't know if it was the Puerto Rican in me, but I took to the sport like crazy. And a team sport was good for me. It forced me to interact with the other kids and learn to socialize better. But I could as easily entertain myself making blueberry mud pies—especially when Crazy Cindy was with her new group of friends. I would pack the mud in a circle, slice it in eight, and then roll tiny pebbles in the mud and place them on top to be blueberries—genius, right? I know, I can't stand it either—ha!

My favorite place was the music room, where they had a piano and a music teacher who taught us all types of Christian songs and silly secular songs. We even had dance lessons! I learned tap because they told me that my legs were too short and stubby for ballet (I know, sad, but funny). I loved tap, and I was good at it. I discovered that I had a natural sense of rhythm, which gave me a lot of joy. I loved rehearsals even more—nerd. At bedtime all I could think about was whatever routine we were practicing. I'd tap out the steps in my head until I fell asleep.

. . .

It was a few weeks before Easter, and the Home was putting on a show in the auditorium. Several of the boys' and girls' dormitories were selected to present a specific number. The Baby Girls' dormitory was selected to do a tap dance to "The Candy Man," and I was picked for the front line!

Easter Day finally came, and I was ready! The stage looked like a cheaper version of a Busby Berkeley set. Now, "cheaper" didn't mean tacky—oh no, far from it. This was a Catholic production, and you know how good those folks are at putting on a show. All the girls were getting their costumes on, bragging about their parents coming to see the show. I knew my mother wasn't coming, but I was hoping that maybe Tia would show up, even though I knew she wouldn't. The nuns had told me that she was taking my cousins to church but would see me the following weekend.

One of the counselors pulled me over to do my hair. God bless America two times it wasn't torture queen Sister Mary-Domenica.

"Please make two pigtails with curls . . . like this," I asked, twirling my hand around in a spiral.

"Your hair won't do that," the counselor remarked.

"Yes, it will. You have to use Dippity-Do and twirl it around your finger . . . like this," I precociously instructed.

"Dippity-Do," she said with a laugh. "I'll just twist it in two and braid it on the ends to secure it."

"Ah, for the love of Pete," I said, kicking my heel against the chair, "it's not gonna stay!"

I was so annoyed.

The audience was in their seats. A bunch of the girls peeked out of the stage curtain to see if they could spot their parents. "Ooh!" screamed one of the girls. "There's my mother!" My heart sank a bit, but I played it off as I stood back while the rest of the girls peeked through the curtains with her.

The music began. We entered the stage, tapping our hearts out. I was so nervous, but I was having so much fun and I was on fire! The whole group was killing it!

Who can take a sunrise (tap 2-3-4)

Sprinkle it with dew (tap 6-7, hand circles) . . .
. . . *The Candy Man* . . . (tap, tap, tappity-tap!)

Then disaster struck. My left pigtail came undone right in the middle of the number! I was mortified! I kept tapping, with my hands in position on my hips, flinging my head back, thinking it would whip my hair back into a curl, which did nothing at all but make it unravel more and begin to frizz! Goodness sakes! I told that stupid counselor this would happen! I started to cry, like annoyingly loud, with my feet still tapping, arms still swinging up and down to the music, not missing a beat.

I looked down at the front row. A few kids were pointing at me, sneering and jeering at my fit. I then looked to my right—Sister Mary-Domenica was trying to catch my attention, waving me off of the stage. "Psst! Rosemary! Rosemary! Come over here! Right now!" She looked pissed! Her face was bright red. I ignored her. I had to. I'd watched way too many musicals and knew that the show must go on—and it did, in perfect form!

Great applause came from the audience—of course! Yay! Applause makes everything better, right? I sniffled back my tears and joyfully took my bow with the group. When we walked off the stage, Sister Mary-Domenica was waiting for me in the wings with steam coming out of her ears. She looked so funny that I almost laughed. I tried to avoid her by slipping off stage left, but she grabbed me by my costume, screaming and wagging her finger in my face. I couldn't tell you what the hell she said. I was concentrating on the parents rushing up to the side of the stage, hugging and congratulating their kids. I shrugged off the feeling of being left out and Sister Mary-Domenica's tirade and made my way to the little after-party that the nuns had put together.

I walked into the canteen room where the party was held. Ooh! There were frosted cupcakes and watered-down Kool-Aid! I *loved* sweets—things were really looking up now! I grabbed a chocolate cupcake and a cup of the fake juice. Norman Greenbaum's "Spirit in the Sky" was playing on the radio up on a shelf. The young Catholic counselors loved this one for sure. "Set me up in the spirit in the sky . . . when I die and they lay me to rest, I'm gonna go to the place that's the best. . . ." One of the girls in our dance class invited me to join her and her mother. I felt too proud to accept and politely declined, but watched her with her mother from afar. The discomfort was similar to what I had felt during my mother's visit, except in reverse. The girl was completely detached while her mother was at a loss, trying to make a connection. It made me think of how Tia was with me when she first came to visit. My good cheer started to fade. Where was Crazy Cindy? She always made me feel better. I looked across the room and saw her with her mother, her brother, and I think her older sister! They never came to visit! She caught my eye and waved me over. On the way, Sister Ann-Marie stopped me.

"You did so good, Rosemary," she said, bending down to speak face to face to me. "You're quite a dancer! What's wrong?"

"Oh nothing. Everything's just swell," I answered with as much sarcasm as a kid could muster.

"I think I know what's wrong. Well, all I have to say is that you kept going. And that's the most important thing. You didn't give up, 'cause that's who you are. And I know next time you'll be even better onstage, because you're a natural talent!"

Her words made me feel wonderful, important, and strong. I know it sounds weird for a five-year-old to feel that way, but it's true. It took a minute for the smile I was feeling inside to appear.

"Thank you, Sister Ann-Marie. Thank you very much."

I still remember that moment to this day—that bit of kindness and acknowledgment. I joined Crazy Cindy and her family. They were intense, to say the least—it explained a lot. Cindy and I got some pastel-colored cupcakes and Kool-Aid, went to sit outside in the sun, and enjoyed the rest of our Easter Sunday—just the two of us.

. . .

I began to ease into a few more friendships since Crazy Cindy was in Group One now.

One weekend, as I was outside showing some of the girls my Jackson 5 moves, I was told that I had to come inside.

Mrs. Vasquez greeted me at the doorway of the Baby Girls' dorm. Mrs. Vasquez, the Home's official social worker, was a short, curvy woman who was in charge of parent-child relationships, foster care, and adoptions. She was always in a tight-fitting outfit.

You could hear her coming a mile away by the sound of her big fat thunder thighs rubbing together. I didn't remember her face at first from when my mother first left me at the Home.

All five of my half-siblings were already there. I quietly entered and waved hello to Amy and Terry. Both of them were nice, waved back, and said, "Hello!" Yay! I didn't wave hello to Betsy. I just gave her a sheepish smile, since she was the one who had told the whole Home that I was their "half-sister," not their real sister. She smiled back, then made fun of my hair—jeez. I never really caught my brothers' names, so I just offered them a slight grin.

Lydia was sitting in front of a small table with a small boy on her lap, maybe three or four, I don't remember exactly. He had dark shiny straight hair, deep dimples, sharp Native American features, and the whitest skin—very different from me and even my other siblings with their dark olive tone and soft wavy hair. We all greeted our mother with a kiss. And then my brothers and sisters began to play with the tiny tot as if they knew him already.

"Say hello to your little brother, Rosie," said my mother.

My little brother—another one?! And they all know him, obviously, and I don't? Weird thing, it didn't hurt. It just annoyed me— pissed me off.

"So," said Mrs. Vasquez, "we wanted to let you know that your little brother Johnny will be staying here at Saint Joseph's with you all. Your mother, with her new baby girl, can't take care of him, and I know you guys will look out for him and make him feel welcome."

Wait! Did she say, "her new baby girl" too? Jeez Louise! Did she ever hear of birth control?

I don't think I said much. I went back outside before everyone else left. I felt like I was going to explode, but on the outside I looked blasé and unaffected.

I walked all the way to the girls' playground by myself. (Being in Baby Girls, I wasn't allowed to venture off by myself without permission—very bold move.) I looked around for Cindy but she wasn't anywhere to be found. A bunch of girls from Groups One and Two were dancing in two lines, imitating the Jackson 5's routine to their hit single "I Want You Back." Man, did I love the Jackson 5! Gosh, I wanted to join in so bad! I stood there, jumping up and down in my skin, watching the routine as the count danced out in my head. Since the tap lessons, I'd felt and seen music differently, even though I wasn't fully aware of it. My moodiness began to melt.

I began to dance, trying to keep up with the older girls, but my shyness kept making me stop each time one of them looked back at me. Then my sister Terry came over. "Hey! Look at my sister dancing!" *Sister?* She called me her sister! And she didn't say "half"! Yay!

Terry was the one sibling that really warmed up to me. Like I've said, we began to click somewhat since we were both very silly, but she had never witnessed my Jackson 5 skills!

Terry walked up to the front line and started to groove. Man, she was a natural. She had such style and an agility that professional dancers would sell their souls for. She just floated on top of the rhythm! I moved over behind her and imitated each nuance to her steps. She turned and looked at me. Oh shoot! I stopped dancing. "Why'd you stop? Come on!" She waved me over. We stood side by side and started dancing together. She smiled at me. I smiled back. Holy freakin' cool-ass moment! I'm dancing with my sister! It was the first time I felt a bond with one of my mother's kids. It was so great that my dancing skills—that were no match for hers—is what sealed it between us! I remember feeling a part of the clan just for that second. I remember bragging to myself thinking, *Yeah, this is my sister. I'm a Perez, too!* Dork.

CHAPTER 9

I WAS to spend the entire summer with Tia! I'm not sure if this one was my first full summer vacation visit to Tia's house, but I do remember that after a while it seemed normal—this was my life, going back and forth, living between two very different worlds. And I remember the heat on that particular vacation. If you just blinked, you would pour down sweat. And the subway ride from Grand Central was beyond suffocating. All those hot, smelly, sticky bodies trapped, pressed up against each other, were stifling. By the time Tia and I made it to Williamsburg, my body was limp from dehydration, and worst of all, my hair looked ridiculous.

Millie told me that when I walked in with Tia and she and Cookie saw the state of my cotton-candied mess plastered to my big-ass forehead, I was sent to the "beauty parlor," aka the kitchen sink, quick fast, for an emergency makeover. The cold water on my head was heaven. Cookie made two cute curly pigtails slicked into form with good ol' Dippity-Do. Millie and Cookie, with their wet sets wrapped in their scarves, went outside to hang out on the stoop. It was too hot for me, plus I wanted to stay close to Tia and watch TV with her. Hair done, television on, Tia by my side as I sucked my thumb—bliss. That was all it took for me to feel like I was back in the flow of life in Brooklyn.

. . .

Saturday midmornings was when Don Felipe, the milkman, and Don Cache, the credit man, would come by. Everyone bought from Don Cache. He offered the best items with only 5 percent down and the lowest interest rate. Whatever you needed, he had it: furniture, kitchen appliances, clocks, etc.

Don Felipe was really nice and funny, and I would always wait for him to come up the stairs with the glass milk bottles clanking against each other. I was his little helper, exchanging ours and the neighbor's empty bottles of milk for new ones. Don Cache was a different story. He was haughty, always in a pretentious business suit and hat and well manicured. Since most people were always late on collection day, a lot of our neighbors would always hide from Don Cache or play sick or do anything to avoid paying him. Tia was different. She would always let him in and make coffee, small chitchat. And she was always on time with the payments.

But this one weekend she wasn't. She had purchased a new stove on credit—the old one was falling apart—and she was late on a payment because she had put some clothes for us on layaway from Dumsy's thrift shop on Kent Avenue. Millie, Cookie, and little Lorraine were watching television. Titi was hanging outside of the window talking to some fine-ass light-skinned boy who was leaning against a car. I was with Tia, helping her cook the early supper. She was moving around really fast, which was weird because she usually took her time when she cooked on the weekends.

During the week, since Tia had various jobs, working at three different factories in Bushwick, she rarely prepared dinner. Doña Ida would cook for us, or Tia would bring home Chicken Delight ("Don't cook tonight, call Chicken Delight"), the only fast food in the neighborhood at the time. But when the weekend came, she threw down. She would be at it the entire afternoon, and I would be right by her side, helping her wash the rice and the beans.

Titi saw Don Cache walking up to the building and her mouth

dropped. Before she could duck back inside, he saw her, tipping his fedora hat with a smile. She faintly smiled back and ducked inside.

"Mommie! It's Don Cache! He's coming up!"

"Whaaaaa?! *Ay Dios mio!* Hide—hide! Everyone hiiiddde!" screamed Tia.

"No, Mommie! He already saw me!"

"*Ay,* my fucking goodness! Dammit to hell! Everyone, *seet*! Rosie! Come here," my aunt yelled, looking panicked as shit. "Answer *de* door. Tell Don Cache that I'm not here. Okay? I want you to tell him that I am not here! Everyone *seet*! *Act normal!*"

Millie, Cookie, and Titi quickly sat on the sofa, placing Lorraine on the floor in front of the TV, forcing a relaxed tone to their posture—as if it were routine. I stood in the middle of the room completely baffled. No one had explained to me what was going on.

Tia grabbed me by the hand and quickly walked me over to the door. "Remember, when you answer *de* door, I want you to say to Don Cache that I'm not here! Okay?" I nodded obediently.

Knock, knock, knock.

"Oh damn it to hell!" Tia loudly whispered as she quickly squatted down in the corner behind the door. "Rosie! Open! Open!"

I opened the door.

"*Hola, Rosita. Como tu ta?* [How are you?]" said Don Cache, tipping his fedora.

"*Bien, gracias, Don Cache. Y tu?*"

"*Bien, bien. ¿Y tu mama? ¿Esta aqui?* [Good, good. And your mommie? Is she here?]"

"Yes! And she wanted me to tell you that she is not here!" I proudly stated.

A huge gasp was heard from the girls over on the couch. I turned my head around toward them like, *What?*

"*Oh, si? ¿A donde?* [Where is she?]" he asked.

"Behind the door, right there," I answered, pointing at Tia.

Don Cache slowly pushed the door open until he felt it hit my aunt's plump-sized body. He peered his head around and saw Tia scrunched down, looking up at him. The look on her face was priceless and so funny that I quickly covered the giggle that was bursting out of my mouth.

"Oh, hello," she said with a wilted, humiliated smile. "*Ay*, my knee. I'm so fat. Would you please help me?"

Don Cache helped her up. Tia was still smiling through her embarrassment. I had never seen her look like that, and it frightened me. This wasn't funny anymore. Oh no! What did I do?!

"*¿Queires café?* [Want a coffee?]" offered Tia.

She didn't wait for a response and quickly went into motion, making a fresh batch of Café Bustelo. Don Cache turned and looked at my cousins, who were still frozen on the couch, then back at Tia, who was nervously dropping shit left and right. He shook his head and slightly chuckled to himself in disbelief. "*Me voy.* I'm sorry, but I have to leave. I'll come and get the money next weekend. I hope you don't mind." He smiled at me, patted me on the head, tipped his hat, and left.

As soon as the door closed behind him, Tia fell to her knees and died laughing: "Ga, ga, ga, ga, gaaaaaaa!" My cousins started laughing with her. "*Ay*, my goodness. Did you see my face when he saw me in *de* fucking corner?" she screamed. "*Ay*, I wanted to die! God bless America two times he didn't take *de* stove!" She then looked at me, saw my worried face, and called me to her. "*Ay*, come here, Rosita. Come."

I slowly walked over to her, scared, wondering if she was going to beat me like the nuns always did. She pulled me toward her and hugged the shit out of me, shoving me into her big, fat, watery breasts as they jiggled up and down with laughter. She didn't hit me. She didn't punish me. She didn't humiliate me. She just laughed and hugged me. Figure that.

· · ·

It was the second weekend of the summer visit. I was still at Tia's. The afternoon was hot and muggy. Tia was in the kitchen making an early supper of *chuletas, arroz blanco, y habichuelas rojas* (pan-fried pork chops, white rice, and red beans). The aroma of the fried pork and sweltering heat was insane.

I was taking a nap on Tia's bed in my panties and undershirt, covered in baby powder from my neck down to my toes to help cool off from the heat. (Baby powder is poor people's air conditioning.) Cousin Lorraine was in her playpen napping as well, and the others were who knows where. (Tia was like that: she always trusted her girls and gave them a lot of freedom to hang.)

Tia came into the bedroom holding a brand-new soft, butter-colored summer frock. She slowly rubbed my back. "Rosie. Look. You like?" Loved! I quickly put it on. Just then, my uncle-father knocked on the French doors to Tia's bedroom. My face dropped. I had not seen my uncle-father, who was still my uncle, in a while, and I still hadn't gotten over the "I'm your daddy" fiasco. He was wearing his army jacket and tight, tapered khaki slacks. Back then, he used to always wear tight-ass pants, so tight that Tia used to call him *huevos apretados*—which means "tight nuts"—behind his back.

"Wow," he said. "You look so beautiful, baby! You ready to go?"

Huh? I froze. I looked up at Tia. Her eyeballs were throwing daggers at him. I scurried across the bed to her, burying my face into her big breasts.

"You came early," she loudly whispered with her thick-ass accent. "*Yo no tuve tiempo de decirle!* [I didn't have time to tell her!]"

"*Oh, lo siento.* [I'm sorry.] I was too excited."

"Rosie, you remember my brother, your Uncle Ismael?"

Duh! Of course I remembered. I didn't respond. I just gave him a stern look.

He then turned to me and handed me a five-dollar bill. Who the hell gives a four-year-old five dollars?

"We can go and buy bread for the pigeons. And I'll buy you a coconut soda!"

"A coconut soda?" I said. "Whoever heard of a coconut soda?"

"How 'bout ice cream? Would you like an ice cream?" he pleaded.

What else was I going to say to ice cream?

While Tia quickly changed out of her *bata*, I peeked past the French doors at my uncle-father seated in that same wingback chair where he'd been sitting when he informed me in an intoxicated whisper that he was my dad. I wanted to look away, but couldn't stop staring at him.

It was about a seven-block walk to Woolworth's department store. We first stopped by the building next door, where Tia's friend Doña Susana was hanging out of her window with her humongous titties surgically attached to the windowsill. Of course I had to break out in song and a little tap dance in homage to her name: *"Ooooh! Hola, Susanna, oh don't you cry for meeee!"* My uncle-father looked at me and cracked up, slapping his knee. For some reason it bothered me, and I stopped dancing.

Next, we headed over to Katz's pharmacy on Broadway—more hellos and a pat on my head and a gumball from Mr. and Mrs. Katz, a sweet, talkative couple who adored Tia, although Ismael monopolized the conversation. Mr. Katz made me laugh as he kept repeating to his wife, "What does that have to do with the price of eggs?" each time she would contradict him or my uncle-father.

Next stop was the corner store, owned by Don Quintin (pronounced *keen-deen*) and his brother, Don Àngel. These two brothers were inseparable. Don Quintin died several years later after going to a cheap dentist; his brother Don Àngel died three months afterwards, everyone says from loneliness. As we exited the bodega, a beautiful curvy woman with a bad blond dye job came around the corner. My uncle-father's head spun around like Linda Blair's head in *The Exorcist*. He dramatically gasped, with his hand on his heart.

"*Perdone me, senorita. Lo siento, pero.* May I please have the pleasure, no, the honor, to have you dine with me tonight, or tomorrow, or the next night? I would wait until eternity to be in the presence of a beauty such as yours."

He took her hand and kissed it, just like Pepe Le Pew in the Looney Tunes cartoon. I kid you not! She declined with an annoying giggle. Before she could escape, he quickly stepped in front of her and said, "I know you must be thinking, *How could I go out with such an ugly man?* Well, I may be ugly, but I make beautiful babies!"

Hold up! Is this man trying to use me to pick up a bimbo? Oh, hell no.

As the bouncy blonde laughed and sashayed away, my aunt slapped my uncle-father upside his head so hard that he stumbled forward. "You are so stupid!" Tia screamed. "I swear to God and *de* entire fucking universe!"

Inside Woolworth's, against the side wall, was a long counter with a deli/soda fountain/ice cream parlor behind it. I jumped on the bolted-down swivel stool with a leather cover on top.

"What you like? A cone? *¿Frijol de vainilla?* [Vanilla bean?]" asked my uncle-father.

What the heck did he say? I think he said, "vanilla." I shrugged my shoulders; I was too embarrassed that I didn't understand it all. The nuns were winning in canceling out my memory of the Spanish language. I looked over at Tia. She came to the rescue. "She likes chocolate. You want a chocolate, *mija*?" I shrugged my shoulders again, then quietly answered, "May I have a hot fudge sundae with chocolate ice cream and chocolate sprinkles instead?" Tia laughed. I giggled back. My uncle-father smiled with us in a sad kind of way, feeling ostracized from Tia's bond with me.

Tia ordered a coffee, no sugar. My uncle-father ordered a Tab. They both were beginning to take their diabetes seriously. He sat there watching me eat every bit of my sundae. Talk about feeling uncomfortable. Then he asked me if I would like to go to Puerto Rico with him someday. I shrugged my shoulders. I didn't know anything about Puerto Rico. I looked back at Tia again. This time her eyeballs were shooting evil darts at him. He didn't say shit after that. We sat in silence for a while. The tension was thick. Of course I had to relieve it with a joke.

"Tia. Knock, knock!"

They both just looked at me, completely baffled, like I was crazy.

"Whaa? Why you say you knocking?"

I started laughing.

"It's a joke, Tia. You have to say, 'Who is it?' "

"Oh! Okay. Who's there?"

"No," I cracked up. "Not 'Who's there?' You have to say, 'Who is it?'!"

"Oh! Okay. Sorry. Who is it?"

"Banana."

"A banana? A banana's knocking?"

"Tia! You're suppose to say, 'Banana who?'!"

"Oh! Okay. Banana who?"

"Knock, knock!"

"*Ay*, this is stupid!"

I was on the floor with laughter. It took me at least ten minutes to finish the damn joke! Then my uncle-father called over the guy behind the counter.

"Excuse me, sir. May I please have a coffee?"

"How would you like that, sir?" asked the waiter.

"Wet, please! Get it?" he continued. " 'Wet'! Get it?"

Complete silence—tumbleweeds blew through the department store. Tia then rolled her eyes. The waiter shook his head and walked away. I went back to digging at my sundae.

When we got back, my uncle-father was standing at the front door, not sure if he should come in or leave. I felt sad for him. I should have made him feel more at ease, but I just couldn't. "Thank you very much for the ice cream sundae, Tio."

"*De nada*, baby. And I'm glad you like the dress," he said, and then left.

I looked down at my butter-colored frock, then at Tia. I ran down the hallway and ripped it off.

Later that night Tia, Lorraine, and I were watching *The Iris Chacon* (pronounced *Eee-dee-ss Cha-cone*) *Show*, a Latin variety show broadcast from Puerto Rico. Her nickname was La Bomba de Puerto Rico (The Puerto Rican Bombshell). Iris was voluptuous, pretty, and had the biggest ass you ever saw in your life. She could barely dance and barely sing (and if she did sing, she would lip-synch—badly). And yet, she was charismatic and entertaining as hell.

"Where's Puerto Rico?" I asked.

"Puerto Rico? In the Caribbean! That's where I was born. *Yo soy Boricua*."

"Bo-wing-wa?"

"Bo-rrrring, Rrring-kwa, kwa."

"Bowwwwingkwa?"

"Close enough. Puerto Rico used to be called Borinquen before Spain took it. I used to take you with me when you were just a little baby. You were so funny, crying, sticking your hands down your diaper to take *de* sand out! You hated sand. Ga, ga, ga, ga, gaaaa!"

"Can we go to Puerto Rico?" I gleefully screamed.

"Oh . . . I don't know. I would have to get permission from *de* Home and your mother, Lydia. I have to start to make dinner."

Her whole mood changed.

I pulled a chair up to the sink and helped wash the rice as Tia began to season the chicken with Adobo (a Spanish seasoning salt that we use for everything!).

My father came by the next day, and the next, and almost every other day afterwards for the rest of the summer. I started to look forward to our "dates." In fact, I started to go it alone, without the shield of Tia. I even started to laugh at his corny jokes and smile on cue whenever he would use me as a ploy when he found a plump pheasant to flirt with. Later at night, I would feel conflicted about not keeping up my wall of defense, yet excited to see him again.

. . .

Much later, I was told that Tia had me sent over to my mother's house that summer. I didn't remember any of it for thirty years. I had totally blocked it out.

My mother, along with her best friend, Lòpez, a sweet, short, jovial, skinny man, took my half-siblings and me to the five-and-dime store to buy the girls a Raggedy Ann doll and the boys a Raggedy Andy doll. I, of course, didn't want a Raggedy Ann doll. I wanted a one-cent plastic whistle. My mother got so upset. She kept insisting that I wanted the damn doll. I politely said that if I couldn't get the whistle, I'd rather not get anything at all.

She tried to shove the doll in my hand, tightly yelling, "Take it! Everyone else wants it! What the hell's wrong with you?" I still politely refused. She got so pissed that she slapped me across the face really hard and pounded me on top of my head, in front of the customers and sales clerks—beyond embarrassing. Lòpez finally intervened: "Let her have the whistle." Lydia huffed, bought me the whistle, shoved it in my hand, shoved me in my back, and told me to wait outside.

Outside I proceeded to toot my own variation of the same tune, "Tea for Two," which I whistled to myself in the bathroom when I first arrived at Saint Joseph's. I added a spontaneous two-step—I was in my own world. A small crowd started to form.

My mother, Lòpez, and everyone else came out, and my mother stopped in her tracks, watching in disbelief. "Look, Lydia. She has talent, just like you," Lòpez said. Lydia got even more pissed and slapped the whistle out of my hand, then huffed down the block, with everyone in tow, telling me to "hurry the fuck up." I grabbed the whistle off the ground and started whistling again. She stopped and turned around. I froze. I was scared that she was going to hit me again. Lòpez started laughing, "She can't help it. She's got it. Like you!" My mother stepped into the bodega on the corner, bought two beers, one for her, one for Lòpez, and guzzled hers.

I was sent back to Tia's the next day.

. . .

At the end of my summer visit, Tia brought home Tina. "This is your cousin, Tina, from Puerto Rico," Tia said. I said hello casually. Being Puerto Rican, meeting new cousins was the norm—ha! Tina was around the same age as I was, cute as a button, short, really chubby, and a brat.

One Saturday afternoon Tia was busy with her usual weekend side job of selling irregular fashion dresses door to door in Williamsburg. Cookie was left in charge of Tina, Lorraine, and me. She was making us a late breakfast of fried eggs with crispy edges and French fries—very Puerto Rican. She set Tina's plate down first. Tina didn't waste any time and started shoving the fries down her throat. Cookie then set my plate down.

"Rosie got more fries than me!"

"She did not! Shut up and stop being so greedy, fucking fat pig!"

Then Cookie, adding insult to injury, handed Lorraine her plate, with double the portion of fries. Tina was outraged! As soon as Cookie turned back toward the stove, Tina reached over and grabbed a bunch of fries off of Lorraine's plate and shoved them into her fat little face.

"Stop, Tina!" screamed Lorraine.

Cookie quickly turned back around and banged Tina on the

head with a saucepan, twice—*bam! bam!* I couldn't believe it. I was scared and upset. It was the first time I had seen an act of violence in my aunt's house.

"I'm gonna tell my father on you!"

"If you dare tell Tio Ismael, I'm gonna beat the shit out of you!"

Tina ran off crying into Tia's bedroom.

Wait. "Tio"? Meaning my uncle-father? Does that mean Tina is not my cousin but my sister? What the hell?! Confused? Think how I felt! I didn't ask Tina if she was my sister or not. Why? I don't know. Just didn't.

Of course Tina told on Cookie to Tia that she hit her. Tia was so upset, screaming at Cookie, crying for at least two hours, pounding at her heart intermittently at the injustice and the agony of it all— drama on the high seas!

CHAPTER 10

GOING BACK to the Home after that summer was really hard. I felt so detached from everyone and everything. Daydreams of Brooklyn and Tia, my father, my "cousin" Tina, my cousins, "Hola" Doña Susana, and Mr. and Mrs. Katz danced through my head.

Thank goodness the new school year had begun. I had just turned five years old.

Kindergarten was awesome. It was part of the Home's Catholic school, which was directly across the street from the girls' dormitory. We had the best curriculum with a teacher who offered full support and attention. And best of all, kindergarten didn't have a nun for a teacher like the other grades did—yay!

It was still a challenge. Like the preschool, it was open to the public, and although the kids from the Home outnumbered the "outside" kids, in my kindergarten class there were only three or maybe four of us from the Home. And the "outside" kids' prejudice had intensified a bit now that they were a year older.

One day the class members were called upon to write their name, date of birth, home address, and telephone number and say all that out loud to the rest of the class. All of the "outside" kids quickly started writing. The rest of us from the Home froze as we looked at each other. We were all good with our full name and date of birth, but that was it! We could forget about the phone number. Since we weren't allowed to use the phone in the Home, obviously we didn't know the number. And our address? Were we going to put down the Home as our "home" address and further the humiliation?

I rubbed my head. It started to tingle with heat and a slight headache.

The teacher began to go around the room asking each kid to tell the class what he or she had written. I looked down at my paper. All I had written was my name. My face flushed with red-hot heat. My throat rumbled with a feeling of dry heave.

"Rosemary. It's your turn. Would you please stand and share your information with us?" asked the teacher.

I slowly stood up. Here went nothing.

"My name is *Wosie Pewez*. . . . My birthday is September fourth."

I paused, scanning the room as I peered over my paper. I took a deep breath.

"I live . . . in . . . Brooklyn, on *Wollybout* Street. And—"

"She's a liar," yelled out this little Goody Two-shoes of a boy. "She lives over there in the Home!"

My face went red with embarrassment. I looked up. All eyes were on me. The kids from the Home were looking at me too, wondering what my next move would be.

"She's lying! She's a liar!" The little fucker pressed on.

"Okay. Calm down. And that's not very nice to call her a liar, now is it?"

"But she lied! She lives over there! She's from the Home!" This freaking kid kept going.

"Okay, that's enough! Now, Rosemary, you know that you live at the Home. Do you know the name of the street we're on?"

I stood there, stone-faced.

"Rosemary?" she continued.

"I'm not a liar. I live over there and at Tia's house in Brooklyn. And that's the truth," I sheepishly replied.

"Rosemary? Now stop that!"

"No! I won't stop! It's the truth! I'm not a liar! And I can't stand him, and I hate you!"

Everyone gasped.

"Rosemary, go over to the corner. Now, please!"

The teacher's aide grabbed my arm as she guided me to the corner. I whipped it away from her. Her face pulled back in shock. I sat there staring at that stupid corner feeling like crap. Why did I lose it like that? I hate myself. Now she's going to hate me. I hope they don't tell Sister Mary-Domenica; she'll probably beat me good for sure. I rubbed my head. Man, it was burning hot.

After five minutes or so, the teacher walked over to me and sweetly whispered in my ear, asking me to join the class again. I shook my head no with my eyes cast down at the floor—I was too ashamed. My head started to throb with pain.

"Rosemary, please."

"My name's not Rosemary. It's Rosie," I quietly stated. "My head hurts. It feels really hot."

"Oh no," she said as she felt my head. "I better get you to the nurse."

Then everything went blank.

. . .

When I woke, I found myself in a clear plastic oxygen tent that was tucked under a white, iron-framed hospital twin bed. I remember being scared and wondering why I was inside that synthetic contraption. I was in the infirmary. I sat there for a moment, taking in the room. It was packed with sick kids only from the Home, ranging from toddlers to teenagers. Some were reading on their beds, others were playing checkers or cards on a small, wooden round table set toward the entrance of the room. And some were watching television! Yay! TV!

I saw a nun enter, dressed in an all-white habit. I decided to ask her what was going on. I slipped out of the tent by tugging at it for a long time.

"Ooh! You're not supposed to leave your bed. You're gonna get in trouble," yelled out another older Spanish girl from Group Three. "You have to go back to bed or you'll get in trouble with Sister Irene."

Too late. Sister Irene, the head nun nurse in charge, had entered the room. Sister Irene was a white, fair-skinned, plain-looking nun with blond, swooping bangs that peeked out from under her habit. "Who told you to get out of bed?" I stopped in my tracks. I quickly climbed back into bed, watching her approach in a stern manner as another nun nurse followed behind.

"You are not to get out of bed unless given permission to do so. You have pneumonia and you are very sick. Understand?"

I nodded yes.

"Roll over."

I did so. Then rolled back.

"What does 'pneumonia' mean?" I asked.

"It means you're very sick."

"I know that!" I coyly and precociously stated. "I mean, what does 'pneumonia' *mean*?"

"Just roll over," Sister Irene said with an amused smirk.

I did so. She pulled down my panties and stuck a thermometer into a jar of Vaseline and then stuck the thing up my butt. That shit was so shocking and hurt so much that my butt cheeks involuntarily clenched so tightly together and the thermometer popped right out—Sister Irene frantically scrambled for it. She finally got a hold of it. There was a momentary stare-off. I started to chuckle—she didn't.

"Roll over."

"Okay. But, excuse me, please, Sister, I don't think you're supposed to do it like that because I'm five now, and I saw on I *Love Lucy* that you're supposed to put it in your mouth, not in your—"

She shushed me, then rolled me over and dug that freaking thermometer up my bum, with the other nun nurse squeezing my ass cheeks together. She read it, her forehead contorted with concern. She turned to the other nun nurse.

"Her temperature went up. Closely monitor her and move her bed over to the other side away from the other kids."

As Sister Irene headed back to her office the other nun nurse pushed my bed to the other side of the room with the help of a skinny, tall black man.

My head started to spin with the fever, and then everything went black again.

I didn't know how long I was out. I felt dazed and dehydrated. This big, ugly, older black kid, who was maybe fifteen or sixteen, was standing in the doorway staring straight at me with his zipperless fly on his hospital pajamas wide open, exposing his private parts, fondling himself unabashed. The older Spanish girl from Group Three quickly scurried over to me and whispered in my ear.

"Don't look at him. He's a pervert, and he'll try to molest you like he did to Sorida from Group Two."

I nodded yes, even though I didn't know what being molested meant. What was worse was that I couldn't stop looking. This was the first time I had seen a male's genitals. I tugged at the older girl's hospital gown and pointed.

"What are those three things hanging there?"

"Don't do that! God! That's his dick and his two balls."

"Oh . . . what's a dick?"

"It's a guy's private part. So, don't be looking or it will make him hard."

Huh?

"Okay . . . why does he have balls inside his skin?"

She laughed. I laughed back. It was more of an anxiety-ridden laugh. I wasn't clear on everything but clearly understood the danger in her warning.

Later that night I was afraid to go to sleep. I kept one eye open, wondering if that perverted kid with the two balls and a dick was going to come and try to hurt me. I wished Tia would come to visit. I wished my mother would come too. But no one came. I was in the infirmary, stewing, for over a week.

A few weeks later, after I got out, Tia finally came to visit. I was so cold to her. She tried to explain that the Home informed her that it was best to wait until I had gotten better. She apologized. I politely accepted, but I was five—the hurt kept me silent and distant.

She began to sing her favorite Beatles song, "Penny Lane," in her high-pitched, tone-deaf voice: "Penny lane is in *de* ears and in *de* minds. Da-da-da-da daa!" I looked up at her and started giggling. She smiled back and patted my hand. I slowly pulled it back but smiled back so I didn't hurt her feelings too much.

CHAPTER 11

BACK AND forth, forth and back, my two lives continued. I was six years old now and had moved up to Group One after I returned from a summer visit to Tia's. I did not see my father that whole summer, nor my mother. There was no explanation as to why, and I didn't ask for one. That's how things were.

Group One was where the girls from first to third grade lived. It was on the second floor of the girls' dormitory building, right above the Baby Girls' dorm. Inside, a medium-sized hallway was lined with metal school-like lockers to the left. Just past the bathroom was the first dormitory bedroom lined with about ten twin beds, five on one side, five on the other. To the far right corner of the second bedroom was the clothes closet; the far left corner was where Sister Renata's bedroom was. Following the bedrooms was the "living room," equipped with a sofa, a rocking chair, a stereo component, and a TV—yay!

Sister Renata, brutal, strict—evil reincarnated, seriously—was Group One's dorm "mother," and she ran it like a Nazi. She was tall, white, pasty, and broad-shouldered, wore ugly black-rimmed glasses, had a slight grayish mustache with sprouting whiskers on her chin, and was strong as hell. I was so afraid of her. There were rumors of her merciless cruelty throughout the Home. While still in Baby Girls, I had witnessed firsthand Sister Renata's infamous demented viciousness.

This girl, in Group One, wouldn't eat her vegetables. "Eat! Now!" commanded Sister Renata as she stood behind the girl. The room went silent. By the fourth or fifth bite the girl vomited all of it onto her plate. Sister Renata pushed the girl's face close to the vomit and said, "Now you're gonna eat all of that mess, and I better not see a morsel left on that plate!" The girl slowly picked up a heaping spoonful of her vomit, lips quivering, tears running down her eyes, and swallowed! Sister Renata looked around the room like General Patton after reprimanding the troops and then walked away. After the coast was clear, the cafeteria's janitor—this kind black man with a slight hunch to his spine—came over with a wheeled garbage can and covertly dumped the girl's plate and placed it back in front of her in one quick move. God bless that man, wherever he is.

. . .

Just as it was in the Baby Girls' dormitory, the day was scheduled—when to get up, shower, eat, play, study, etc.—but the number of chores had increased. Sister Renata made sure that everything was done to the letter and didn't hesitate to use her long wooden paddle, which she wore under her habit, to enforce her demands. She would resort to a ruler if she didn't want to exhaust herself. Miss Millie, a skinny thing with an ugly big-ass mole on her face, helped Sister Renata run Group One, but Sister Renata really didn't need her.

Some of the girls in Group One I already sort of knew from the playground. Of course Crazy Cindy was there! Yay! When she first saw me carrying my clothes to the clothes closet, she screamed with glee, gave me a quick hug, then scurried off to play with the other girls. Puerto Rican–Jew Evita Feinstein was in Group Two across the hall from Group One—she was older than us, so I didn't see her as much. There was Lil Tillie, skinny with frizzy hair always in two twisted pigtails, and Fat Dina, a short, chubby, stocky girl with black hair that had the texture of a Brillo pad. Fat Dina looked like a Puerto Rican Tasmanian she-devil from the Bugs

Bunny cartoons—no lie. Most of us girls were afraid of her, or at least intimidated by her. Crazy Cindy wasn't of course. If she was scared of Fat Dina, you couldn't tell because she antagonized Fat Dina every chance she got. That made absolutely no sense, since Fat Dina could flatten Cindy in a hot second.

My first night in Group One was very memorable.

The Metro-North train whistled down the tracks in the distance along the Hudson River. Sister Renata led us into the bathroom. We all lined up, naked—still hated that—for showers. Most of the girls had begun developing and covered their breasts in modesty. It was four or five to a shower. The shower was covered with this brown, moldy filth. I was grossed out and found a clean spot, quickly washed myself, and dashed out. Sister Renata, standing guard, made me go back and stand in the middle of the guck and shower again, saying I hadn't washed properly. It was so nasty that I wanted to vomit, but didn't dare in fear that she would make me eat it.

Bedtime. We all knelt at the foot of our beds with our heads bowed as Sister Renata led the Lord's Prayer. Lights out.

I think Crazy Cindy's bed was across the room and one down from mine. She was whispering nonstop to some of the other girls. I kept looking over at her hoping that she would glance my way. But she didn't. I didn't want to seem like a crybaby. I was in Group One now, and crying was not tolerated by the nuns and the other girls—everyone knew that. I turned over on my side, stuck my thumb in my mouth, ran my hand over the donated wool army blanket, and tried to sleep.

"Who's that talking?" yelled Sister Renata, walking out from her bedroom dressed in a granny nightgown and nightcap. Cindy quickly played like she was asleep—same ol' Crazy Cindy. Sister Renata walked over, stood at the dividing doorway, and scanned each bed with her scowling, beady eyes. "If I hear a peep out of one of you girls, you will all be in trouble," she said, then headed back into her room.

After a few minutes, Cindy finally called out to me.

"Psst. Psst. Rosie! Psst."

A smile jumped up from my heart and spread across my face. She's still my friend! I knew it—happy good feelings inside!

"Pssssst! Rosie. You sleeping?"

"Yes."

"If you're sleeping, why'd you answer me?"

She cracked up at her own joke. I couldn't help it and let out a low snicker.

"Shut up!" screamed one of the girls in a whisper. "You're gonna get us all in trouble!" She was one of the top dogs. The room fell silent.

After a moment, a rapid machine-gun fire of loud tight farts rang out in the darkness—*pop, pop, pop, pop, pop!* A few heads lifted to see who the culprit was. Cindy's body shook with giggles as she tried to bury her guilt-ridden laughter in her pillow. "Shut up!" screamed the alpha female. Sister Renata rushed out of her room, this time with her paddle in her hand. "Everyone! Up! Now!"

All the girls quickly jumped out of their beds, forming two lines, waiting for further instructions. I was a bit slow and wary getting up. Everyone was shooting dirty looks at Crazy Cindy. She tried to shrug it off, but I knew she felt bad.

"Give me fifty squats!" screamed Sister Renata.

"What the heck is a squat?" I innocently and slightly sarcastically asked one of the girls.

Smack! Sister Renata's manly hands went right across the kisser! Shit stung like a biatch!

"Watch that mouth, young lady. Now get in line!"

After about twenty tiring dips or so, Sister Renata told us to go back to bed, except for Cindy and myself. "I want fifty more, and then you can stand there and wait until I get back." She turned and walked back to her room.

With every few deep knee squats, Crazy Cindy would fart and

quietly laugh at the same time. I then joined in with a dip and a fart of my own—we died laughing! Dag it! Out came Sister Renata like a bat out of hell. She grabbed both of us by the back of our nightgowns and stood us in front of the metal lockers in the second bedroom with our noses inches away.

"You will stand there for an hour with your eyes straight ahead, no talking, and your heads better not touch that locker."

An hour? Uh, hello, I'm only six years old here!

She pulled up a rocking chair and sat to the side of us with that paddle on her lap. After a few minutes, which felt more like an hour, my eyes started to close shut and my head leaned forward. Bam! Sister Renata banged my head into the metal locker. My big-ass forehead instantly swelled up with a pounding headache. Sister Renata then marched back to her room.

Ten minutes passed by. I was completely exhausted. My head involuntarily leaned forward onto the cool metal of the locker. Cindy gently nudged me awake.

"Don't. Or you'll have to stay longer. . . . And she'll bang your big forehead up again." She giggled quietly, wanting me to join in. I didn't. I wasn't amused.

"Sorry," she added softly.

"It's okay," I whispered back.

Pause.

"Do you like Mod Squad better or The FBI?" asked Cindy in a matter-of-fact way. "I like Mod Squad better because. . . ." She paused for a moment, squinting her eyes shut with her butt sticking out. "Ooh, a perfume fart. That one's gonna stink." She then stuck her hand down the back of her panties, pulled it back up, smelled it, and said, "Yup, it stinks." A sneeze-laugh snuck out of me along with a spray of snot. Cindy burst out laughing! Dag it!

Out of nowhere, Sister Renata was standing right behind us and slammed our heads against the lockers again! Bam! How the hell did she get behind us so fast? Cindy glanced up at her. Sister Renata was standing there without her nightcap on. Her hair was short and bundled into small knots that looked like spark plugs sticking out of her head. Cindy's body shook as she tried her best not to laugh. Sister Renata banged Cindy's head again against the locker real hard—then again. Cindy looked straight ahead, responding with a defiant smirk. Bam! went her head a third time! Man, I was terrified of Sister Renata even more now. And my heart was breaking for Cindy. This was the first time I saw her get angry. Cindy's nostrils flared. She looked like a completely different girl. She took a deep breath and looked straight ahead.

Twenty minutes passed. We finally got to go to bed. I was dazed with exhaustion and too much in pain to be angry. I pulled the blanket over my head, closed my eyes, and stuck my thumb in my mouth. Sister Renata went back to her room.

"Psst. Psst."

Oh my goodness! Is Crazy Cindy for real? I can't! I just can't!

"Psssssssssssst!"

"What?" I screamed in a loud whisper.

"Good night, Rosie."

"Good night, Cindy . . . good night, John Boy," I added.

"Oh my God, you're still corny!" she quietly chuckled.

"Cindy! You can't use the Lord's name in vain!"

"Oh my God!" she laughed, burying her face in her pillow.

I quietly chuckled back. I stuck my thumb back in my mouth and felt a soothing satisfaction that we were once again best friends.

. . .

Sister Renata was on my ass after that. She was like that. If she didn't like you, she'd single you out through endless punishments. Spankings, restrictions—which meant being grounded for the most part—and withholding food were her favorites. It was unfair because I was really well behaved and liked doing the right thing.

Like, if you threw a gum wrapper on the ground, I'd pick it up and properly throw it away . . . like, even at six years old, I would offer to help the other kids with their chores. But Evil Reincarnated didn't take any of that into consideration.

My bed wasn't made well enough, so she gave me a spanking . . . then ripped apart all of the other girls' already made beds and made me remake them as well as mine.

When I was caught watching television with my thumb in my mouth, she gave me a quick scolding and numerous whacks to my hands with a ruler, plus restricted me from dessert for two days.

I should have said "May I?" instead of "Can I?"—a military-style lecture.

I was impertinent to one of the counselors, and so all of the girls had to stand in front of the lockers for an hour . . . after I got a spanking—bare-assed again. And a week's restriction, plus no dinner.

Being ten minutes late walking back from school got me no dessert . . . after a spanking.

I was accused of showing off by correcting a girl's grammar (it's a sin of pride), so I had to kneel down and pray in front of my bed for an hour or so . . . then was put on restriction for a week.

I said a bad word—a pop in the mouth with the back of her hand, then a bar of soap shoved in it, followed by bathroom cleaning duty for two days and a week of restriction.

On and on it went, day after day, week after week. Always in trouble for minor things, I was like a nervous bunny, busy developing strategies to avoid and navigate around Sister Renata's moods so that I could avoid further beatings. And I was always apologizing for *everything*—very Catholic.

Now, if I knew a punishment was justified, I'd suck it up, but come on, people! And the beatings took their toll—especially the face slaps. Slapping a child in the face should be against the law, seriously. It is demeaning, hurtful, and insulting, and the damaging consequences are both immediate and long-term. I began to have screaming tantrums that would begin at the first slap and last for hours. It got so bad that I would get extra spankings in an attempt to shut me up, which most of the time didn't. After a while, the screaming stopped and I resorted to long bouts of intentional silence. The self-righteousness I displayed drove Sister Renata crazy. What really sucked was that I kind of liked her . . . in a way. Yes, she was the devil's daughter, but she was also self-assured, very smart, and at times caring.

Once, there was a huge storm ripping through Peekskill. The sky looked like a scene out of *The Wizard of Oz*—branches flying every which way as the rain came down sideways. By nightfall, all of us were terrified. *Ba-boom! ba-boom!* went the thunder in the dark night. Everyone screamed with fear and jumped onto each other's beds for some kind of safety. Sister Renata ran out of her bedroom, with that silly cap on her head, holding a bottle of holy water.

"Come here, children! Come over to me!" she said as she started to sprinkle the bottle of holy water on us! The girls rushed toward her. Although I thought the whole holy water thing was silly (I didn't buy it for a minute—I don't know why, but I didn't), I was so afraid of thunder (still am), but more afraid of Sister Renata spanking me for not believing, that I rushed over too. "It's only God and his angels bowling. That's all it is, children." Another huge crackle of thunder struck, shaking us all over again. "Everything's okay. God just got a strike! Hoorah!" Sister Renata screamed with her fist up in the air in celebration.

How could this same lady be such an evil queen!

. . .

A couple of months had passed and the main office called up to Group One: I was to go down to the Baby Girls' dorm to meet my mother on "important business." As I headed out, Betsy and Terry were walking up behind me.

We walked in. Mrs. Vasquez, Amy, and my three brothers were already there. And so was my mother, with my infant half-sister, Kathy, on her lap. This must be the other one that Mrs. Vasquez had talked about a year earlier. This was the "important business"? Meeting another sibling who would be part of the system? Sad. I kissed my mother hello, kissed Kathy—she was so cute, with auburn, curly hair, thin dimples, and the palest white skin ever— hung for a few minutes, and then left. I heard later that she was placed in the Home or in foster care. I really didn't know, because I don't think I ever saw her in the Home again.

. . .

There are priests and there are brothers. The difference is that brothers are not ordained and are subordinates to priests.

Brother Bob was the most handsome brother at the Home. He looked kind of like Gregory Peck—tall, dark-haired, slim, and just dreamy. All the girls had a crush on Brother Bob. It wasn't just his gorgeous looks. This guy was so sweet and extremely kind, a strong contrast to the penguins. In fairness, the brothers got to live with the priests, and priests did have nicer living conditions and better food—they didn't have to share mealtimes with us either. But then again, if you're supposed to be a servant of God, that kind of stuff shouldn't affect how kids are treated—you feel me, people?

It was Sunday. The winter was just beginning, and it was cold, very cold out. There were maybe seven girls, most of us from Group One, set to go with Brother Bob in the Home's beat-up four-door sedan on some type of trip to somewhere that I've blocked out. We all had winter coats or snowsuits on. I was in this ridiculous, thick-ass one-piece snowsuit that was white with blue, no, maybe pink, trimming. I still had my potbelly, so I looked like a miniature Michelin tire man.

These trips with Brother Bob were somewhat regular because I remember how everyone would fight over who got to sit up front with him. All the popular girls, all four of them, which included Fat Dina, pushed their way to the front seat. Although I really wanted to sit up front too, I wasn't the bully type. Besides, the back was usually where we sat anyway—Crazy Cindy, Puerto Rican–Jew Evita Feinstein, and myself.

That day we were playing "cooties." Over and over again, Crazy Cindy would end up losing. It drove her insane. By the eighth or ninth time, frustrated, she grabbed Fat Dina's winter hat off of her head and threw it on Puerto Rican–Jew Evita, screaming, "Cooties!" Evita then screamed and flung the hat on me: "Cooties!" Before I could respond, Fat Dina turned around, saw me with the damn hat, lunged with her big fat paw, and punched me hard in the gut. The force flung my body against the passenger door, which unfortunately was not shut properly, and I flew out of the car as it drove pretty fast up a hill, with me now trying to hang on by grabbing at two big, gold-encrusted religious candles that were lying on the back board of the car.

Whoosh! Out I went, and my body skidded down the hill like a rock skids on water, screaming my head off at each bump against the pavement. The skin on my hands was burning off from the scraping friction against the street. I tried to stop with my feet, and I heard two loud cracks. My head dropped in wrenching pain—*boom!* My big fat forehead banged on the concrete as my skin scraped off all the way to my hairline. (I know—not the forehead!) I lifted my head in aggravating pain—*bam!* My head slammed on the pavement again, busting my nose flat. Blood was pouring out of me. I remember looking up at Brother Bob, running in a panic down the hill as I screamed and cried. Everything looked red, and I don't remember hearing any sound, not even my own screaming—everything was silent and in slow motion.

Brother Bob scooped me up in his beautiful, slender, muscular arms and carried me back to the car. He made all the girls climb in the back and placed me in the front! Yay! Okay, so part of my forehead was scraped off, my nose was busted, my lip was split, blood was pouring down my face, my feet were probably broken, and my knees were banged up—but I was in the front, with fine-ass Brother Bob! I also remember not feeling pain anymore and still not being able to hear any sound. As we rushed to the hospital, Brother Bob wrapped his arm around me and held me close to his body, and I looked out the front windshield at the row of houses—everything looked red and hazy and beautiful in a strange, dreamy way.

They told me that I was unconscious for several days, but it felt like twenty minutes or so. When I opened my eyes, everything still seemed dreamlike. There was a nurse with dark brown hair standing over me, gasping gleefully. Then the pain came. I became very conscious and confused. I licked my bottom lip, feeling the stitches against my tongue. I put my hand to my head. It was wrapped with bandages. "No, no, no. You can't touch," the nice nurse said. "You're in a hospital. You had a very bad accident and were asleep for a very long time." I looked up even more confused. I didn't remember a thing—and wouldn't until years later. I told her that I dreamed I was in The Wizard of Oz and I was Dorothy and Toto was my dog. "I was singing 'Somewhere Over the Rainbow' to you. Every day while you were asleep." She replied all heavy and stuff.

"Wanna hear a funny joke?" I asked, trying to change her mood. "Okay."

"Why did the chicken cross the road?"

"I don't know. Why?"

"Because he felt like it! . . . Get it? . . . Boy, tough room."

She let a bit of a smile seep out and then left before she started to cry. I lay back, wondering what the hell was wrong with her. Then my thoughts turned to Tia. I wondered if she came to visit me. I closed my eyes, stuck my thumb in my mouth, and went to sleep.

. . .

Several days later, I think, I was back at the Home in the infirmary. I remember having to wear these braces on my legs with weird crutches to help me walk. My nose was taped, my bottom lip was smeared with Vaseline over the stitches, and—adding the ultimate insult to injury—I had a helmet on my head. Yes, folks. I had a pad-ded helmet on my big-ass head to protect me from further concus-sions. I think it was blue or red, I don't remember. And of course, "Helmet Head" quickly became the joke. I see the humor in it now, but come on, people!

I hated the pain even more. The middle of the night was the worst. The pain ringing through my head was agonizing, and the piercing pain in my knees didn't help either. By two or three o'clock in the morning, I couldn't take it and would have to wake Sister Irene up. I hated waking her up too. After a series of frustrated huffs and puffs, she would rip off her blankets and get me an aspirin or my kiddy pain pills. God, she was so annoyed by me. I really hated that.

. . .

Sister Renata came into the infirmary with Mrs. Vasquez, and they gathered around my bed. Mrs. Vasquez told me that the nice nurse from the hospital wanted to adopt me when she found out that I was a kid from the Home. That's why she was so emotional over me! If I wanted to be adopted by her, they would ask Lydia and take it from there.

I was totally insulted. I felt like she pitied me, and I didn't like that feeling.

Adults would come in on the weekends from time to time and look over the kids to adopt, as if we were a bunch of puppies on display in a storefront window. I always felt sad how some of the kids would run up to these strangers with their eyes pleading and their forced and rehearsed smiles, hoping to be saved. I found it even more despicable how the adults would only consider the cutest picks of the litter. Yes, I wanted out (and quite honestly, used to fantasize about some famous rich person adopting me), but I resented that we were subjected to this type of desperation. I refused to participate. I wasn't some depraved child who needed saving. Or was I? Was that what people thought of me? Forget that. I had a mother, even though she hated my guts, but she was going to like me someday—I just knew it. And I had Tia! And she loved me, even though I hadn't received a visit or gone on a home visit for several months. Besides, I was going to get out of there and get my own house and be successful and everything was going to be all right.

Well, at least that's what I told myself. I had to tell myself that, or else I'd be just like the majority of the kids in the Home who seemed to have given up or to never think about wanting much more than what was presented—and that was unacceptable.

I shook my helmet head no, slumped down, folded my arms, and stared straight ahead at the wall.

. . .

I was back at Group One. The crutches were off, so was the helmet, and so was my cheeriness. Even Tia noticed when she came to visit or when I went to visit her.

It was winter and very cold, which made the pain from my accident worse. I had to take a little blue pill to help me sleep. Well, that was if demonic Sister Renata gave me one. I literally had to beg her for a pill and succumb to her heartless antics. Every single night we went through this frustrating dance. One night I hit my boiling point.

"Sister Renata, my knees hurt, really bad. I need a pill, please."

"No, you don't. Go back to bed."

"Please. It really, really hurts."

"No, it doesn't! It's all in your head. Now go back to bed."

"Nooo! I need a pill!!!!"

Smack—across my face! I banged my fist on the wall in a rage. *Smack!* The bitch hit me again! "I fucking hate you!" Bad move. She went to grab me, and to my surprise, I smacked the mess out of her face—hard!

Why the hell did I do that?!

I ran . . . well, hobbled . . . like hell. She caught me, spun me around, and cracked me across the face again, and again. After the third or fourth slap, I smacked that witch again!

I know! Stupid!

With one swipe of her muscle-bound arm, she scooped me up and carried me to my bed as I kicked and screamed. She ripped my nightgown up, pinned me down, and proceeded to beat the crap out of my butt and the back of my thighs with the paddle. I finally couldn't take it anymore, and my body went limp. My butt and thighs were welting up, with blood seeping out of the cracks. She finally stopped. "Don't you ever even think about hitting me again or I'll beat the living daylights out of you! I'm bigger and stronger. Don't you ever forget that!"

I remember those words to this very day.

All night long I stared into the darkness of the dormitory feeling my hatred for Sister Renata grow.

The next morning I began a full-blown, intentional, and tactical silent war. This was way different from my previous silent treatments. I literally would not speak to anyone, especially Sister

Renata. I took my punishment of restriction from everything like a pro, without uttering a single word. This went on for several days.

I was sent to Dr. Tisby, the Home's psychiatrist, a short, fat, roly-poly man with a ridiculous bushy mustache, who smoked an old-fashioned pipe all of the time. Dag. This was a real threat, and I was scared. Everyone knew that if you were ordered to Dr. Tisby's office, a file would begin on you, and after several visits you could be sent to Graceland, a "hospital" where they would put you on "meds" and you would come back walking like a zombie. This was a fact, not some Home legend. Seriously. I remember seeing one of the girls come back all drugged out. "What's the matter with her?" I asked one of the older girls. "She was at Graceland. She's on meds." Scared the crap outta me.

His small office was painted beige, no, yellow, I think, with a big desk and chair, another chair in front, and a smaller child's play table to the side of the room. First we played checkers. Then he casually asked me about simple things, writing every single word I said down on a yellow notepad. Then the questions got a little bit heavier. Did I get along with the other kids? Did I feel like I fit in at "outside" school? How did I feel about my mother, my father, my other siblings? And blah, blah, blah.

Then he finally got down to the real business at hand.

"Why do you think you hit Sister Renata?"

I was about to tell him the truth about the physical abuse, but thought if I did, he would send me away quick fast.

"Because I lost my temper. I know it was wrong."

He nodded as he wrote again. My leg was swinging back and forth like crazy. He finally put his pen down and looked at me.

"It's good to hear that you feel that way. So, do you think you should apologize to Sister Renata and end all of this *meshugaas*?"

"I know that word!" I said in a hushed excitement. "It means 'crazy'! Right?"

"Yes, well, 'craziness,' " he chuckled. "How do you know this word?"

"From Doña Betsy and Doña Rosie! They're Hasids. That means they're Jews."

He smiled. I smiled back. Then I got nervous again.

"Are you upset about something, Rosie?"

"No."

"You appear to be upset."

I had to think fast. I didn't want him to think there was anything wrong with me.

"I'm just nervous 'cause you keep writing everything I say down, 'cause you're trying to see if I'm crazy, right? So I don't want to say anything, if you don't mind, please."

As soon as those words came out of my mouth, I regretted it. I looked back down at my feet swinging back and forth. He chuckled and took a pull from his stinky pipe.

"That's very perceptive of you."

"What does 'perceptive' mean?"

"It means you're observant and insightful. That you understand what's going on. You can go back to the dorm now."

My mind was racing. I hoped I wouldn't get sent up to Graceland. I hoped I did well. I hoped he liked me. I made the long walk back to Group One. No one was there, everyone was outside playing. I found Crazy Cindy drawing out a skelly court with white chalk.

"They gonna send you to Graceland?" she excitedly asked.

I shrugged.

"Did Dr. Tisby make you play Go Fish and checkers and write down everything you said?"

I nodded my head yes.

"Did you tell the truth?"

I shook my head no.

"That's good. 'Cause you gotta play it right or they win. He's so fat, right, right?"

"Yeah." I laughed. "And his stinky pipe made me want to vomit!"

"Oh snap! You talking now?"

I was required to see Dr. Tisby once a week. I knew that eyes were watching me, especially Sister Renata's. It was game on for her.

CHAPTER 12

A GIFT came by way of Miss Connie. I was informed that she
had become my full-time Volunteer (nowadays called a Big Sister),
which meant that I would have weekend sleepovers at her house,
and she was coming to pick me up the next day. Some of the other
kids at the Home would get a Volunteer as well—some didn't. I
never knew why that was—it seemed so unfair too. I had packed
my little suitcase over and over, not knowing what to bring, even
though I only had maybe a couple of clothing items. She and her
husband, Bill, picked me up in their car. Bill was fine as hell.

I think their home was just outside of Peekskill, north of the
Home. The house was so charming, right out of a *Leave It to Beaver*
episode. I completely loved it. It was like I had stepped into my
daydreams of a normal "TV" life. Everything was in its place, intentionally designed and warm and cozy. Bill was quiet and seemed
uneasy. He didn't know how to relate to me or to the whole situation and was walking around on eggshells. It became clear to me
that this was not a joint decision, and it made me feel awkward.

Miss Connie told me to bring my little plaid suitcase up with
her to my room. My room? I was to have my own room! Oh joy!
Actually, it was their guest room, but I didn't know that at the time
and thought she had the room made just for me. I sat on the bed
and looked around. You can't imagine how special and lucky I felt.
"Oh my goodness," I exclaimed, "this bedspread is so fluffy and
soft."

"It's a goose-down comforter."

"What?! It's made of a goose?"

She cracked up. "Just its feathers. Like it?"

I nodded yes, smiling emphatically.

"After you unpack, come downstairs."

The two of them were sitting on stools in their small kitchen. Miss Connie was eating some chips or something like that. "Are you hungry?" she asked.

"No, Miss Connie. . . . Well, yes, I am, please," I timidly answered.

Miss Connie laughed. "You're not at the Home. Sister Renata's not here, you can relax. And please stop calling me Miss Connie! It's just Connie, okay?"

She then handed me some of her chips. Bill shook his head. "Oh, shut up, Bill. Pay him no mind. He just thinks I'm too fat, and he doesn't want me to make you fatter." That pissed Bill off.

"Let me fix you a drink, dear. You need one," Connie sarcastically said. She filled a short crystal-looking glass with ice cubes, then poured some brown stuff from a tall bottle that I had never seen before. Wait! Yes, I had! That was what the wives on TV made their white husbands when they came home from work. Ooh, I loved this suburban experience! Wait. "Fatter"? What the hell do you mean, "fatter"? I beg your pardon, "Connie." I guess the look on my face was intense because Connie cracked up, pointing her finger at me.

"What is that look about, missy?"

"I'm not fat. I'm pleasantly plump, thank you."

She laughed.

"Oh, Rosie. You are so funny. I'm sorry. I didn't mean to call you fat. I'm just obsessed with my own weight problem."

"Weight problem"? Hmm, first time I heard that phrase.

Bill went into the den with his drink, swirling the ice cubes around in it, saying he'd be back for dinner. Ooh! They had a den, just like Darrin's den in *Bewitched*—don't you just love it! Connie reached into a jar of pills and popped one in her mouth.

"What are those?" I asked.

"My diet pills. Don't tell Bill I took one. He hates that I'm fat, but it's not my fault. It's my genes."

"Your jeans make you fat? That's ridiculous!"

"No," she laughed. "Not my 'jeans,' but my 'genes,' g-e-n-e-s, meaning what my body inherited from my family. Like you have dimples, and so does your sister and two of your brothers. You probably inherited them from your mother or father or someone in your family. Understand?"

I did. I just loved how she spoke to me, like I mattered and I could be part of the conversation. She then pulled out one of her Virginia Slims cigarettes. And of course, yours truly was right on cue singing out with the appropriate commercial jingle and strut to boot!

You've come a long way, baby, to get where you got to today!

Connie fell out laughing! "Oh my, you are the most, Rosie! I swear to God you just kill me!" I gasped with my hand over my mouth. "You're not supposed to swear to God. That's a sin!" This only cracked her up more.

At bedtime Connie came in to tuck me in. I didn't know how to feel about it—it was so intimate. I tensed up with this weird half-grin of anxiety and happiness. Weirdo. I think I made her feel uneasy because she quickly left the room after just a touch to my cheek with her hand. Dag it! I wanted that good-night kiss so badly, even though I didn't want it. She shut all the lights off! In the Home, there was always a little light on. I was scared for a quick moment, but then sank deeper into that plush pillow and fluffy comforter. I swore to myself that all of my beds, in my amazing apartment—like Marlo Thomas's apartment in *That Girl*—would have goose-down comforters.

We spent the next morning at the International House of Pancakes. Bill pulled out Connie's chair, and she expected him to without asking—like in the movies! She put a napkin on her lap. I did the same. I watched her daintily pick up her coffee cup and sip tiny sips. I took in everything and mimicked her to the tee, making a concerted effort not to look too obvious.

We spent the rest of the day at the house of her best friend Miss Jan, I mean Jan, near Mahopac Lake. Jan was skinny, white, blonde, and strong and always wore jeans. She lived with her kids, five or six dogs, and a couple of horses. When she opened the door, the dogs came charging out and toppled me with kisses. I fell in love with each one of them instantly. The immediate connection was natural. They followed me around the same way I would follow Tia room to room during a home visit. I knew that they knew I understood them and would love them back the same way they loved me. Jan took me to her stable next to the house. The connection with those big, beautiful creatures was just as intense, but I had to work for their respect. They were very wary of a newcomer. I stayed there brushing and petting them for hours, earning each ounce of it.

By the end of our fantasy weekend, I was filled with melancholy. Although I knew I would come back from time to time, I didn't want to go back to the Home. Who the hell would? I wasn't able to fully enjoy the last day. I don't think Connie knew how to handle my mood. She was quiet and cautious, which made me feel worse.

CHAPTER 13

I WAS told that I was going on a home visit to my mother's house! I didn't believe it. Why would I? I was seven or eight, I think, and had never been (since the whistle incident that I had blocked out). Why now after so much time? Plus, even though she would visit us at the Home—rarely, I might add—she would also stand us up a lot of the time.

We rode the Metro-North down to Grand Central Station by ourselves. I don't think my two older half-brothers came along, I only remember Terry, Betsy, and Amy. I was carrying my little plaid suitcase, and I was nervous as hell because I had always gone with Tia.

"This way. Come on, Rosie. Keep up!" Amy said in a way a big sister would.

"Do you see her? I bet she's not coming," said Betsy, then adding, "Look at Rosie's forehead. It's so big and ugly, right?"

"Don't say that. That's not nice," Amy scolded.

"But it is," laughed Betsy.

I looked away, swinging my suitcase back and forth, trying to act like it didn't bother me.

After a while—and I mean a long-ass while—Lydia was running toward us with her friend Lòpez, waving her hand up in the air. Everyone ran up to her and kissed her hello. I hesitated, too timid to be so free and forward as they were.

"The fucking train was late," my mother said. "*Ay*, my God, I'm fucking sweating!"

She looked down at me and smiled. Whew! She likes me now. She extended her cheek, and I kissed it as I'd done before.

"Let's go," she commanded. "The fucking train ride back is going to be so fucking crowded with the fucking rush hour."

This lady had a mouth on her like a truck driver. The entire subway ride was fucking this and fucking that. My mind was blown away by all of the profanity—it excited and scared the hell out of me.

Lydia lived in a duplex apartment somewhere in Brooklyn. I don't recall where exactly. We entered through the basement-level entrance. My mother had a fear of living above the second floor, in case of a fire. The front door was made of wood that had a pointed top. The staircase to the bedrooms was at the entrance. The decor was sparse and second-rate, with the predictable plastic-encased furniture. I didn't care, I was too excited.

A lot of people were already there, kids and adults. The adults were drinking hard, laughing and talking really loud, and the kids were running around like a bunch of crazy banshees, so excited to see my siblings when we walked in. From their casual reaction and similar looks, I assumed they were some type of family members. I later found out they were cousins. The two babies, Johnny and the baby girl Kathy, were there as well—I assumed that they'd gone back to live with Lydia, since I never saw them at the Home, but I found out later that they were in the system as well. They were transferred to foster care.

Everyone was admiring Kathy's new pierced ears. She had tiny little colored studs, with gold-plated posts. Lydia kept commenting on how she was such a good little girl because she didn't cry when Lydia pierced them herself with a needle and an ice cube. I looked at my half-sisters' ears—all pierced too. I remember touching my unpierced ears and looking at my mother's ears, which were pierced as well. My mother caught me staring at her. She then formally introduced me to everyone: "This is Rosie." Rosie? Not "This is my daughter"? Great.

I wandered off to the back room where the television was—of course. I sat on the floor off to the side, wanting to sit closer to everyone else. ABC's *Wide World of Sports* was on. I believe this was the first time I really took in who Howard Cosell was—I loved him! Everyone was doing his or her best impersonation of him. I don't remember who was boxing, but I remember the excitement coming from all of my cousins—young and old—and I was transfixed as well. The brutality would upset me and thrill me at the same time, yet I couldn't turn away. Weird.

Lydia came in with coffee and crackers. (I know, not appropriate for a girl under ten, but what can I say, we're Puerto Rican.) The coffee was mostly milk—steamy, hot, with the color of a light smooth mocha. I dipped my cracker. That soaked wafer melted in my mouth, and I was in heaven. Oh! How I lived for that sweet java taste. I'd been doing so since I was four, when Tia gave me my first cup, which was mostly sweetened hot milk, so I could feel like a big girl.

After a couple of hours of nonstop chatter on my part, from the caffeine high, my mother picked me up and sat me on the kitchen table. "Give me a brush and the Dippity-Do. I want her to look real pretty tonight." Oh my goodness! My mother was going to do my hair! I was so excited, but took a deep breath, readying myself for the agony. "Whaa? Whaa *happin*? You okay?" she asked. "I'm just bracing myself for the pain." She looked at me and cracked up. I laughed too, beaming inside that she got my sense of humor.

"*Mirale el pelo negro—que malo* [Look at this black hair—so bad]," she snidely remarked with a chuckle to her family and friends, who were all standing around the table. "*Que feo.* [How ugly.] She got this nappy hair from her father, not me."

Oh no, she didn't!

Everyone laughed—except me. I couldn't believe that my own

mother had just made a horrible racist statement about how ugly and nappy my hair was. Oh yes, honey. I knew it was an insult. Any person of color, young or old, would've known it was an insult. I was crushed and pissed. My hair texture had never bothered me before, since Tia and my cousins had hair with a texture similar to mine, even though they did burn their hair with lye relaxers at times. They never, ever made a comment like that. Hearing it from my mother just killed me. My whole freaking mood changed—but it didn't affect her one bit.

Her touch was surprisingly gentle. She pulled all my hair back into a high ponytail, leaving some out in the front to form a curled under-bang, covering my big-ass mofo. A bang! Hello? Why didn't someone think of that sooner? I looked so cute, I must admit. My hair looked just like Sandra Dee's in *Gidget*—okay, maybe only a little bit. I felt so special that my mood began to turn around again.

Just at that moment, there was a knock on the door. In came my cousin Lourdes—aka Cookie. "She's all ready, Cookie," my mother answered with a disgustingly happy tone. Ready? Ready for what?

"Come on, Rosie," my mother continued as she tenderly picked me off the table and set me down. "Go get your suitcase."

"I can't stay?" I asked my mother, holding down the big lump in my throat.

"No, you're too little. We're gonna have a party for the grown-ups, but you can come back in a few days."

Man, this woman had me on an emotional roller coaster! I sulked the whole way back to Tia's, wondering why the others, my half-brothers and -sisters, got to stay. They were all underage as well, right?

· · ·

Tia had moved to 147 Linden Boulevard in East New York. (That's east Brooklyn for all you hipsters.) The apartment was much bigger, but it was smack dab in the middle of a bad neighborhood. It was the first time I saw a heroin addict nod out on the street. Funny thing was, after my sleepover at Miss Connie's, it was the first time I had realized that Tia was in fact poor, but I didn't care.

Poor Tia. My attitude was the worst. I wouldn't talk much and just moped about. Thank goodness Titi, Cookie, and Millie were so lively. They got me out of my funk. Once they put on the record player and the dancing started, my smile returned. Especially when we all gathered around the television set to watch our newest addiction . . . wait for it . . . *Soul Train!* Oh my goodness, did I live for that show or what? The girls would point to their favorite outfits worn by the *Soul Train* dancers—"Ooh, *lookit* her platforms. . . . I'm wanna get me those pants!" We'd all get up and try to copy the *Soul Train* dancers prancing down the Soul Train line too! Loved it!

Speaking of addiction, Millie, Titi, and Cookie were a bit older now and were into partying any chance they got. Although Tia allowed them to smoke weed in the house but not cigarettes (she hated the smoke), out of respect they wouldn't do it in front of her and would take me with them to the park, sometimes in the late afternoon, sometimes at night, as they held court, smoking weed and cigarettes, drinking Wild Irish Rose or cans of beer from brown paper bags, cracking jokes. I loved it! And I loved sitting up on the swings or the concrete picnic tables laughing my ass off as they talked about boys, sex, and rock and roll—well, dance and soul music too, but you know what I'm saying.

One day, when Tia and I were alone in the apartment, cooking *pollo guisado*, I finally asked her the big question.

"How come I can't come live with you? I hate the Home. I hate it so much."

"*Ay,* I know. I wish you could, but . . . forget it."

"No, please, Tia! I want to know why!"

"Because I can't. I would love to have you be with me, always, but your mother won't let me take you."

"Why? She doesn't want me. She hates me. She wouldn't even care."

"*Ay*, don't say that, Rosie. That's not true."

I rolled my eyes and turned back to stirring the pot. I felt bad for being like that with Tia, but I couldn't help it.

I was sent back to my mother's house for the last two days of that visit. I was a gloomy piece of work, to say the least. I was finally having fun at Tia's and honestly didn't want to go back to Lydia's. My mother told us to get dressed, we were going over to a friend of her and her husband's for drinks. Lydia had on this tight-fitting dress that showed off her amazing hourglass figure. She hated my outfit and kept sucking her teeth every time she looked at me: "She's so fat. My God, look at her belly, and that hair, my God!" All of her comments were directed to her husband, as if she were trying to reassure him that she really didn't like me as much as her other kids, since I wasn't his. I took it all in and said nothing.

We got to the house. It was overdecorated to the nines—very seventies, hip and tacky. There was this glass coffee table, shaped like an hourglass, that captured my attention. I thought it was so cool-looking. I smoothed my hand across it, admiring its slickness. "Don't touch!" my mother yelled, so loudly that my hand jumped up and my elbow crashed onto the glass coffee table, shattering it. Everyone froze. I immediately started to cry, purely out of fear of my mother's reaction, and boy was it a doozy.

"Oh my fucking God! Look at what you fucking did! This fucking girl! My God! This fucking, fucking stupid girl! Get up! Up! Get up!"

She grabbed me by my arm so hard that I thought she was going to rip it right off. I yelped in pain. Durin pushed Lydia back and told her to let go of me. Say what? This man who barely said one word to me was coming to my defense? Holla! Lydia pushed me back down to the floor. I was beyond embarrassed.

The subway ride back to Lydia's house was torture. Besides the fact that my shoulder was killing me, she went on and on about how I ruined the entire night. Back in the house, after her husband dipped out to see his mistress, Lydia beat the shit out of me with a belt, then told me to go to bed, she was disgusted with me.

When I went upstairs, my oldest half-brother was lying under the covers on my mother and stepfather's bed watching television. "Hey, Rosie. Wanna watch TV with me?" I sat down on the edge of the bed. "Wanna see something?" I turned my head around, and there he was, stroking his erect penis. He burst out laughing. "Wanna touch it?" I immediately felt threatened, thinking about the kid in the infirmary with the dick and two balls, and all the rumors of sexual assaults I later heard from the older girls at the Home, by priests, by their family members on home visits, and even by the maintenance workers. I rolled my eyes with as much bravado as possible and flatly responded no. I turned back to the television, not knowing what I should do. I couldn't move—my head was spinning. I finally got up, saying something like I was going back downstairs or something. I went to the bathroom instead and stayed there until one of my half-sisters came pounding on the door, waking me up: "I need to pee!"

Lying in the full-size bed with Terry, Amy, and Betsy, I was sad and scared. I felt like I had no one to turn to, no one to tell what had happened, no one to stick up for me. I kept thinking, *Why did my brother do that? Was it because I was his half-sister and not his full blood? Did he just not care that much about my feelings and could take advantage? Was that why none of the rest of them offered any type of sympathy when Lydia was treating me like shit?* Maybe they were avoiding a beating as well. Lydia used to beat the crap out of some of them too, but come on, people, they could've at least asked or given me a look to see if I was okay.

That visit, with my mother's abuse and my perverted half-brother's demented stunt, affected me greatly. I didn't make the connection at the time, but it did change me. I began to train myself to care less about whether my half-siblings liked me, let alone claimed me, even though I still liked them. Weird. There were times when I would interact with Terry or Amy, if they initiated it. When I saw the rest of them at the playground or the cafeteria, I acted as if I didn't see them and kept it moving. It wasn't easy, but I did it. Whenever Lydia came for a visit—or, I should say, if she came—I was the last one to show up. If I got a home visit to her house, I would jump when I saw one of my cousins at the door to pick me up and take me to Tia's. Even though I was too small to fully grasp it, my heart understood where I belonged, where I needed to be.

Back at the Home, I was becoming more and more of an enigma to everyone, even to myself.

On the weekends that I didn't get to go to Tia's, I found relief in the visits to Miss Connie's house or on the Home's field trips to Bear Mountain that Mr. Neil and Ed Yano, the head counselors, would take us to. I would get lost on the nature trails, singing to myself the latest radio hit tunes, picking flowers, etc., and both took a liking to me. They explained the Vietnam War and the politics behind it. This was the first time one's personal politics were really discussed. They explained their liberal motivations for working with disadvantaged kids. Mr. Neil told me kids like me made his career choice worth it.

Mr. Neil and Ed both agreed that I stood out, as well as a few other kids, but that I was very different from most. They said that was a good thing. Say what? They even went further, stating that I could change the world because I was so smart and an innately good person. Whoa! Their words made me feel special, and I needed that badly. I stuck to them like glue after that, soaking up all their worldly knowledge and sharing what I knew to show them that I was in fact capable.

The other kids began to perceive me as uppity or having an attitude problem, since I wouldn't interact with them as much. I wasn't uppity, no. I was just sad and didn't want to be sad all the time. I wanted to enjoy myself and needed to feel safe and validated and stimulated mentally and emotionally. However, I must admit, I certainly had an attitude problem along with a raging temper if provoked—and I hated it.

The conflict inside really bothered me. I liked being that kid Mr. Neil and Ed Yano saw. But I couldn't control my temper a lot of the time. If you disrespected me—forget about it. If a girl started in on me for whatever reason, I would snap—and I mean snap. I would curse her out in a second, punch back if she even dared to touch me. I became a sneak and a liar too, and I hated being like that. So conflicted.

And being friends with Crazy Cindy was a conflict as well. She brought me so much joy and fun, but she did lead me down a path that I knew better than to go down. Like how we used to sneak down to the kitchen and steal food whenever we were starving from all of our punishments. Every time I would stuff my face with pie, I would wash it down with a huge amount of guilt. But that was nothing compared to other things we got ourselves into.

One day, while playing Red Light, Green Light, One-Two-Three, with the big girls on the bottom grove, Cindy ran over with one of the bad girls. "She got cigarettes. Wanna come and smoke with us?"

Smoke? Hell no! Well, maybe I'd just come along and see.

As we tiptoed back into the dorm, Lil Tillie, with the two permanent braided pigtails, was sitting up on her bed. "What's going on? You going to the kitchen?" "It's none of your business, Silly Tillie. And you better not tell on us either, or I'll get you back!" snapped Cindy.

Poor Lil Tillie. She was the nicest thing on the planet.

The bad girl decided that we were going to commit the crime in the clothes closet away from everyone. She lit up and passed the cigarette. I shook my head no; I didn't want to do it. "She's such a baby. I told you not to bring her!"

"Shut up, stupid," I barked back.

I picked up the book of matches and lit one. Watching the flame transported me as it burned all the way down the matchstick, burning my fingers. Cindy took a pull on the cigarette and held it out to me. I gave in. Ugh! It was disgusting. I was gagging, and then we all heard a noise. We froze.

"Someone's coming!" The bad girl and Cindy ran out. I was frozen, standing there like an idiot with the damn cigarette in my hand. Crazy Cindy ran back in. "Come on!" I panicked and flung the cigarette over my shoulder and ran out. Unbeknownst to me, it landed in one of the bins filled with clothes and lit the bins on fire.

After the firemen left, Sister Renata lined us up and walked up and down, scanning all of us with her beady eyes and her paddle.

"We have ways to find out who did this. You can either step forward now or pay the consequences later."

No one budged. Sister Renata motioned to Miss Millie. Miss Millie waved over the first girl in the line. "Hold out your hands!" Miss Millie smelled her fingers (nuns' forensic techniques!). "You're good. Stand over there. Next!"

One by one, Miss Millie sniffed out each girl's hands. She got to the bad seed's hands. Sniff. "You are in big trouble." She motioned her to stand on the opposite side from the girls who had been checked and cleared. Sister Renata bent her over and whacked the hell out of her tiny butt until she saw red. "And that's just a sample of what's to come!" I shook. I couldn't bear the thought of another violent beating.

Crazy Cindy leaned backwards from the line, trying to get my attention.

"Psst! Psst! Stick your fingers down your butt."

Cindy actually stuck her fingers down her pants like she was digging for China.

She went up next. Miss Millie took a whiff, and her head jerked back from the stench. Cindy cracked up in her face. Miss Millie motioned her to the "not guilty" side.

Next up was Lil Tillie. Miss Millie smelled her fingers—guilty! Guilty? What the hell? "But I didn't do it," cried Lil Tillie. "Quiet!" snapped Sister Renata. She then bent Lil Tillie over and began whacking. I shoved my fingers so fast up my ass it wasn't funny.

It was my turn. Miss Millie smelled my fingers, looked suspiciously up at me, then over to Crazy Cindy, who gave her this perfect beguiled blank stare. Miss Millie looked back at me; I was shaking and couldn't meet her eyes. "Not guilty!" Did the fingers in my butt work, or did she let me off the hook? She was always kind to me and hated how Sister Renata beat me.

As we were leaving, we could hear the screams and cries from Lil Tillie and the bad girl. I was disgusted with myself. What was going on? Who was I becoming? I thought about Mr. Neil and Ed Yano, who perceived me as good, and I worried that I would disappoint them. I didn't want that to happen. I felt desperate to hold on to that part of me. I went over to Crazy Cindy and told her how bad I felt that Lil Tillie took the fall for us. Crazy Cindy just shrugged it off. "So? At least we didn't get caught."

CHAPTER 14

I WAS eight years old and was summoned to the office of the head nun, Sister Minetta-Mary. Dag it! What the hell did I do this time? This was serious business, being sent up to see the big boss. Sister Renata accompanied me, not looking or speaking to me either. I was silent during the long walk to the head nun's office.

Sister Minetta-Mary's office was simple and carpeted, with leather-studded chairs and a mahogany desk. Sister Renata told me to sit on one of the chairs; she sat in the one beside me. Sister Minetta-Mary came out. Man, she was older than dirty-dirt. She had an authority to her that showed she had put her time in too.

"Hello, Rosemary. You know we care about you girls here. We teach you manners, give you a fine education, a roof over your head, and your recent and continuing impertinent behavior is what we get in return? You're usually a very good girl."

She paused dramatically, folding her hands together.

"You're in our outside-school program, correct?"

"Yes, sister."

"Those privileges are not given to everyone. You do know that?"

"Yes, sister."

"Rosemary, I think you're a good child who's lost her way. Perhaps you need a change of environment. There is a new program called a Group Home—there will be one for girls and one for boys. Eight girls and eight boys will be picked that we feel are either well behaved or academically advanced enough to live in a real house in upstate New York. It will be a great opportunity. You are being considered. However, one more stunt and you will be taken off that list and all other privileges will be taken away."

Yay! I couldn't believe my luck! Man, I'm going to be really good now!

"But this is not why we have brought you in. Sister Renata, please ask Mrs. Vasquez to come in."

Mrs. Vasquez? All I was thinking was, *Not another damn kid.* Mrs. Vasquez and her swishing fat thighs entered and sat down. The big sister continued.

"Rosemary, you have a father who is different from your brothers' and sisters' father. Did you know that?"

Of course I knew that. My half-brothers and -sisters and my mother made sure to remind me constantly. Of course I knew I had a different father after he made that drunken confession to me four years before. Yes, I knew! The whole world was constantly reminding me!

"Your father would like to meet you and has expressed that he would like to take a bigger role and interest in your life. We can take things slow and see how you feel after you have met him today. Does that sound okay to you?"

Uh, no! I don't want to meet my father—who I have already met! And what nerve of him, especially since I had not seen him in almost a year after I started to fall in love with him because of our weird and wonderful dates he used to take me on! No! This is not okay with me! The head honcho didn't wait for me to answer.

Mrs. Vasquez walked me out onto the balcony. Ismael was sitting on a bench that faced the railroad tracks. He got up, took his hat off.

"Hello, Rosie. I'm your father, Ismael."

What? Why was he acting like I had never met him before? I started to get really angry but tried really hard not to let it take over me. Mrs. Vasquez left, leaving us alone.

"Hello, Rosie. I'm your father. I had met you before in—"

"I know who you are!" I rudely interrupted.

Awkward pause.

"Oh. I'm glad you remember. (*pause*) Did you know that I was the first one to call you Rosie? Yes. It is true. (*laughs*) You know, I used to have a girlfriend named Rosie and a girlfriend named Marie. And you have both names!"

He chuckled up even harder. I looked at him and rolled my eyes. I felt like I couldn't breathe.

"There's a restaurant down the hill," he continued. "Sorrento's. I thought we could have some lunch there."

I looked down at the cement staircase, swinging my leg back and forth, praying to God that this would be over soon.

"You know, I wanted to come see you sooner, but I was away on the ship. . . . Plus, your mother wouldn't allow me to. You see, you have her last name, Perez, not mine, Serrano. But if you change your last name to mine, Serrano, I can come see you anytime you like. . . . Or take you to Puerto Rico to visit me and my family—"

Family? Like I'm not your family?

"You see, I was not on the birth certificate and—"

"I don't want to change my name. I'm fine with Perez."

His face dropped. He leaned back on the bench and made a deep sigh. I rolled my eyes at him and looked away.

Sorrento's was this tiny Italian restaurant at the bottom of the hill, directly across the street from the train station. The lighting inside was dark, and each table had a small lighted lamp on top. Ismael ordered eggplant parmigiana for both of us, with a salad to start. I thought that was so weird, not only that he ordered for me, like they do in the old movies and I always wanted someone to do that for me, but also, eggplant parmigiana happened to be my favorite Italian dish.

"You know, if you change your last name to mine, then me and Minguita—"

"I'm not changing my name. I'm Perez. I wouldn't do that to my mother."

Say what? My father just nodded his head yes. I watched his eyes flood with tears and then watched them roll down his face.

We ate in silence. The waiter came by our table and gestured to our half-eaten plates.

"Are you finished, sir?"

"No, sir. I'm Puerto Rican."

As bad as that joke was, I chuckled. My father looked up at me and smiled.

Dad, banking on my change of mood, decided to just spill the truth. He told me that word had gotten back to my mother about our "dates" back in Brooklyn. And she had heard rumors of him claiming me as his, saying that he was going to have my last name changed. Lydia was pissed and told Tia that if my father pursued any legal actions, she would make sure that he and Tia would never be able to see me again. He got scared and stayed away, but finally got the nerve to stand up to her and told the Home that he was in fact my real father.

Bullshit. Yeah, it was great that he finally stood up to my mother, kind of, but all the other stuff was immature, selfish drama on the part of both my mother and my father! They were acting out their own bullshit over a failed romance, and I was the one getting hit the hardest by being left in the Home as their saga continued. And Tia was hurt too. If they both put their nonsense aside, I would have been back at Tia's, and she and I would have been happy like we had been.

"May I be excused, please? I need to use the ladies' room."

My father stood up and pulled out my chair for me, like the men would always do for Bette Davis and Barbara Stanwyck in the old movies. I liked that, but couldn't let on.

Inside the bathroom stall, my heart was pounding. Why didn't I say yes and agree to change my last name? I didn't understand at the time that that would have been my ticket out of the Home. I could only feel anger toward him for not seeing me for such a long time. I saw this as something that would further separate me from my mother. It was too much for me to comprehend. I splashed water on my face, quietly snuck out of the restaurant, and ran back up the hill to the Home, leaving my father sitting there like a clueless idiot.

After hiding out for a while in the dormitory, I started to think about what the head nun had told me about being on the list for the Group Home. Man, I hoped I hadn't blown it by pulling this shit with my father. I decided to go back to the main office and face the music. If I was going to get punished, I wanted to get it over with, take it like a champ, and hopefully still be considered for the program.

My father was there waiting and immediately ran up to me and hugged the shit out of me, thanking God that I was all right. Sister Renata started screaming, pointing her finger in my face. My father turned to her and firmly told her not to yell at his daughter. And he never wanted to hear her speak to me that way again. Ooh! Pops got heart! I was shocked. Sister Renata was fuming. Too bad he didn't understand that I was going to pay for his actions on top of mine.

My father told them that he was going to have me walk him down to the train station. He took my hand as we started down the hill. I pulled it back. He stopped, turned to me, and just smiled this sweet smile. We continued down to the station, not saying a single word.

The train pulled in. My father turned to me and smiled. "I'll see you very soon. I love you very much, Rosie. I am your daddy, and you are my life, and I'll never forget you, ever. And I want you to meet your sister Carmen and your little brother Tito. You call me if you need anything." He got on the train and turned around to me, pumping his fist up and down in the air as he cheerfully cried out, "Choo-choo!" I had the instinct to laugh but shook my head with a smile in disbelief instead.

Ismael changed after that visit. He replaced a lot of his limited idle time wasted on philandering—not all of it, mind you—with time spent with me. He began to visit on Sundays at the Home or come to Tia's whenever I would go down for a home visit. The visits to Saint Joseph's always included a meal at Sorrento's Italian restaurant. I loved those "dates," loved how he continued to pull out my chair for me and order my meals too. I began to melt for him again—my guard was still a bit up, but I certainly wasn't as icy as I was before. I couldn't be, not with his charm and corny jokes. He was still a merchant marine, and when he was out at sea, he would write me many letters from all around the world, always ending with, "Your loving father, Ismael." I cherished those letters and kept them in my locker all the way in the back so that no one would steal them.

. . .

My father's apartment was inside of a nice limestone building, on Linden Boulevard in East New York, ten minutes away from Tia's. There were a bunch of kids playing stickball in the street. It was my little brother's birthday party, and the smell of roasted pork and *pasteles* reeked through the open first-floor window. On the way there, Tia told me that Tina, who they'd told me was my cousin, was really my sister and her real name was Carmen. (Tia had wanted to call Carmen Tina since she was born on Valentine's Day and . . . anyway, just some Puerto Rican weird shit.) She also told me that Carmen was not my father's wife's kid, but that my little brother Tito was. My father had been married to her during the conception of his two love children, Carmen and me—again, more dramatic Puerto Rican weird shit. Tia made me promise never to let on that I knew about Carmen's real mother.

The apartment was huge, decorated in gold and brown tones,

and the plush, tacky, faux traditional Americana gold-and-maroon-colored sofa was covered in plastic. Birthday decorations covered every inch of the living room. I took in all of the presents that were stacked up on the mahogany living room coffee table; it seemed unreal. We would only get one present, possibly two, at the Home. I looked down into the small dining room. The table was cluttered with half-eaten plates and half-empty large platters of Puerto Rican delights. I started to put two and two together.

Here was my father, with a family all his own, who had a house in Puerto Rico and an apartment in Brooklyn, his son had all these gifts and shit, and he kept Carmen, another love child, and me stuck in a "home" with sadistic nuns. The iciness that I had felt for him before began to come back. I took a deep breath and tried to talk myself out of the dark mood that was creeping up inside of me.

A short, well-dressed, well-groomed, red-haired, fairly attractive woman walked in with a plate of hamburgers and French fries.

"Jello, Rosie. I'm Angel, jor father's wife. And I so 'appy to meet jew. I made jew de 'amburgas and de Fren-fry." I looked at the plate of American food. I was so insulted. Why did she assume that I would want a damn hamburger and fries? Because I was in a damn home run by American nuns and priests who tried as hard as possible to wash away every ounce of ethnicity in me?

"No thank you, I'm not hungry," I said as I rolled my eyes.

Angel looked like I had punctured a pin in her happy balloon. My father came in smiling from ear to ear and kissed me on the cheek.

"Hello, baby! I'm so happy you are here. You look beautiful! Welcome. This is your home. And this is my wife, Angel. And this is your sister, Carmen, and your brother, Tito—Hey! Tito! Carmen! Vien' aqui!"

Tito was bucktoothed, sandy blond, and cute as hell. I couldn't stop staring—he looked so much like me! No one on my mother's side looked like me. He smiled at me and then ran off. Carmen, who used to be Tina, was bubbling over with excitement.

"Hello! I'm your sister Carmen! You used to be my cousin, but now you're my sister! Papi says you don't know Spanish, so we're not supposed to speak to you in Spanish. But I know Spanish!"

Uh, thanks for the clueless insult—annoying idiot. I rolled my eyes. Carmen looked up at our father.

"She doesn't like me, Papi." Carmen pouted as she stomped her foot.

"Sure she likes you! You're her sister! Why don't you take her outside to meet her cousins and all of your friends?"

"Okay! Come on, Rosie!"

"No thank you."

Carmen ran to the back of the apartment, crying her bratty head off. Angel ran after her. I leaned in closer to Tia. I wanted to kick myself in the ass for being such an ass, but I couldn't help it. Dad looked up at his sister with a reassuring smile. Man, this guy is so damn positive, it makes me sick. "Don't worry, Minguita, everything's okay. I'll see you tomorrow."

Tomorrow? Tia's leaving me here? Oh, hell no! I looked up at her. "I'll stay for one minute to eat, then I go," Tia said. She stacked my plate with rice and beans and the crispy skin of the roasted pork. I ate, not uttering a single word. Tia seemed to be a little embarrassed by my behavior, but smiled it off.

It was time for bed. My father pointed me to a full-sized bed, and Carmen got into the twin pushed against the wall. Dad came over, smiled, and patted me on the head. He went over to Carmen, tucked her in, and kissed her good night, then left. My heart sank. I wanted a kiss too. I pulled the covers over my head to hide my thumb-sucking. The sheets smelled musty and old, even though they were clearly clean. It grossed me out. I poked my head out to suck in some fresh air.

"Rosie. You awake?"

I didn't answer her. I wished she would just shut up and let me sleep.

"I always told my father that I always wanted a sister, and now I have one."

Your father? He's my father too, you spoiled brat.

"I can't wait until you come to Puerto Rico. They speak Spanish there."

Okay. I'm two seconds away from punching this girl in the face.

"Rosie? Rosie. You know that was my *abuela*'s bed you're in. *Abuela* means 'grandmother' in Spanish."

"I know what *abuela* means! I'm not an idiot!"

There was a silent pause after that. I hoped she'd shut up now.

"Rosie?"

"Jeez Louise! What?"

"I just wanted to tell you that my *abuela* died last week in that bed. She was dead there for a day before they took her to the cemetery. She had a big forehead like you too."

Oh my goodness! I was so freaked out that I didn't even have time to absorb the forehead insult!

"Why the hell did you tell me that for? Now I won't be able to sleep!"

"I'm sorry. I was just telling you that she died there and—"

"For the love of Pete! Would you please shut up and leave me alone! My goodness, you're so irritating!"

I knew I was a jerk, but come on, people! And she went for the forehead!!

The next morning I woke up to Carmen's voice crying out from the kitchen, ratting me out to Angel and my father. Now I really couldn't stand her. I slowly walked in. I felt embarrassed and awkward. Everyone went quiet. My father finally broke the silence. "Good morning, baby! Come sit next to me." I sat next to him and didn't utter a word.

Tia came by shortly afterwards, with my cousin Titi. I could hardly look anyone in the eye when I said good-bye. On the train ride back, I just kept thinking that I blew it and that I'd probably never see my father and his family again.

. . .

Later that summer, still at Tia's, she told me that we were going on a plane to Puerto Rico, just the two of us, to see my father! Wow. Maybe I didn't blow it after all! I burst out crying happy tears. She told me I had to swear not to tell anyone, especially the Home or my mother, that we were going. She would get in trouble, and I would never be able to go again.

Getting packed and ready to go was pure chaos. Tia was a mess. "Where's my shoes?! Where's *de* American Express?! Where's my dress?! Where's *dis*?! Where's *dat*?!" We bolted out of the house and climbed into a gypsy cab. Tia was in a panic the entire ride to JFK (or was it La Guardia? I don't remember which one we flew out of), screaming at the driver, "*Ay*, my goodness! We're gonna miss *de* flight!"

The plane was packed with Puerto Ricans. I think I saw maybe four Americans (white Americans). Two were in first-class. Tia let me take the window seat. As we began to take off, Tia closed her eyes in prayer and crossed herself twice. "You have to pray for God to let us land safely without crashing and dying."

"What? We're gonna die?"

"*Ay*, please. Don't be so dramatical, Rosie. Pray." I bowed my head with her, crossed myself twice, and prayed my heart out.

When the plane landed, all of the Puerto Ricans, including Tia, began clapping in unison. I started to clap too. A white man sitting directly across from us was snide, rolling his eyes at our provincial gesture of gratitude for landing safely. His judgment felt just like the "outside" kids at "outside" school. Well, he wasn't going to dis

Tia like that and get away with it, with his corny pink knitted pull-over and white shorts. I leaned over Tia and gave him a nasty look.

"Excuse me, sir!"

Tia pushed me back.

"No, Rosie. Don't be like that. It's not right. Pay him no mind."

Puerto Rico was so damn hot and humid. As soon as we got off the plane, my hair went *poof*. I looked like one big powder puff. We shared a broken-down cab with three adults and one other young girl, all Puerto Rican, and we were all squished up, sweating all over each other. The nonstop storytelling, jokes, and sing-alongs lasted the six hours it took us to get to my father's town, Agua-dilla. It was great fun that helped distract us from the scary-ass ride. It was before the freeways were built, and we had to cut up and through mountains and drive along the narrow streets along the sides of the cliffs in the dark of night. It was terrifying as hell, especially since the driver drove like a maniac.

The cabby left us off at the end of a driveway to a peach-colored single-story house. I heard this strange sound, like a million crick-ets singing out into the night air. "Those are crickets, Tia?"

"No, those are Coquís. They're little frogs that sing in the night. 'Co-key, co-key,' you hear them saying that?"

My father came out in his boxer shorts, a white V-neck T-shirt, and house slippers. "Hello, baby!"

My heart was jumping so fast inside. How should I greet him now that it'd been made official, with that whole scenario back at the Home, that he was my father, and especially after how badly I had acted at his house? *"Bendición,"* I mumbled.

He grabbed me and gave me the biggest smothering, annoying hug ever. Okay, I loved it, but I didn't express it. I wanted to, but I couldn't.

Inside, everyone else was asleep. Dad made us coffee. (I know, weird to make us coffee at such a late hour, but that's how they roll down in P.R.) I don't remember much of how the single-level house looked, except that it was small and there was a patio and a mango tree in the front. Dad brought my suitcase into Carmen's room and told me that I was to stay there with Tia. Carmen was bunking up with Tito in his room. They each have their own room? Wow. They're so lucky. Carmen's room was filled with Barbie dolls, like about fifty of them! I'm not kidding. And she had a queen-sized bed. Wow! She had so much stuff in there. I felt jealous, but I told myself to knock it off.

"What's wrong, Rosie?" asked Tia.

"Nothing . . . Look at all these Barbies. It's ridiculous," I said as a lump reached my throat.

"Don't be like that, Rosie. I know it's hard, but you should never be mad at someone for having things. They are just things. It means nothing."

I got in bed first. Tia was still in the bathroom. My father poked his head in, saying, "Good night, baby. I'll see you in the morning." "Good night, Daddy." Whoa. That just slipped out. Simple. Natural. I looked over to him, standing at the door. "That makes me so happy to hear you call me Daddy, my baby." I quickly rolled over on my side, giving him my back, and stuck my thumb in my mouth.

. . .

In the morning, I woke up to the sounds of La Playa Sextet playing on a hi-fi stereo record player. It was one of my father's many favorite bands. My father, still in his boxers and T-shirt, was sitting at the head of the dining table eating a large slice of Italian bread and butter that he constantly dipped in his *café con leche*.

"Morning, baby. I saw this group in 1962. Oh, they were fantastic. Let me show you the album cover. You hungry? Angel, bring some breakfast for Rosie, please."

As he went to get the album cover, Angel brought me a plate of fried eggs and French fries. No pancakes. I looked up at her and smiled and felt very appreciative. She hugged me. The eggs were made perfectly: crispy, bubbly edges, with the yolk just slightly cooked underneath. I only ate the egg whites and fries. I always hated the yolk.

"Come over here, baby. Here's the album cover. I saw this group in 1962. [Yes, he repeated himself—he did that constantly.] Wow. Man, could they jam! You like jazz? I love jazz. All the greats, I love them."

He looked at me, waiting for a response. There was nothing. He put on Nat King Cole's "Nature Boy." My eyes widened as I recognized it immediately. I love him!

"That was recorded in 1948. I love Nat King Cole—very classy guy. You know a Jewish man wrote that song? Oh yes."

Next was Benny Goodman.

"The King of Swing! He's Jewish too. First man to let blacks play in a white band. He could play almost like a black man too, and his drummer, Gene Krupa—great drummer. Yeah. I love Benny. But Tony Bennett's my favorite. You like him?"

I nodded yes. Actually, I loved him. And loved Benny too. I recognized him from the old movies. "Jimmy Stewart played him in this movie," I peeped. Dad beamed!

Tia, my father, and I headed into town. As we walked down to the end of the road to catch the *gua-gua*, my father took my hand. I didn't pull it away. My hand felt so little in his. Of course, my father knew everyone on the minibus, including the *gua-gua* driver. Dad held court, spewing his infamous corny-ass jokes.

I was in awe of Aguadilla, known as the *Jardin de la Atlantico*. It was a beautiful, tiny, quiet, sleepy, poor, beach bum, surfing town on the shores of the northwestern tip of Puerto Rico. The town was so tiny, with its one traffic light, that you could drive around it within five minutes. The town's main square, named La Plaza de Rafael Hernandez—after Puerto Rico's most famous composer—was surrounded by small pastel-colored shops that stood side by side, with a chapel at the head of the square. Directly across the street was one of the beaches. It was beautiful! I ran to the water and stood at the edge of the shore, mesmerized. Tia tapped me on the shoulder.

"This town is where our people are from. Boricuas. You know Christopher Columbus, who discovered America, came here. Oh jes! He did! *Ay*, I hate sand. Let's go."

I looked around for Dad. He was standing just a few feet away, watching, waiting, desperately wanting to be a part of the bond that Tia and I had. I forced a smile his way. That was all he needed. He clapped his hands together, and with a little hop and a skip, he walked over to us. "How about I buy you a coconut soda? Would you like that?" Not the damn coconut soda again. "Yes, please." Well, what else could I say to this guy?

We later went up to see my great-aunt, Amelia Serrano, who was my grandfather's sister. Ismael's father, my grandfather, passed away when my father was a young kid, and many have said that he never got over it and suffered even more when his mother passed when he was in his early twenties. So, my great-aunt Amelia, who also was a gifted piano player, therefore became the pillar of the Serrano clan. Everyone called Amelia, Tia Aya (pronounced *eye-ya*), and she was black as the night with starkly bluish-green eyes, skinny with a muscular wry build, and she held a command. She was so strong in her character, so strange-looking; I couldn't stop staring. Her husband was extremely tall and dark-skinned, strong, silent, with a sweet demeanor. They had two sons and a daughter named Rosie! I felt like a part of the family, instantly.

The house sat up on a little hill on the side of the mountain. It was pastel peachy-pink and had a large kitchen. There were vegetables and fruit all over the tiled counter in the center. Ropes of garlic wrapped around each doorway. I asked Tia Aya why there was garlic everywhere.

"To keep the evil spirits away," she said.

The look of terror that washed over my face made everyone laugh.

"You have evil spirits here?"

"There are spirits everywhere, Rosita. Good, bad, indifferent."

"You mean like witchcraft or something like that? That's against God."

"There's nothing evil or spooky about anything if there isn't anything evil and spooky in your soul."

Tia Aya then looked at me, smiled, and winked. I smiled back. Even though she freaked me out, I liked her so much. I wanted to stay with her, learn everything I could from her, but the influence of the Home and Catholic dogma was eating at me, trying to convince me she was bad for not believing the way they did. I forced myself to block out the Home's creed.

The backyard was filled with mango and avocado trees. A couple of chickens were squawking about in the back of the yard, along with the cutest little black-and-speckled-white pig. His name was Miguel, and he captured my heart. I smiled at him, and he waddled up to me and smiled back and playfully butted me with his snout up against my belly. I was in love, just as I was in love with all the doggies and horses at Miss Connie's friend Jan's house. I played with Miguel the entire afternoon.

Then Tia Aya came out back, grabbed one of the chickens, and broke its neck! Right in front of me, and acting as if nothing out of the ordinary had happened! I screamed at the top of my lungs. She looked up at me, kind of chuckled, and started to pluck out the feathers.

The next morning, Tia and I went to see my other great-aunt. She lived in a two-room wooden shack with a dirt floor. When we knocked, this skinny, hunched-over, 110-year-old woman opened the door. She had shocking white hair and no teeth. She touched my face with her arthritic bony hands and told me I was pretty. We only stayed for coffee. Tia didn't want to exhaust her.

Tia and I drove all the way back to the outskirts of San Juan to spend the last night at the house of her oldest brother, Tio Monserrate. He lived there with his wife, Blanca, and their two kids, Albin and Mickey. Albin was around sixteen; Mickey, who was about fourteen, looked just like Tia! Tia was acting so strange. She cried the whole five-hour drive to his house. Then, when we got there, she stayed outside on the sunporch and wouldn't go inside. When she saw Mickey, she started to quietly cry again. Years later I found out that Mickey was her son and that my uncle kept him after they put Tia in a "hospital" after her divorce. Tio Monserrate was supposed to give him back when Tia was released, but never did and legally adopted him. Tia never got over it. She cried the next morning and on the plane ride back. I promised that I would never forget her, that I would never make her cry, ever.

. . .

When I got back to the Home, I hated it more than ever and was even more determined to get out and have a successful life and career, like Mary Tyler Moore on *The Mary Tyler Moore Show*. I had been to Puerto Rico. I had met Tia Aya and walked along the shores of my ancestral home and heard about the island's saga. I had met Tio Monseratte and Titi Blanca. I had climbed mango trees and played with Miguel the pig. I had fallen asleep to the sounds of the little Coquís. I had met my history, and it made me feel present and validated. I knew now that I belonged to something, and it gave me strength to believe I could do anything.

. . .

It was Sunday. I was eight years old and waiting to hear about being picked for the Group Home upstate. The Home was putting on another *Peanuts* play. I was cast as Lucy. I wanted to play Peppermint

Patty, or Kathy. I had moved on from wanting to be Linus since he was a thumb sucker and I was trying desperately to stop sucking my thumb.

My mother was coming for an afternoon visit. Since she would stand us up the majority of the time, I didn't bother to go up to the main office to wait for her. But during rehearsal, I was told that she did in fact come. I immediately judged myself for not rushing out.

It was a typical visit: I kissed my mother on her extended cheek, ate the Puerto Rican delights that she so deliciously cooked, and uttered about two sentences. I told my mother that I had a rehearsal and couldn't stay. "Oh," she said, with a slight pause. "I was going to pierce your ears today. You don't want to stay and get pierced?" Looking back on it now, it was the first time I saw her hurt. I didn't register it at the time. Instead, I declined and went back to the auditorium.

At the end of rehearsal, I saw my mother waiting for me at the entrance of the auditorium with ice cubes and a needle and thread. When I saw that needle, I didn't want anything pierced—shit was big! She insisted. She pleaded. I relented. She sat down and placed me in between her legs, with my head on her lap. First was the freezing of my earlobe—that was agonizing enough. I kept telling her that I had changed my mind. "No, it's gonna be okay. Be still," she said as she squeezed her legs tightly, squishing the air out of me.

Then came the needle—it hurt like hell! I yelled my head off. I'd had enough and tried to push off her knees so that I could get myself out from between her thighs. Bad move. She pushed me down, grabbed my hair at its roots, punching my head at the same time, and told me to "hold the fuck still!" She dug that freaking needle all the way through. Shit hurt like hell! But I was more pissed than hurt. She did the other ear, pulling the thread through, tying it at the ends, and then smearing on a huge goop of Vaseline. "There," she said, smiling and sweating with satisfaction. "You look so cute. You like it?" I nodded yes. "Make sure you move the string back and forth so it doesn't get stuck." I nodded yes again and told her I had to use the bathroom. I hid there and didn't return for the rest of the visit.

Later that day and all through the night, I kept showing off my pierced ears, bragging that my mother had done them. Weird.

Thinking about that incident afterwards, I wonder if she did it because she knew my father had told me that he was my father and that I had gone to his house and met the rest of my family. I wonder if that was a desperate action to not lose me completely, to tell me in her own nonsensical way that she loved me and was worried and maybe even jealous. She was like that. She had weird moments of misguided sincerity that would break your heart.

At least that's what I told myself. It was way better than the other side of the truth.

I had to do that a lot, to see more than what was on the surface in order to still have hope and find the good in people and not become hardened like some of the kids had become in the Home. Yet, I also had to stay strong and let the abuse from my mother and the Home roll off my back. I had to believe that I was going to get out of this place one day and live with Tia or even Dad. And if that wasn't going to happen anytime soon, I was still on the list for the Group Home, and I wasn't going to mess that up with acting out.

CHAPTER 15

THE EIGHT girls were chosen for the Group Home—eight to sixteen years of age. The prerequisites were high grades, good behavior, or both. I was selected—yay!—as well as my half-sisters Betsy and Terry. We were all gathered in one of the dorms and told that the Group Home would change our lives significantly, meaning it would be a better-designed stepping-stone from institutional to civilian life. You see, the pressure of "making it" after leaving the Home was intense. The nuns always stressed the importance of getting accepted to college, being able to support yourself, getting married, etc., so that we would be prepared for the outside world once we left. Many fared well. But a few didn't. We would constantly hear stories.

Some kids whose parents took them back permanently didn't always make it. They couldn't readjust, or were subjected to abuse. They would end up on the streets, in jail, or even back at the Home if they were still under the age of eighteen. Some who were orphaned or abandoned and who spent most of their lives at Saint Joseph's, then were released into society once they turned eighteen with no one to go to, didn't always do well either. Post-traumatic stress disorder and other psychological factors would hit them as well—hard. They would end up on the streets too, or drug addicts, or emotionally disabled—some to the point of not being able to function as well as they knew they could. This haunted me.

I, being the youngest—only eight years old—asked Mr. Neil, if I was scared to go to the bathroom late at night, would there be a light left on? That question was probably more about the big change and the pressure of succeeding in the program. The eldest girl blurted out, "God, she's such a baby. I don't want to go now." Mr. Neil told her she didn't have to go; she could stay in the Home. She quickly recanted. I marked her comment, so I could make sure I kept my distance. It wasn't that I was afraid of her; it was that I didn't want any irritating drama that would suck me in. I did the same with Betsy. All of her jabs were button-pushers. I didn't want to mess this opportunity up. At least I had Terry and Olga Lopez. Terry and I were more like friends than sisters but it was still a good thing. She would crack me up so much and loved hanging with me just to make me laugh. Olga, well, Olga was a star at the Home. She was extremely smart, never got into trouble, and the nicest, funniest, and nerdiest person ever—so, of course we clicked.

We drove up in a station wagon, about two hours upstate from Saint Joseph's. Terry and I melodramatically sang along and acted out almost every song played on WABC Musicradio, trying to out-funny each other, especially on the song "Feelings" by Morris Albert—talk about drama on the high seas. I took in the pertinent road signs—the Route 9 post, the bridges, the gas stations—just in case I needed to get back to Tia's house.

The modest two-story, five-bedroom house, complete with a single-car garage, sat on top of a small mound that spread out over a quarter-acre of plush green grass. It was in fact one of the cheaper houses in the middle- to upper-middle-class rural-suburban neighborhood lined with well-manicured lawns. What the hell did we care? It was awesome in comparison to the dorms. The bedrooms were crazy big. The basement, which was the designated playroom, had a pool table that doubled as a Ping-Pong table and a hi-fi stereo record player. Four bicycles sat waiting for us in the garage. And there was a big fat television (yay!) in the corner of a tacky red-and-gold-decorated living room—happy-happy, joy-joy!

A couple of the maintenance workers we were all familiar with from Saint Joe's were still painting when we arrived. I overheard one of them complaining about the long work hours with no overtime. This tall, chubby, middle-aged black man caught me listening from the corner of his eye and quickly interjected, "This is not about us. This is about giving these kids a new start. If ya'll want to go, then that's on ya'll. I know I'm gonna stay and finish what we started for these damn kids." I cocked my head to the left and inquisitively stared at him. I wondered if he was sincere or felt compelled to say that because he was caught.

We went outside to see the rest of our new world. The green grass, the big full trees, and the freedom were exhilarating, but I couldn't take it all in. I worried that our new neighbors might not accept us. I worried about Crazy Cindy. Although I was ecstatic to leave Sister Renata and the Home, even if it was for the Group Home and not Tia's or Dad's house, leaving my best friend behind was very painful. It seemed so unfair to me that she didn't get to go. I mean, if someone needed another chance at life it was certainly Cindy. We just hugged and said good-bye. It was weird. You would think it would've been a more tearful moment, but I think we were both so sad to the point of being numb. And I kept worrying about being farther away from Tia and Brooklyn—would she be able to find me? But I didn't spend too much time worrying because it was so damn pretty outside and there were no nuns, not a damn one in sight—God bless America two times!

The next-door neighbor, this white man whose house was separated from ours by half an acre, was hanging out of his second-floor window when he saw us walking by and screaming out, "Heil Hitler!" with a Nazi salute, repeatedly—I kid you not! My internal reaction wasn't, *Oh God! This man is such a racist.* It was, *Great, the whole neighborhood knows that we're from the Home. Here we go again.* Looking back, it was naive of me to think no one would know—eight girls, various ethnicities, all from the city, most not related, living in a house with white Group Home parents. Thank goodness not every family in that neighborhood was like that neo-Nazi. There were a few really nice people up there. Even the Nazi's teenage son didn't share his father's racism—we actually became friends.

The first Group Home "parents"—and yes, there were many to come, how's that for stability—were these white, gray-haired senior citizens who greeted us with serene, laid-back smiles. The geezers were all about being relaxed and eating lots of good food. Yay! There was so much food served at dinner. And we got to serve ourselves! No lining up, no unison prayer with that insane clapping at the end, no nuns—nothing! Just food! And we were allowed to have seconds and thirds—double yay! Seriously. I would daydream about food—good, high-quality, fattening food—a lot. I mean, I even went so far as to steal food from the Home's kitchen! I remember salivating and staring at the "outside" kids' homemade lunches, wishing I had a Ring Ding or a sandwich with more than one slice of meat.

We had great counselors who came to the house almost every day: Maurvive, Beth, Janis, and this man whose name I've forgotten. All were white, smart, caring, and dedicated. Maurvive had a sheepdog named Citizen that she brought over daily. I took to him like crazy. I'd never expressed love the way I expressed love for that dog. I even used to have him sleep in my tiny twin bed with me. She eventually gave Citizen to us after she moved on a year later—everyone considered him mine after that.

Beth taught me poetry and spoke with me about my dreams for my future. Janis introduced me to Todd Rundgren, Paul Simon, Led Zeppelin, and Paul McCartney and Wings. And one of them introduced me to Burt Bacharach! I loved, loved Burt Bacharach! The girls gave me shit for it, saying that I wanted to be white for liking something other than Gladys Knight and the Pips.

Unfortunately, Grandma and Grandpa didn't last past two weeks. Two of the older girls found marijuana in their bedroom, and they freaked out! The girls jumped on their bikes and tried to ride all the way back to Saint Joe's—a two-hour car ride down the Hudson—to tell the nuns. They ended up flagging down a cop along the road. The cops found two brown paper shopping bags filled to the brim with pure homegrown weed. Scandalous! The geezers were arrested that same day. Although I was brainwashed, I mean a believer, in the Catholic Church—sorry, cheap shot—I didn't want to see them go. Their sedate approach was such a nice change from the strict, uptight regime we had been subjected to.

Saint Joseph's sent over a woman named Miss Carmen until they could find replacement parents. Miss Carmen was cool, but she followed most of the Home's instructions to a tee, like enforcing the monthly chore chart that hung in the kitchen. We were each assigned a set of daily "charges," as the chores were referred to, that were inspected and double-checked every single day. Good thing Beth and Janis stayed on. Especially Beth. She would take me riding in her Karmann Ghia around the countryside as we'd listen to Joni Mitchell and talk politics—Kissinger, President Carter, etc. I loved that. Beth also talked about her weight constantly, which made me understand Miss Connie's diet pill–popping and made me aware of my own fixation. I had gotten so chubby—okay, fat— from eating all of my feelings. The other girls would taunt me about my chubbiness, especially Betsy. It started to get to me, and I began to get obsessed with my weight. No, I didn't diet. Are you kidding me? With all that good food we had up there? I just felt like shit for being so fucking fat. It was all that I could think about, especially after being used to everyone telling me I was so cute. I know, shameless, but true. One day Beth taught me this poem, which still whirls in my head:

Isn't it a pity that I'm not the prettiest girl in the world, but sometimes when I feel like kicking up my heels in the sun . . . I'm the loveliest one.

Well, something like that.

I had turned nine years old. Tiffany and Brett Rivera were selected to be the next Group Home parents. Tiffany was white, always wore a low ponytail and no makeup, and was very moody. I liked her most of the time, but never let on to how much her grumpiness annoyed me. I was getting good at placating people. Speaking of assholes, Brett was a big one. He was pompous, arrogant, short, and rather chubby with a potbelly. Yet, he thought he was fine as hell, which he wasn't, and that his shit didn't stink, which it did. I couldn't stand the guy, he creeped me out at first glance. I never wanted to be alone with him and made sure I never was. He knew it too, which created a constant tension between us.

Brett and Tiffany did do a good job of keeping order, but Brett held the threat of their authority over us constantly. The GH parents were required to keep a record of absolutely everything that happened each and every day—from what we wore to what we did outside and with whom, to all of our disobediences—in a huge journal kept under lock and key. This record was sent down to Saint Joseph's at the end of each week for review. If a problem developed (based solely on the Group Home parents' account, mind you), you were sent to Dr. Tisby for further evaluation. And Dr. Tisby could send you back to the Home in a hot second and possibly Graceland Hospital. That was power, and Brett loved to exercise it. At least Tiffany did have good intentions despite her cranky disposition.

That Christmas I didn't go home, either to my mother's or to Tia's. Why? I don't know or maybe I forgot why. In any case, I felt unwanted but played it off, as usual. My half-sisters, to my surprise, didn't get to go home either. Tiffany made a wonderful Christmas morning for us and the few other girls who stayed behind. She decorated the house, with our help, to a tee. The Christmas tree was big, bright, and perfectly trimmed by all, with a bunch of

Left: Papi's government photo—that's when he was bringing brutally sexy back! Holla! *Right:* First apartment in New York. *Left to right:* Abuela (Grandmother) Carmen, Dad, friend, his wife, Tia (seated, don't know who she's holding), Augusto on the floor.

My glamorous mom. This is how I remember her looking every day. [CREDIT: *Courtesy of Sally Pabon*]

Left: Saint Joseph's Catholic Home for Children, aka "the Home," looking appropriately gloomy. That's how it has always felt to me. *Right:* To the left is the girls' dormitory, to the right is the nuns' quarters, and underneath, the cafeteria.

When I went back to the home forty years later, the nun in the middle recognized me and told me that she used to sneak me cheese sandwiches because she felt so sorry for me when food was withheld as punishment. She added that she remembered me as "so nice, so funny, so sad."

The Group Home in Wappingers Falls. Middle-class suburbia at its best. Good times and not so good times.

"My" first dog, Citizen. I loved him to pieces.

Me and my two half sisters with Group Home parent.

My pretty sister Carmen in Puerto Rico, the summer she got tits—ha!

Me, my little cousins, and Tia. Happy times!

Me in high school.

A night out at Florentine Gardens with college friends and a *Soul Train* dancer (middle).

Me and Tito in his house in Puerto Rico.

Tupac and me at the Soul Train Music Awards in 1993. We were kindred spirits. I really miss that guy. [CREDIT: Wire Image]

Left-to-right: Me, Debi Mazar, Madonna, and Marion Wade at the GMHC AIDS Dance-a-Thon.

Below left: 1988, *Do the Right Thing.* With Martin Lawrence (in red shirt) in a piece-of-shit rental apartment. *Below right*: Heavy D & the Boyz. On the video set for "We Got Our Own Thang." [CREDIT: Brian D. Perry for Beezo Photo Archives LLC]

Me and my cousin Sixto on the set of the TV series *House of Buggin'*, starring John Leguizamo.

On the set of *White Men Can't Jump*. That movie was the most fun I've ever had filming. [CREDIT: Twentieth Century-Fox Film Corporation/Photofest]

Tia's first ride in a limo! She got her hair done for it.

My ex-husband, Seth Rosenfeld.

Puerto Rican Day Parade, Johnny Leguizamo and me. I was the Madrina (Godmother).

Tia and me in her first apartment I was able to pay for!

My mother, Lydia—after her AIDS diagnosis. Her looks were gone but not her spirit.

Oscar night! Me, Dad, and Carmen.

presents underneath. And of course, I kept playing Johnny Mathis's *Winter Wonderland* album nonstop—love him! It felt like a Christmas that people on television had. And I was so happy that Tiffany got me a bathrobe that fit. Because of my weight gain, my other robe could barely close—God, I got so fat. Brett ended up ruining the day for me because he kept asking if my "bad, nasty attitude" was the reason why my mother didn't ask me home for the holidays. Who does that? Sick ass.

. . .

Spring arrived. Terry and I snuck out the window onto the ledge of our bedroom to watch the tiny clusters of stars twinkle in the night air. We were in the middle of our one-liner corny joke contest—don'tcha love it! We were supposed to be downstairs watching television with the rest of the household. Although it wasn't a rule, we all had to do almost everything together, all the damn time—so annoying. Brett came looking for Terry, calling out her name—not mine. I instantly got suspicious. Terry was around fourteen or fifteen years old and had a body that wouldn't quit. I had noticed him noticing her hourglass figure on the sly.

We got busted. After a long-ass reprimanding, he told me to take my shower downstairs and go to bed. Wait. Why only me? And why downstairs when our bathroom was upstairs, five feet away? Terry looked shaken, like she knew what was coming. "I'm gonna take a shower too." Brett grabbed her arm, telling her to stay put. I freaked out, mind racing to think of something to stop this!

"You're not allowed to grab her like that! I'm gonna tell Mr. Neil!" I said.

"Go to the bathroom! Now! Or you're on restriction!"

"No," I flatly stated.

"What did you say to me?"

I paused for a moment, scared shitless. . . .

"You just doubled your punishment! Two weeks' restriction. . . . Come here. Now!"

I shook my head no. Brett then stood up. His size and anger scared me. Terry held her hand out.

"No," she blurted out. "Go, Rosie. It's okay."

Oh no! I pretended to go down the staircase, but quickly ducked into the upstairs bathroom. Then I heard *smack . . . smack . . . smack!* Then silence. Dag, I just had to find out what was going on. I slipped out of the bathroom, went back to the top of the stairs, and stomped on one step over and over, pretending that I was coming back up. I walked back in.

"I forgot my bathrobe."

Terry's eyes were cast away. I took my time getting my bathrobe, glaring at Brett. He looked back at me—"You little shit," he said—then got up and walked downstairs.

Terry and I went into the bathroom. She began brushing her teeth with her eyes looking straight into the mirror as if nothing had happened. I started to quietly cry. She turned around and wrapped her arms around me, slumping with an exhausted, muffled sobbing, making sure that no one could hear. She then pulled back and made a funny face. I smiled back and left it at that. I never asked her what happened, ever.

Within less than a year, Brett and Tiffany were gone without an explanation. I didn't find out the real reason why until forty years later. One of the girls reported to Mr. Neil that Brett had raped her, and she was afraid that it was going to happen again, to another girl he'd been eyeing. I thought of Terry. And the worst part is that no cops were called. They arrested the senior citizens for smoking a fatty, but no cuffs came out over the rape of a child. Sick.

And to add insult to injury, Maurvive came to take Citizen, my sheepdog, back to live with her. I was devastated. I barely interacted with any of the girls after that, except Olga Lopez and Terry.

Terry started to act like a real sister to me after that. She taught me how to ride a bike after many attempts and crashes into the big fat tree at the bottom of the hill. She taught me how to fight too. I used to just slug with one arm, which didn't always prove to be effective, especially with my other half-sister, Betsy. Her attacks went from verbal to physical. Why? Who knows? Even though I always fought back, her size and power were too much. She would beat the shit out of me, especially since I wouldn't stop fighting back.

Terry could kick some ass. It came naturally. Plus, she used to help one of our brothers train for the Golden Gloves, though he never made it. She would take me out back and begin jabbing me in the face until I learned how to take a punch and, more important, how to move my head out of the damn way. Duh! Imagining that I was Muhammad Ali helped me stay in there, because those punches hurt like hell. Every time I got in a shot I would quote Ali—"I'm a bad man!" Terry would die laughing. The next fight Betsy and I had, I didn't win, but I surely didn't lose. I got some good licks in, especially a nice body shot to the stomach—we never had a physical altercation again. I gained her respect, sort of. I wish it had come in a different form, but I got it. And I began to understand my love for boxing. It takes dedication, hard work, guts, and belief to go toe to toe with someone. Whether you win or lose, you know you had what it takes to just step in that ring and face your fears.

CHAPTER 16

TIA HAD moved again, this time to Suydam Street in Bushwick. Half of the area along the East River was a cluster of factories that Tia would slave at. The other half was residential, mostly poor. Bushwick was more segregated too, racial incidents were rare, and you knew which blocks to play on and which ones to stay away from. Weird thing, there was a lot of intermingling going on, especially with Puerto Ricans—hence Juan Epstein from *Welcome Back, Kotter*. (Okay, that was corny, but true.) But for Puerto Ricans, blacks were a no-no. You were scorned, and people gossiped that your unborn baby would come out with nappy "bad" hair and dark skin—not kidding, folks.

On a home visit, walking to the corner store for my mother, my oldest half-brother—the one who showed me his thing—pulled up in front in a car packed with his friends. One of them, this black kid, smiled at me. I smiled back and waved hello. My brother jumped out, smacked the shit out of me, and pulled me in close and whispered, "Don't you ever look at a fucking *moreno* [black guy] like that, humiliating me in front of my friends!"

"But he's your friend!"

"I don't give a fuck what he is!"

I loved Bushwick. Really. I especially liked it in the wintertime because there was nothing to do and no place to go—and I mean nothing, like *carajo land* for real. All you could do was go to a bowling alley down the block or a skating rink all the way over in Ridgewood, but who the hell wants to go bowling every day in inches of snow? On visits, Tia and I would hole up in our third-floor, shotgun three-and-a-half-room apartment for days, cooking, playing records, watching television—all the bad *novelas, The Honeymooners* marathons, old movies, especially Jerry Lewis. (God, she hated him, except when I'd imitate his iconic dance down the stairs in *Cinderfella*.) Ooh, and she hated when I played Queen, which I'd love to do just to get a rise out of her. "Why *dat* guy [Freddie Mercury] has to be so weird all *de* time?"

I loved the summers too. In the summertime, Cookie was in charge of me while Tia went to work. She had moved in with her baby's daddy on Melrose Avenue and Flushing in a dilapidated tenement that she kept clean as hell. We spent hours listening to Frankie Valli's "Swearin' to God," People's Choice's "Do It Any Way You Wanna," and so on, doing the Hustle in her kitchen for the longest time while my wet set dried. She would use the money Tia gave her for my lunch to take us to the matinees in Ridgewood or at the Commodore movie theater back in Williamsburg while she and her friends joined the majority of the audience in lighting up "loose joints"—I didn't realize till years later that I'd be high as a mofo from the contact. I saw almost every gangster and inappropriate R-rated movie offered during the '70s: *The Godfather* (parts 1 and 2), *Dog Day Afternoon, Hustle*. Before we saw *Rosemary's Baby*, Cookie told me that it was a film about me.

Some of the best times I had on Suydam Street were just hanging on the block, mostly on the stoop all day into the night, cracking jokes and hanging with the kids on our street—Luis, Vinnie, Anthony, and Jeanette, who became my new best friend. My cousin Lorraine was best friends with Jeanette's sister, Joanne. Lorraine and Joanne were the party girls. We were the "cool nerds" and loved holding court with our witty, stupid, corny repartee. Jumping rope, playing stickball, or listening to the latest gossip from my cousins and neighbors was mad fun too. I loved when my father would hang with us too. Whenever he would visit after his ship would pull in at the West Side Highway piers, he would love to hold court, as usual, and flirt with all the old fat ladies on our street.

But there were three things I hated about Bushwick. Number one: my mother moved there as well, about twelve blocks from us. Although I spent most of my visits with Tia, sometimes she would tell me that I should go see my mother. Number two: the danger of the neighborhood constantly kept you on guard if you stepped off your block. And number three: the hard drugs that Bushwick was infamous for and the effect they had on my cousins. Yeah, they would smoke weed and drink a bottle of cheap liquor, but Bushwick introduced them to heroin and cocaine. In fact, they used to call Knickerbocker Avenue "Heroin Alley"! I remember kicking used hypodermic needles to the side so that we could play jacks in Knickerbocker Park (now called Maria Hernandez Park).

It was sad, because during the day Knickerbocker Park was where the older Italian gentlemen came to play shuffleboard in their fedoras; elderly ladies sat in rows on the park benches or on their folding chairs, feeding the pigeons, knitting, and gossiping; teenage girls with their hair and makeup done up coquettishly strolled by hoping for a whistle from the boys playing baseball or basketball with their shirts off; and mothers sat by their strollers, watching their kids play tag. It was quite lovely and peaceful, but come nightfall, forget about it!

My oldest cousin, Titi, loved to take me along whenever she hung out. Her girlfriend was having a house party at her new highrise apartment in Queens. I had never seen an apartment like that before. I only saw tenements and projects. Everything was new— new stove, new refrigerator, new bathrooms. And it was the first time I saw someone make *habichuelas rojas guisadas* (stewed red beans criolla style) from a can—shocking! Even Titi was shocked. Her friend kept apologizing for it, saying she was a career woman, too busy to soak beans overnight and then slowly stew them all damn day. And the beans came out slammin'! Go, Goya!

Then the night came, along with six or so guests. I was the only child in the room. Salsa and soft white lighting was replaced with a red lightbulb and the grooving R&B sounds of Bobby Womack. That was when the joints and alcohol came out. Titi made me go into the bedroom, saying that I could watch anything I wanted. She'd be back soon, and then we could go home. I didn't want to stay there, but I was excited that I could watch *Police Woman* starring Angie Dickinson—I loved her!

It was getting pretty late, and I was worried. I quietly peeked through the bedroom door and saw a woman tying a thin, brownish rubber hose around Titi's bicep. Then a man leaned over and put a needle in her arm. From all of the R-rated movies I had seen with Cookie, like *Panic in Needle Park* starring Al Pacino and Raul Julia (love), I knew exactly what was going on. My heart sank to see my cousin-sister getting high on heroin! I had to focus. I had to get us out of there and safely back to Tia's.

I quickly went into Titi's purse, looking for money so that we could get back on a bus or the subway. She had about six dollars on her, enough for two tokens or a gypsy cab. I tucked the cash in my pants and timidly walked down the hallway.

Titi had started to nod out, her eyes slowly closing and opening. "I want to go home," I said. She was too gone to respond. I tugged on her arm. "Come on, we have to go!" Her friend tried to lead me back to her bedroom, slurring, "Go . . . TV, 'kay. We'll . . . be . . . go . . . 'kay, baby?" I shrugged her hand off of my shoulder and started to cry—loudly. Everyone panicked! They all started stumbling about, shaking her awake. She finally came to, kind of. She tried to hold her hand out for me, but it fell off the table, making her head slam facedown on the table. *Boom!* She was so high she didn't feel shit.

Her girlfriend helped my cousin up into the bathroom. I watched her pee red into the toilet. I thought she was dying! "No . . . no. . . ," she slurred. ". . . My period. You didn't (*heroin pause*) yet, right? (*another opioid pause*) No . . . you're . . . nine, ten?"

"I'm nine."

Her eyes started to close again. I looked down between her legs at the red-colored water floating in the toilet. She looked at me for a moment, smiled, then slumped over and was out. I sat on the bathroom floor next to her for over an hour, shaking her every now and then to make sure she was still alive. And not a single person checked on us.

Titi continued to nod in and out on the bus, with drool running out the side of her mouth and a big knot on her forehead, mumbling over and over again between her brief moments of clarity, making me promise to not tell Mommie. God, she was so annoying. Seriously. Then, one after another, passengers came over, asking me, "You all right? You need me to call somebody? Is that your mommie? You need the police?" I was so embarrassed; I knew they were judging both of us—*ghetto Puerto Ricans*, they probably thought to themselves. They didn't know me, didn't know I was a fairly nice, Catholic-raised nerd; nor did they know my hip, well-read, and loving cousin. In their judgmental point of view, they only saw a pathetic heroin junkie and a pissed-off little girl next to her.

Tia flung the front door open, pulled me toward her, and smothered my face into her big wobbly titties, screaming at Titi, "It's fucking two in the morning, *punueta!*" Titi paid her no mind, stumbled to the living room couch, missed it, fell facedown on the floor, and passed out. I slept with Tia that night. I could feel her hurt as her breasts heaved up and down with each breath. I swore to myself that night that I would never be an addict, ever. And I never told on Titi either, ever.

. . .

I didn't like living in the Group Home with all its drama, but I liked being upstate and part of the community. I loved the school we went to. The teachers were so nice, and there were so many activities. I loved participating in the school chorus, lived for the school's bake sales and plays, and loved recess and the sports activities the best. I liked riding my bike up the hill to play touch football with the neighborhood kids. Loved sleigh riding down the long hills in the winter and having a big Christmas. Loved sleepovers with the very few real friends I made.

Eileen was in the same grade as me at Brinkerhoff Elementary. She lived about a mile up and around the hill from the Group Home in a ranch-style house. I would hang with her almost every day after school, and we are still in contact. Although I was a class clown at school, I was very shy about making real friends. Eileen was a patient, funny, and good person. It took a while for us to create a bond, but once we did, we were besties! We spent endless hours together watching *The Muppet Show* and singing the theme song at the top of our lungs, having sleepovers, baking cakes and cookies, and listening to Elton John and Kiki Dee's "Don't Go Breaking My Heart" over and over again. Nerds.

I loved Gene, Eileen's mother, very much too. Witnessing the connection she had with her kids used to make me happy. I would sit in their kitchen baking with her and Eileen, in awe of their relationship. They probably had no clue I was doing this, but while they were being entertained by my flawless repertoire of corny jokes and crazy stories of Brooklyn and the Home, I'd absorb that special, subconscious mother-daughter exchange without a blink in my delivery. They were the only people upstate to whom I told the whole truth about being in the system. Eileen and Gene made me feel safe like that.

At first the kids had no idea I was from the GH, but once they found out, a few treated me subpar. I got into a couple of fistfights, mostly with boys, defending my honor, which only validated their prejudice. I remember one boy taunting me and calling me a jerk; he took my shyness as an easy target. I had never heard that expression and took it for the insult that it was, so I smushed him in the face. He smushed me back. So I kicked him in the balls and punched him in the face. I was sent to the principal's office. He didn't punish me. He just talked to me, told me I shouldn't have done that and to go back to class.

Too embarrassed to go back inside, I stood at the door staring at my fourth-grade teacher, Mr. Kenney—fine as hell. He caught my eye, came out, and sat with me.

"Who cares what he thinks. Sometimes I'm a jerk."

"You are? What's a jerk?"

He laughed and hugged me. I was freaked out by his touch, but excited because I was in love with him. He was so dreamy, like Robert Redford.

"Mr. Kenney, would you marry me?"

"I'm very flattered, but I'm too old for you." He chuckled.

"No, you're not. Audrey Hepburn married Humphrey Bogart in *Sabrina,* and he was really old."

"Humphrey Bogart? What do you know about Humphrey Bogart? Let's go back inside. And don't let silly things bother you so much, 'kay?"

I wanted to participate in everything Brinkerhoff offered. I did what I could, but was seriously limited. Not just because of my emotional roadblocks but mainly for financial reasons. I couldn't join the Little League team after I made the tryouts because the Home wouldn't approve the purchase of my uniform. Even if I did, I knew I would have to walk the five miles back and forth because there was no one to take me to the games. There were too many girls with other requests in the house that took priority. I joined band after the Home said they would pay for my instrument, but then they didn't. Sat there for about three weeks playing air-clarinet—humiliation. The music teacher kept me on as long as she could, but finally she had no other choice but to ask me to leave—beyond humiliating.

I hated not being able to afford things that kids should have for free, like the arts and recreational sports. And I hated not being able to join in the fun, like going to Dairy Queen after school with the rest of the kids. Refusing defeat, I started to work for the first time, doing yard work, cleaning out garages, anything. I didn't have enough for Little League, but I had enough to purchase my own movie tickets, French fries, pizza, Dairy Queen's Hot Fudge Brownie Sundae with walnuts—love—and Nestlé $100,000 chocolate bars without having to take the other kids or their parents up on their offers to buy these things for me. And when I made the after-school softball team, they gave me the team's T-shirt and I did that five-mile trek back and forth, without asking for a ride, singing songs along the way so I wouldn't get pissed off about the long-ass trip.

Mr. Mackie, my fifth-grade teacher, made learning fun, championed my good grades, and even let me dance during breaks—not kidding. He asked me to show the class how to do the Robot like Michael Jackson did on *Soul Train*. And you know I did! He was the first person to address my speech impediment in a positive way and got me to go to speech therapy—God bless America two times! Bad thing was that the speech therapist, who was white, had me sounding like her. Some of the girls in the Group Home accused me of acting like a wannabe after that. What a bore. Seriously. If you liked rock and roll, you wanted to be white; if you read a lot of books, you wanted to be white; if you had manners and were polite and blah, blah, blah—so pathetic and boring.

Unfortunately, I still had issues and continued to act out.

In Mr. Mackie's class, I asked to go to the bathroom after some extreme blowout with one of my classmates. Alone inside the bathroom stall, I lit a piece of toilet paper hanging from the toilet paper dispenser with a book of matches. I ripped off the flaming tissue before it rose up into the rest of the roll. It felt good, fun, and cool. I lit another piece, ripped it off, and lit another. This time I wasn't fast enough—the flame rose up and the dispenser caught fire!

I tried kicking the damn thing off, but it was too hot. Before I knew it, the dispenser started to warp from the heat. I thought to myself, *If I get caught, I'm done for and I'll be sent back to the Home in a hot second.* I figured that after all the toilet paper burned out, the fire would stop. So I ran out, snuck into another bathroom on the other side of the building, quickly washed off the smell of smoke, and in a quiet panic walked back to class.

The fire department came. Thank goodness only the dispenser went up in flames. Everyone was questioned. I clammed up—had to. I felt like crap. I thought about the cigarette incident and not being accountable. I thought about Mr. Neil and Ed Yano and their high regard for me and their expectations of me. I thought about Sister Minetta-Mary and her lecture on the chances that I'd been given. Man, why was I such a good girl and yet did such bad things like this?

I got my A game on after that. I stopped being late for dinner from playing baseball or touch football with the neighbors. I did my chores and homework at top speed. I didn't talk back. And I did more and more odd jobs, not just for the money, but to keep myself out of trouble too.

CHAPTER 17

SAINT JOSEPH'S sent Sister Mary-Grace—just her—to take over from Miss Carmen, who stayed on as a counselor. Everyone knew Sister Mary-Grace when she was just a novice at the Home—curly auburn hair, tall, slim, white, good breeding, and never known to raise a hand toward a child. She asked us to call her Grace. I think she didn't want us to feel embarrassed by having to call her "Sister" in our new community. That simple gesture was the beginning of my trust in her.

And there was an order she brought instantly to the house that felt safe and light. Some of the girls didn't like her. Maybe it was because she was so sure of herself that they mistook that as arrogance. I think it was because she demanded the best from us constantly, in regards to our character and ability, without fear or intimidation—that's powerful.

And Grace got us a new dog! A half pointer, half springer spaniel named Freckles. I loved this dog more than I loved Citizen, more than I loved anyone, even Tia. (Well, that's how I felt at the time.) Freckles loved me instantly and unconditionally too. We were thick as thieves. She followed me everywhere I went, licked my secret tears, and slept with me nightly. Every morning when I got on the yellow school bus, Freckles barked for me and chased it down the road. I felt like I would never see her again each time I left her. After school, I would frantically look out the window for her as the school bus pulled up to the GH, even though I knew Freckles would be waiting for me at the mailbox. Each time I would see her,

I'd breathe a sigh of relief. When I went on a home visit to Tia's, I moped about, endlessly longing for Freckles, until Tia distracted me with something like cooking *bacaloa* salad.

At school, we were given an assignment to write about who we loved the most. I wrote about Freckles. At ten years old, I got the school alarmed, writing that. Good thing Dr. Tisby didn't make a big deal out of it when I was forced to see him because of this. Grace didn't either. She told me it takes a special and intelligent person to understand and appreciate an animal, and that a dog always recognizes a true heart. She told me that someday I would come to love a person as much as I loved Freckles. I didn't believe her, but that statement solidified my connection with her, made me feel like she got me.

One day, while shopping at the Grand Union for the weekly food supply with Grace, Miss Carmen, and the rest of the girls, Miss Carmen asked me to get several cans of French-cut green beans. I went over to the veggie aisle and picked up the dented cans. I always hated that they were left on the shelf and no one was ever going to pick them up. I knew I'd get shit for it but scooped them up anyway.

"Why do you do this all the time? Put them back now!" yelled Miss Carmen.

I stood there with a pleading grin, refusing to budge. Grace gave me a look and shook her head with a smile. Got her!

"Please, can we buy them? Tia buys dented cans all the time. She says it's worth the chance. There is usually nothing wrong with them, and they're half-price, so you get over."

" 'Get over'? For goodness' sake, what the heck does that mean?" Grace laughed.

"She's right. Nothing's wrong with most of them, and they are discounted," the cashier interjected.

"You see! I'm a genius!" I gleefully yelled out.

"Okay, genius," Grace said sympathetically, without pity, "we'll take your dented cans, this time. Go wait in the station wagon."

"Can I stay to make sure you won't put them back . . . pretty please, with sugar and a big fat juicy cherry on top and hot chocolate fudge drizzle for good measure?"

I sealed it with a cheesy grin and a little shimmy and shake of my butt. Why? Who the hell knows? I did shit like that all the time. (Olga used to say I would act like Fozzie Bear, Miss Piggy—the personality, not the looks, people—and Bugs Bunny combined just for a good laugh.)

"Rosie, you are a pip!" declared Grace.

"A pip!"

Then, of course, I had to break into a spontaneous rendition of Barbra Streisand's "I'm the Greatest Star" from *Funny Girl!*

Who is the pip with pizazz? Who is all ginger and jazz?

"Get in the car, Barbra!" laughed Grace.

"Barbra! Do I sound like her? Do I—"

"Stop! Go! Now!"

I hung out with Grace constantly. I couldn't wait to come home and share my day with her. She taught me how to bake better than the nuns without standing over my shoulder barking orders. She introduced me to Charles Dickens and Emily Brontë—which were tough reads and depressed the hell out of me, but I loved them. She checked my "attitude" without making me feel defensive, then later praised the slightest improvements I'd make. She made me feel okay about being a cornball—seriously. We just hung out, you know? We enjoyed each other's company and had fun.

When all was beginning to get right with the world, Grace decided to leave—not only the Group Home, but the order too! She didn't want to be a nun anymore. She had met a man and fallen in love. Scandalous! Although inspired by her choice to listen to her heart, I was seriously broken up by her departure. I remember her sitting with just me the day she was leaving, saying everything was going to be okay, things would carry on. Nothing helped ease the pain—except for Freckles, who became everything to me even more after that. The other girls thought my "obsession" with Freckles was weird. I didn't care. I would disappear with her for hours, walking through the woods and singing happy songs to cheer myself up before I got back to the house. (My pride prevented me from showing how affected I was.)

After Grace left, we went through several different Group Home parents.

There were Abby and Michael, wholesome and very Americana—cheerleader marries soft-spoken jock.

We had three new girls from the Home after one of the original girls left, another got pregnant and married, and the aunt of another took custody of her and brought her home. These new girls were much more hard-core and gave Abby and Michael hell.

One night, as retaliation for a punishment, the three new girls snuck downstairs after dark and taped Kotex pads stained with ketchup on their door to spell out "fuck you"—a new low point for sure.

Abby and Michael were pretty much gone after that.

Then came Priscilla and Elvis.

Priscilla was mushy fat, and Elvis was skinny as a rail. Most of us couldn't stand either of them. Priscilla had gotten into a fight with one of my half-sisters. Elvis stepped in and put my half-sister in a bear hug. My sister flipped out. Scared, I grabbed the kitchen knife, stood up on the dining-room chair, and pointed it at Priscilla's throat, telling her she better tell her husband to let go of my sister or else. Priscilla, not threatened in the slightest, rolled her eyes and told me to get down. I sheepishly backed away and quickly apologized—feeling like an idiot.

They were gone shortly after that.

Next came Sharon and Bobby, two Italian American sweethearts from Long Island. We all felt that these two actually cared about us. Sharon was great. Bobby was too, at times. Most of us thought he was closeted from day one. Sharon eventually found out that he was in fact gay and left with their daughter, who I adored, without giving us an explanation, but we all knew why. Scandalous!

Bobby stayed, for a while, but was soon gone after that.

Several other GH parents came and went who were nasty or ill equipped or both. I just checked out. I spent even more time with Freckles, as well as with Eileen and other friends from school. After a while, I became well known as a social butterfly, living the casual, joy-filled suburban life of sleepovers, Pop Warner football games, and weekend house parties with the kids upstate. And I loved every minute of it! Because of this, the girls in the house thought I was stuck up. I didn't think so and was bothered by their perception. I didn't mean to be so separate from them. I just wanted to escape— television wasn't enough anymore—and unfortunately, the other girls were unintended casualties. Well, except for Olga and this new girl, Mita. Especially Olga, since she and I had kind of the same mind-set. She and I hated our predicament, knowing we deserved better, yet we never saw ourselves as victims and took full advantage of what was being offered to us by way of education and our social environment.

I remember one of the girls trying to tell me off, saying that I thought I was special. Man, I was getting tired of this shortsightedness. I answered, "Yes. I do. And why don't you? 'Cause you should too." That ended that.

Work took me farther away from the house too. Because of President Carter's CETA (Comprehensive Employment and Training Act) program, I got my first real paying job on a kids' talk show at a local cable television station as the special effects generator operator, then was promoted to one of the hosts because of my "undeniable personality"—that's what my boss told me. What can I say? Holla!

Speaking of government, I took to the U.S. Constitution like crazy, just as I did with political science later in high school. I was fascinated by it all. I thought how great America was, how we all have a chance to rise above the situation we're born into, and that we have a government that helps give those less fortunate a fighting chance. Not all the girls appreciated CETA as much as I did and quit the program after their first paycheck, but me, I went whole hog and stayed with it to the end. I've always felt different—not better than, but different. Even at an early age I felt and knew I was supposed to contribute something important to the world. Seriously. Maybe this is what the girls in the GH misconstrued. Maybe they couldn't see or understand that I had an agenda. My Mary Tyler Moore aspirations were still intact and I wanted to be as ready as possible.

CHAPTER 18

I WAS twelve now—yes, twelve—and still in the Group Home. Most of my half-siblings were back at home with my mother. I knew not to ask why I wasn't included because it was understood that you had to wait for an official invitation from your parent to go home. You'd think I wouldn't care. Even though I didn't want to live with her at this point, I wanted to know that she wanted me. However, I did ask the Home if I could skip her house altogether during home visits and go directly to Tia's instead. They of course had to pass the request through Lydia. Her reaction probably wasn't a good one, because it took a while, but she eventually said yes, as long as I promised to visit her house at least for a night and that she'd retain her parental rights over me. That whole process angered me. Giving so much power to someone they all knew was mentally ill and had suspected of physical abuse seemed crazy to me.

Yes, they knew she was crazy but never told us. And they did in fact suspect the physical abuse. How? I really don't know, but speaking for myself, I think it could be from the bruises I would come back with from her freakin' punching me or slapping me or almost ripping my arm out of its socket. No, I never told them that she did it, but come on, people! And when I found out myself about Lydia's mental issues, it was a difficult pill to swallow.

I used to think that my mother was just intense—ha! But seriously, I did. I thought she had a violent temper and was extreme about everything. Like when she would say something funny, she would repeat the joke over and over for an hour or more, and climax into this laughing frenzy. Or how she carried her gun with her just to get a carton of eggs from the corner store. But I started to suspect her mental illness when I caught her talking to the kitchen wall—no lie.

I had woken up early, like around six o'clock in the morning, and had to use the bathroom. I tiptoed so that I wouldn't wake my mother up. She didn't like us using the bathroom so she would put a pot in the middle of the bedroom floor for all of us to piss in. I know. And yes, I found it to be so disgusting. So, I walk into the kitchen where the bathroom was and froze when I saw her carrying on a conversation with the freaking wall. She was actually having an argument with it. "Oh, so you think I did that to her? No? It wasn't me! . . . What? How can you say that?!" Not kidding, folks.

I never told anyone about it. It scared me, and believe it or not, I didn't want to embarrass her. But then, on a home visit, when I was ten, I arrived at my mother's to find she wasn't there. My older half-siblings were laughing, telling me, "She'll be back. They took her again to the crazy hospital for a couple of weeks. You know Mom's crazy, right? She's schizophrenic. You never saw her talking to the wall or to the benches on the subway?" I guess being kids, possessing all that information was too much, and all they could do was laugh about it.

Schizophrenic?

I'd sit in the school library looking up the meaning in countless books, worrying constantly if I could be schizophrenic too. By the time I was twelve, I had asked Dr. Tisby during our sessions, in what I thought was a coy manner, if mental illness was hereditary since the mother of my "friend" was nuts. When he raised his eyebrow at me, I finally just came straight with him. He returned the gesture—very delicately, I might add—and admitted that my mother was in fact mentally ill, asking me how I felt about it. I remember trying to act all grown-up, saying I was more concerned about her, which I honestly was, and that I was okay with it, which I wasn't. Leaving his office, I felt sad and powerless. I didn't understand why they still allowed her to maintain her parental rights. Why didn't they let my aunt or my father gain custody? Was Lydia that good at fooling them into thinking she was a great parent? I guess so.

I remember this one time when Mrs. Vasquez called me into a meeting at the Home with Lydia. She wanted to discuss my relationship with my mother, ask me why I wanted to skip the home visits with her. It was all a sham, and I knew it. It was my mother's ego—she didn't want anyone thinking ill of her, and mostly, she didn't want to lose any potential government assistance that she would've gotten for me if and when I'd go to live with her. Trust. She knew my father and Tia were still trying to get me out of the Home.

Lydia started things off by saying she was hurt—I was her favorite, she loved me more than any of the other kids. Say what? My mouth dropped on the floor, and when the waterworks came, my eyes went rolling. Then the trickling of tears, followed by sniffles of snot. I mean . . . and the Oscar goes to. . . ! Mrs. Vasquez asked if I wanted to sit "on Mommie's lap." I'm freaking twelve, I never sat on my mother's lap, ever! Barely even got a hug from her. After much unrelenting pressure from Mrs. Vasquez, I sat on the edge of Lydia's knees. Talk about awkward! "Now, doesn't that feel good to sit on Mommie's lap?" That was it! I slid off and asked to be excused to go to the bathroom and purposely took forever, knowing that by the time I got back, her train would be coming and it'd be time for Lydia to go.

But I digress.

Things were way tense between Lydia and me. I would still stay the first night at her house, but now I wouldn't wait for her okay to be sent over to Tia's. Sometimes I would stay the night because there was a good card game of Spades being played, or there was a party going down, or just to hang with Terry and Kathy. But most of the time I would walk in, say hello to everyone, hang for a bit, and then come up with a batch of lies, saying, "Tia needs me, sorry," or anything to get me over there quick fast. And Lydia wouldn't stop me or walk me over either. Yep, I would walk all twelve blocks by myself, day or night, through the dangerous streets of Bushwick that scared the hell out of me. And talk about lies . . . I was becoming an expert.

This one time, on the Metro down into the city, a girl who went to my school was on the train with her parents.

"Rosie! Rosie! Hi! Going to Brooklyn? [I never lied about being from Brooklyn!] Is your father here? I would love to meet him!"

"No. I'm actually going alone. Father couldn't send the car. The divorce, you know, it's been tough . . . but please don't tell anyone. It's so embarrassing and . . ."

Before I could finish, she grabbed my hand and led me over to her parents. Gosh dag it! She whispered to her mother the details about the "divorce." My mother had placed me with the Catholic Church until the proceedings were over, much to my father's chagrin, and he was spending a lot of money to get me out, and blah, blah, blah. The fake tears came streaming—not too much, mind you, and on cue! I was panicked the rest of the train ride, wondering if they really fell for my crock of shit.

When I got back to school after that summer, everyone was asking if I was okay, and many were offering their homes to me until the divorce was over. The girls from the GH were pissed at me and called me a liar, which I was, saying I was ashamed to be in the system (true again), which meant that I must be ashamed of them too (not true at all). But it didn't matter at this point. The lying was horrible—period. It made me feel low, but being a kid, I kept on lying because I couldn't see a way of stopping and coming clean.

So things were bad between my mother and me.

The subways were hot as hell, packed, and on constant delay.

It took me forever to get to my mother's house, anxiety attack the whole way knowing she would be pissed because she hated if I was late, which meant I'd have to stay longer and calm her down so that she wouldn't prevent me from going over to Tia's. (I know, fucking exhausting!)

I walked into an empty house. *Oh good, everyone's out*, I thought. Ugh! All I wanted to do was take a shower. I turned around and found Lydia sitting in the kitchen looking tight. Dag it.

"*Bendición, Mommie.*"

I kissed her extended cheek.

"You're late. (*A long-ass awkward pause*) You got a little fatter, huh. (*She sucks her teeth*) God, look at your hair, just like your father's."

"Sorry, Ma."

"Why are you sorry? Get the food stamps from my bag and go get meat and two cans of beans from Key Food."

"Now?"

She cocked her head to one side with a smirk as if to say, *I know you didn't just ask me that.* I turned to put my suitcase away. Lydia pounded her fist on the kitchen table.

"Where are you going?"

"To put my bag away."

"Did I say you could do that? Go get the food stamps. And make sure you get me the right meat."

"What kind do you want?"

"Oh my God! This girl! I'm making stew, so what kind of fucking meat do you think I want?"

"Oh, sorry. I didn't know. You want cubed beef?"

"Fucking genius over here!"

God, she makes me so freakin' nervous.

I returned with the groceries. As I started for the bathroom, hoping to finally take a shower, Lydia pulled out the package of meat.

"Oh. My. Fucking. God. You see this! See it? This says seventy-two cents per pound. I told you I wanted to only spend less than three dollars on this meat."

"But you didn't tell me . . ."

Smack! Right across my face! She hit me so fucking hard that my cheek instantly welted up in the shape of her hand!

"I didn't tell you what? What? Seventy-two cents times four pounds is what?"

"Um . . ."

"Two eighty-eight! I wanted the sixty-nine cents per pound, which would cost what? Two seventy-six! Two seventy-six!"

I went back to the store, frantically checked the math on the meat over and over, and headed back.

When I walked in, Lydia was sitting at the table with the cans of beans looking tight. She took a deep sigh and said . . .

"These. Cans. Have. Dents."

"I know, but I was trying to save you money. See, Tia buys them all the time 'cause the dented ones are half-priced and are usually still good, so you get over. Genius, right?"

She grabbed both cheeks, squeezing hard. My face was throbbing like crazy, especially the side that was still swelling from the previous smack.

"Don't you fucking patronize me."

She kept squeezing. I stood stoic, took it like a pro, knowing it would piss her off more but I didn't give two shits at this point. She stared me right back in my eyes with a devilish grin and said, "You think you're slick, Rosie."

I went back to the store, came back with undented cans of beans. She didn't even look in the bag, and then she casually asked me to season the meat and asked how school was going—freaking crazy and exhausting.

The next morning I got up extra early to sneak out to Tia's. Lydia was already up, finishing covering her face with makeup. She was surprised when she saw the bruising on my cheeks.

"*Ay* my God. What happened to your face?"

"You hit me last night."

"What? No. I didn't hit you. Why would I do that?"

I just shrugged my shoulders. She did that a lot, denying the abuse the next day, even with the rest of her kids. So what would be the point to further the discussion? Then the kitchen light blew out.

"Fuck! Come with me to the store."

Lydia got her pistol, wrapped it in a plastic shopping bag, then placed it in a large brown paper shopping bag. Inside the store, she told me to keep watch.

"For what?"

"For the fucking store owner!" she loudly whispered. "Grab a couple of circular lightbulbs," she continued as she held open the paper bag. Scared out of my wits and mortified, I shook my head no, refusing.

"That's wrong, Ma."

"You think you're better than me? Huh? You rather us sit in the fucking dark? Put it in! Now!" I did so—feeling so ashamed. "This fucking girl. Let's go! Act normal!"

Back at her house, she became pleasant again, laughing at our supposed caper. I went into the bathroom, brushed my teeth, got my suitcase, and headed for the door. "See you later, Ma."

"Oh! Okay, see you. Tell Minguita I said hello."

Tia gasped at the bruising on my cheek. I told her that a fly ball hit me in the face during a softball game back at the Group Home. I always lied to Tia too, but only about the abuse by my mother and Sister Renata.

The incident was easily pushed down inside when I went to see John Travolta in *Saturday Night Fever* at the movie theater in Ridgewood on Myrtle Avenue. Loved it! First time I screamed out loud at the big screen. I had such a crush on John—I had daydreams of the two of us getting married. I know, I know, all the rumors, but who gives a shit, really. He's an actor who can act his ass off, and that's all I care about; his personal life is his business to worry about.

. . .

Another home visit in Bushwick had come. I went to my mother's house first to do my usual hellos and good-byes. Lydia wasn't there. She had disappeared for that entire first weekend to hang with her sisters—who I'd only met one time, mind you, she did that a lot too—I decided to stay because my half-brothers were getting ready for a "pot" party!

The party was crazy. Jimmy Castor's "It's Just Begun," Manu Dibango's "Soul Makossa," Barry White, Al Green, the Brothers Johnson, Donna Summer, Chaka Khan, Labelle, and especially Dr. Buzzard's Original Savannah Band, played endlessly. I danced for hours! There was a perpetual cloud of marijuana smoke that lingered till dawn. Everyone except the two youngest and myself were smoking, drinking bottles of Night Train or malt liquor, and the party continued into the next day!

I was exhausted and went to bed early that next evening in the back room in one of the three beds all eight of us shared, including my half-brothers' best friend, Armin, who our mother took in. (Yes, she took him in, but didn't ask me to come home—but, whatever.) I think only my three half-brothers were home. I don't know where the girls were. Just as I was about to fall into a deep sleep, the oldest brother, the same one who showed me his thing years before, lay down next to me and began to caress me sexually, telling me to lie still.

"It's okay. I love you, Rosie. Just relax."

I wanted to scream but couldn't. When he tried to put his hands down my panties, I got up as calmly and quickly as possible. He tried to stop me, but I was too quick. As I was rushing to the bathroom, the other half-brother asked me what was wrong. "He tried to molest me!" I loudly whispered.

Shocked, he told me he'd go and talk to him and work it out. Inside the bathroom, I overheard them talking in a hushed panic. "You think she's gonna tell? I told you not to try it on her. You should've waited for one of the other girls to come back!" Say what! I calmly walked out, quietly put my clothes on, and snuck out the first-floor window.

I didn't want to go home to Tia because I was so freaked out and knew she would ask a million questions. What was I going to tell her? I ran to my friend Candy's house next door instead. She had confided the previous summer that her uncle had molested her, so I knew she would understand my hysteria.

She wanted us to run away. Being pragmatic, I convinced her it wasn't a good idea. We broke night instead, walking around Bushwick with two male friends of hers—one of them was eighteen and fine as hell. Candy told them what happened while they passed a bottle of Night Train and a joint around—not to me, of course.

Five o'clock in the morning, my oldest brother, the molester, found us hanging in Knickerbocker Park and tried desperately to apologize, begging me not to tell. Then the fine-ass eighteen-year-old got up in his face and threatened to beat him up, calling him a nasty motherfucker. I got so scared. My brother never backed down from a fight, but to my surprise he dropped his head in shame and walked away. Weirdly enough, I felt sorry for him.

Candy and her two friends walked me back to my mother's house—I wanted to get my stuff and haul ass to Tia's. The fine-ass eighteen-year-old kissed me good-bye on the lips and told me I was beautiful. (That was weird, especially since that was my first kiss and I was only twelve.) Armin was waiting outside on the stoop. He told me that Lydia was home and knew what had happened, it was okay for me to come in, and she had my back. Really? Cool!

When I walked inside, I was greeted by a crack across my face so hard that I fell to the floor. "How dare you! You think he would do that to you? You think he would pick you, when you're the ugliest? He can pick any of your sisters who are way prettier than you! Huh? Fucking liar!" I was pissed, shocked, and hurt!

She then made me scrub the kitchen floor with a toothbrush. This is true, folks, and I dare any one of my "brothers" to question it!

Later that night, I jumped out the window with my suitcase and went to Tia's. My mother never checked on me either. I was in bed for a few days, only getting up to use the bathroom. Tia was so worried. I kept telling her that I was just feeling ill. I don't think she bought it, because this time I was way beyond depressed.

CHAPTER 19

BACK AT the Group Home, the depression and anger grew.

School had already begun, and I believe I was thirteen now. One of my teachers accused me of cheating on an essay because I would never pay attention in class, would always be late, yet would score high on my essays and tests—what can I say! She gave me an F, I cursed her out and accused her of being prejudiced, and she reported me to the vice principal. I wouldn't back down and was made to write an essay on the spot in front of everyone. After reading it, the vice principal turned to the teacher and made her apologize to me. I smugly replied, "I accept your apologies." I got detention for it.

That put an even bigger chip on my shoulder, which only backfired on me, but I couldn't stop it. After-school detention became a regular event. My grades started to drop. I couldn't concentrate during class. Taking tests was a blur of confusion, and the low marks made me feel stupid and inept for the first time. I got even more depressed—worried about my chances of getting into college.

Grace came back for a visit.

I felt embarrassed by how little regard the new girls had for her. There were only maybe half of us who were still there from before she left. No one even asked Grace to sit down. As I got milk and cookies for us, she kept looking around at the chaos and lack of empathy in the room. Grace grabbed my hand, looked me directly in the eye, and said:

"Listen to me. You can make it! I knew it when I first laid eyes on you. Study hard, be good, and get yourself out of here! Do you hear me? You must stay focused. You must do that for yourself! Promise me!"

I nodded yes. My eyes flooded. I wanted to reach out and hug her so badly, but I couldn't—I didn't know how. She gave a final squeeze to my hand and got up and left. That was it; she was gone again, just like that.

When the GH parents and the Home refused to give me a forwarding address for Grace, I finally snapped. Okay, I had a nervous breakdown, to be exact, but who's counting.

I went into hysterics and tore my room to pieces, breaking everything. I stopped when I realized that I had broken my 45 of "Penny Lane" in two. I locked myself in my closet for an entire day and fell oddly silent. I could hear everyone looking for me but kept quiet hiding. I even peed on myself a bit but couldn't bring myself to come out. I felt too bottomless to move.

Then, as the sun was setting, a haze of sunlight seeped through the closet's wooden shutters. I felt some kind of presence. Maybe it was God, maybe not. But, I prayed earnestly for the first time in my life (I'd never really bought the whole Catholicism thing), telling God that he had to come through for me or I'd never believe in him, ever.

I softly sang to myself the Commodores' "Zoom" repeatedly and everything from Earth, Wind, and Fire to Todd Rundgren, and then fell into a deep sleep. When I woke, I calmly climbed out of the closet and quietly cleaned my room, blasting the Rolling Stones' "Paint It Black," hearing the song in a whole new way. When asked where I had been, I shrugged my shoulders and said I was in my room the whole time. I didn't feel like I owed them any further explanation. All I cared about was that I had a new mission. I was going to get out, like Grace suggested, and that was that.

I made a call to Mr. Neil on the sly and convinced him to advocate for me to live with Tia. He couldn't get my mother to agree, so instead, he set it up so that I could be transferred to a "foster home." I told this girl from school, who went to the same church as I did, to pray for me. (At the Group Home, we were allowed to go to a church of our choosing. After my deal with God inside the closet, I became really religious—evangelistic.) She told her mother. They became my foster family. That didn't work out so well. They desperately wanted to save me by being even stricter than the Home. And to add insult to injury, they told me I had to leave Freckles behind even though they lived just up the street— God, that hurt. I resented them for it and made them pay—I acted out badly. Shocked and confused by my behavior, they agreed with me to end it before things got really ugly.

I got transferred to another Group Home further upstate. That didn't work out so well either.

First day, one of the girls started an argument with me over something stupid. The Group Home mother, who was cool as hell, broke it up before it got violent. During dinner, this girl Mandy started to growl like a pit bull at me when I asked her to pass the peas—I kid you not! I was like, "Uh, hello?" Then she started talking to the air and answering it. Oh boy. I knew she was crazy at that point. Then later, in the wee hours of that night, some of the girls woke me up. "Mandy's digging your grave!" Yes, folks, she was out back digging deep! The next morning she was taken away to a special "hospital." Mandy was schizophrenic, and the change in the house, meaning me, triggered voices in her head and paranoia. I felt guilty, responsible for her madness. Why? Who knows? Half the house hated me after that. Well, in fairness, I was a bitchy snot during that time to boot.

Thank goodness there was Nigel and his sister Michelle, the counselors—cool and supportive to all. Michelle was laid-back and insightful. Nigel was the best: smart, had that Isaac Hayes cool vibe about him, a stand-up guy who never got excited, never had to. He would say stuff to me like, "How's that attitude working for you? 'Cause it ain't working for anyone else," or, "The world is waiting for you to arrive. You ready?" Nigel and Michelle had integrity and self-worth that I admired greatly. It affected me immensely, which allowed me to be nice and act like the nerd that I was around them and with the kids in the neighborhood outside of the Group Home.

Once again, I dived into the social scene, making a lot of friends at school and church, barely staying in the house. I must say, I loved being a social butterfly again, especially upstate. It was mad fun. I especially loved hanging with these two black girls, upper-middle-class, who lived a couple of houses up. They were part of the cheerleading squad and were smart, polite, corny, and fun! It wasn't a rarity in upstate New York—well-to-do African Americans who weren't that different from the white people up there—despite how they choose to depict black folks in movies.

The girls in the Group Home would make fun of these girls behind their backs, calling them Oreos. Once again, they gave me shit for hanging with them and the white cheerleaders, constantly. When I became the manager of the cheerleading squad, they really had a field day calling me a wannabe. It was such a bore! By this point, I didn't give two poop-poops about it.

. . .

I was obsessed with Woody Allen and Neil Simon movies. *Annie Hall, Sleeper, The Prisoner of Second Avenue,* and *The Odd Couple* were some of my favorites. Back in Brooklyn on a visit to Tia's, that was all I wanted to go see. It drove Cookie crazy. Especially since we had to find theaters that were still playing some of their older hits as well as the newer ones. So, of course, she took me to see *The Deer Hunter* and *Midnight Express* instead. Okay, I loved those movies too, but *Annie Hall,* people!

Tia and I went down to Puerto Rico for the summer. My father had lost his house in Aguadilla that winter and moved into a government housing apartment in the same town—three bedrooms with a balcony made out of rebar and cinder blocks to protect it from hurricanes. I wondered if my father was embarrassed about everything, but no. He took it all in stride. He told me it was just money, and he didn't need money to make him happy.

We went up to Tia Aya's for the day to escape the concrete slabs with patches of grass in between.

They had freaking killed Miguel the pig for the holidays!

"It was his time. But no worries, he went painlessly. A nice clean bop on the head," said Tia Aya's husband, like it was funny.

Killing Miguel was the same as if someone had killed my precious dog Freckles, who I'd painfully had to leave behind. I had a fit! I fell to the ground, rolling in the dirt like Giulietta Masina in *Nights of Cabiria* (love!). I rolled too far and fell down the tiny hill at the edge. I could hear my father laughing his ass off up top. Brushing off his help to pull me up, I hastily pushed past him, tripping on a rock, which only made him laugh harder.

When I went inside and sat at the kitchen counter wiping my tears, Tia Aya, paying me no mind, pulled out one of Miguel's shoulders that she had salted and saved, stuck it in the oven, and asked me to baste it. I stormed out the front door, feeling a dry heave of vomit swell up in my throat.

Dad came out to sit with me in the driveway. We just sat there saying nothing. Then he started to sing his favorite Tony Bennett song.

" 'I left my heart in San Francisco.' . . . You know, my second favorite Tony Bennett album was—"

"*Beat of My Heart*," I rudely interrupted, "and Candido played on it, and you told that story a thousand times! Gosh! Get some new material!"

Dad chuckled instead of being hurt, like I regretfully thought he would be. I slowly started to laugh with him. I then looked behind me, felt someone watching. It was Tia, tucked behind the door. She quietly smiled and then ducked back inside.

Carmen had gotten tits that summer, slimmed down, and was buck wild. She was hanging with these girls who were just as bad. They kept making fun of my poor Spanish, calling me a Yankee—typical Nuyorican versus Puerto Rican hurtful drama. Carmen, in constant competition with me, would add her two cents by making fun of my conservative way of dressing. I would get back at her by stealing her boyfriends, like Tuti, who I broke up with after one day, because he kissed horribly. Carmen spent that whole break trying to get me back.

César was the finest guy in the *Municas,* and he asked me for a walk to the "woods." Scandalous! I was never allowed to walk around Aguadilla unaccompanied by a man, which usually meant either my father or at the very least my younger brother Tito. Plus, I didn't know that going for a walk in the woods meant sex, but quickly figured it out when he asked me to go to third base without even getting to first.

Carmen had followed behind with one of her girlfriends to spy on us so she could tell on me to Dad. So, as César was sucking on my neck, trying to maneuver his hand down my tit, we heard blood-curdling screams. Carmen had stepped on a fallen beehive and was swarmed. She and her girlfriend were screaming, running circles around each other. Hilarious! Thank goodness, because I only had barely been to first at that point—nerd—and I was terrified when César was touching my tittie.

As I was dabbing calamine lotion on Carmen's numerous bumblebee stings, she noticed the big-ass hickey on my neck. Oh my goodness! We both knew if Dad saw this he would be pissed! She told me she was an expert in hickey removal: she heated a spoon on the stove and pressed it into my monkey bite. Shit blew up and blistered on the spot.

"Just put some Cover Girl on it," Carmen said.

We did. It didn't work. Then we heard Dad come in.

"Oh my goodness! Get me a Band-Aid, please, and my white button-down collar from my suitcase!"

I buttoned the shirt all the way up and turned up the collar. Talk about not being obvious.

"Why you got that hot shirt on?" Dad later asked.

I just shrugged.

"Come out to the balcony with me."

I went out. It was a blazing summer night. I was sweating to death. He looked at me, paused for a moment, then started to chuckle a bit. I rolled my eyes back at him, which only made him laugh more.

"So . . . anyway, you know, it's your life, Rose, and you can do what you want, but you know, I just want you to respect yourself and me, 'kay?"

"What? What are you talking about?" I answered, all snotty and paranoid and shit.

"Nothing. . . . This is a small town, you know?"

Awkward pause.

"Remember when I told you I'd be so proud if you married in white?"

"Oh my goodness, Dad! I didn't do anything! I swear!"

"That's good. . . . No, I'm just saying. . . . It would be nice, for me . . . and for you too, to be respectful in the things you do."

I looked down at the cemented courtyard, feeling weirdly happy, proud even, that my pops was setting me straight.

"Come on. I traded one of my Sarah Vaughans for Dinah Washington for you! She got a Grammy for this album!" Dad said excitedly. He was part of a record/social club where albums were traded and no money exchange was allowed. " 'What a difference a day makes. . . .' Oh, I love how she interprets that song. I'll get the record to wash!"

"Can I wash it, Pop?"

Carmen was sitting at the dining-room table in front of the tiny kitchenette, desperately wanting to know the *bochinche*. I covertly smiled, letting her know all was copacetic. Dad poured the dishwashing soap in a circle over the record, and I very gently washed it in a circular motion, making sure not to scratch it, just as he had taught me. He then started to laugh. "Please forgive me, but please take that shirt off. You look so silly in that hot thing."

We all cracked up with that one.

That night he kissed me good night for the first time, and before he left the room he turned and said, "I like that. 'Pop.' Thank you, baby. 'Night."

Oh happy-joy-joy!

CHAPTER 20

I TOLD my aunt that I didn't want to go back to the Group Home, I had to leave and live with her or something bad was going to happen. The tensions between the girls and me were escalating, and I didn't want to go live with my mother either—besides, she still wasn't exactly offering. Tia and Titi called the main offices at Saint Joseph's late that night. The nuns told her I was lying about the friction in the house and that was that. Say what? I had to come back or they were going to call the authorities. I've always had great disdain for the system, but now it was at its all-time peak of contempt. Why not give me to my aunt? She had a home, constant employment, never had an incident of abuse or neglect, loved me, would do anything for me. Seriously!

I don't know if it was conscious or not, but when I got back upstate I got into a fistfight with one of the girls from the Group Home the next morning on the school bus in front of the house. It was a bad one. She bit my breast during the fight, and I went so crazy that I blacked out during the actual brawl; when I snapped out of it, I found myself on top of her, banging her head against the pavement. I didn't even know how we got off the bus and onto the street!

I couldn't fathom or connect that I was the same person who would do that to someone. After an interrogation, punishment, and blah, blah, blah, it was decided that I needed to be transferred out and live permanently with Tia. My mother agreed later after it was decided that she would retain legal rights and that I would spend at least two weekends a month at her house—which also meant that Lydia was the one to receive the welfare compensation for me. I was glad that it was all finally happening, but I was also hurt that my mother didn't insist that I live with her, even though I didn't want to.

A month before I was to leave the Group Home for good, I was called down to Saint Joseph's to talk to Crazy Cindy. She'd had a mental and emotional breakdown, and no one could reach her.

Cindy had started to hang out with a bad group of girls, getting into a lot of trouble. Also, she began to go on home visits. I heard through rumors that she would come back in disturbed moods and ready for a fight. She had gotten into an argument with this counselor who shouldn't have been working with emotionally disturbed kids. The fight escalated into a brawl, and Cindy proceeded to stomp, literally stomp, this woman's face in. The nuns sent her to Graceland, and the rumor was that she had received shock therapy. I didn't know if it was true or not, since she was still underage. But the rumors began because, when she returned, her eyebrows were shaved off, her eyelashes were plucked out, and she had stopped talking, except for asking to see me. I was kind of surprised, since we hadn't spoken since our first fight a year before—but not really.

Ours was not the only Group Home that Saint Joseph's had. There was another one for boys and an additional one of girls. The other girls' Group Home was about a thirty-minute drive from our GH, and fly compared to ours. First of all, they had a pool. Second, they had more than one TV! Third, and most important, they had liberal GH parents who were very supportive and lenient. Cindy was friends with this girl, from that other GH, who was pretty and popular. I had found out that Cindy was going up to visit her somewhat regularly. Say what? I didn't even know kids from the Home were allowed to visit! And if so, how come Cindy didn't want to come see me?

One weekend our Group Home had gone over for a visit to

swim in their pool. Cindy was there. I was hurt. She tried her hardest to make me feel better, acting silly, making jokes, but I couldn't shake the feeling. She began to play-fight with me to bring me around. It turned into something more serious, and I really started to pound her. Everyone knew that Cindy could beat me up easily, she was a great fighter, but she didn't fight back. She just let me hit her until I started crying and stopped, apologizing in between my sobs. We hugged it out by the end of the day, but I knew we would never be the same after that.

As the van pulled into the Home, I began to wonder how Cindy was going to receive me even though she had asked for me. I also worried how far gone she was mentally and emotionally.

Walking back into the girls' dormitory gave me a feeling of disgust and fear, yet I felt above it, like I had survived. And of course I bumped into Sister Renata.

"Hello, Rosemary . . . I said, hello, Rosemary. And what may I ask are you doing here?"

"I have permission. And my name isn't Rosemary, sister."

"Nice to see that temper of yours hasn't changed."

"Thank you, sister. Nice to see yours hasn't either."

"You're lucky you're not here anymore, or I'd give you a good crack right across that smart mouth of yours."

"You're not allowed to hit us anymore, sister. Didn't you know about the new child protection laws?" I said beguilingly, blinking my eyelashes up and down.

She gave me a contemptuous look and left. Yay! I know it sounds horrible of me, but it felt so good.

I found Cindy sitting alone on her bed in Group Two. I sat down on the bed next to her. I didn't say anything at first. I tried not to stare; she looked so strange and sad.

"What happened to your eyebrows?" I eventually asked.

"I shaved them, stupid." She chuckled.

"Oh. Your eyelashes too?"

"I plucked them out," she said with a shrug.

"Why?"

". . . Don't know. Just felt like it. . . . It looks stupid?"

"No . . . yes . . . only a little bit."

We both laughed. Then we both got quiet, looking away for a moment.

"Remember when we pulled off Sister Renata's veil and she was bald?" Cindy weirdly said, as if she were continuing a long-ass conversation.

"Yeah!"

"She really beat the shit outta us that time. You know, it's 'cause they can't have sex. Their pussy gets dried up and makes them go insane."

Although it was an old joke of hers, we both laughed.

"What happened?" I sincerely asked.

". . . The counselor. She called us trash and told me I was crazy and ignorant. When she pointed her finger in my face . . . I didn't mean to do it . . . but . . ."

"I know you didn't. I understand."

I did understand. No, I wouldn't have gone so far as stomping her face in, but I got it. Cindy offered a faint smile, then pulled out a Polaroid picture of her and a guy wearing an orderly's uniform.

"He works at the nuthouse. We did it."

"No way! Really? Did it hurt?"

"No. Not really. You did it yet?"

I shook my head no.

"Of course not, corny," she said. "You know everyone calls me Fish Eyes now?"

I busted out laughing. She laughed too. Then we hugged each other as she cried quietly on my shoulder.

An hour or so had passed as we spoke about stupid things like her new inappropriate boyfriend and César trying to fuck me down in Puerto Rico.

"You look different," she said all out of the blue.

"It's the bangs," I explained. "No more big forehead sticking out," I added.

She laughed.

"No. You do look different, like an 'outside' girl. You're gonna make it. I always knew it."

Tears fell heavy from her bald eyes. I cried too. Why didn't they pick her too? Why did they leave her here to end up like this?

"Hey, Cindy, don't get into any more trouble, please. Or they win. Remember?"

She nodded. Then she grabbed my hand and told me I was still her best friend.

On the way back to the Group Home, I kept telling myself that I had to keep it together and not lose it again or I might snap like Cindy did.

I never saw Cindy again after that visit. I had tried for a time to stay in touch. We had spoken a couple of times on the phone, but when she was released from the Home, I never heard from her again. But I never stopped asking for her and surely never forgot her, ever.

. . .

I think I was fourteen by the time all the paperwork was done. I'm not sure. Nigel, our counselor, was waiting for me inside the van to take me on my final ride to the Metro train station.

I thought I'd be doing cartwheels. This was the end of a life that I'd wanted desperately to leave for years, but the sadness from the other girls, who I thought hated my guts, threw me. Especially when the girl I had the big fight with started crying as she waved good-bye, mouthing, I'm sorry. I waved back, apologizing too.

I jumped in the van.

"How's life working out for you, Rosie?"

"My life's a black hole, Nigel. But thanks for asking."

We both sort of laughed.

He looked at me and then asked me what I wanted out of life. I told him that I wanted to go to college, get a job as a legal secretary to pay the bills, then try to get a job at a marine-life study lab as an assistant and eventually get a nice apartment of my own and bring home groceries in a brown paper bag like Mary Tyler Moore and Marlo Thomas.

"Why limit yourself? Why be the legal secretary and not the head of the firm? Why be an assistant and not the head scientist? Why not shoot for a house instead of renting from someone else?"

I stared back at him. I always thought that I was imagining and expecting the best for myself. I was challenged and also perplexed by my own low expectations. Maybe it stemmed from constantly hearing my school guidance counselors and other adults always cautioning me not to dream too high. Say that to a kid a hundred million times and they just might begin to believe it.

"Yeah, well, 'when your head says one thing and your whole life says another, your head always loses.' That's Bogart, *Key Largo*."

He liked that one, sort of smiled back at me.

"Life dealt you a shitty hand, Rosie. There's no doubt about that."

"Gee, thanks. Cheer me right up, why don'tcha?"

He shook his head with a laugh.

"You can always ask for new cards."

"Yeah, right. . . . How?"

"Just by asking. You'll figure it out. Especially when you get tired of holding on to that hand."

Whoa.

As the train took me toward my new beginning, I wanted to purge all those years stuck in the system through screams and tears. All that came was a big lump of some kind of emotion that hung silently heavy in my throat.

. . .

Tia was quietly giddy as she pushed her plump body up to the third floor. She opened the door and gestured with her hand, drawing my attention to the small hallway that separated the tiny kitchen from the back two bedrooms.

"Look, Rosie! For you."

I didn't know what to say, how to respond. Tia had turned the little hallway into my own bedroom—a small bed pushed to one side and a small dresser to the other. This was the first time I'd had my own room—seriously. Okay, so it was in a hallway, but you've gotta start somewhere. (Sorry. That's so sad, it cracks me up.)

"This is for me?"

"*Jes*, all for you. I'm so happy you're here. I hope you'll be happy with us again."

It was too much. I didn't know how to take in that amount of joy. I sat quietly on the bed for a moment.

"Thank you, Tia," I said, trying unsuccessfully to hold back the tears.

"But why you cry? You're here now! Don't cry. Please."

CHAPTER 21

I WAS quiet for most of the first several weeks back. I stayed in a lot, close to Tia. When she was at work, my days were spent listening to Burt Bacharach, featuring Dionne Warwick, and my *Romeo and Juliet* album, the 1968 movie version starring Olivia Hussey (love!), moping about for hours longing for Freckles, or sitting still on my bed, not knowing what to do or where to go, waiting for Tia to come home, just like Freckles probably did with me. And when I did get up, I cleaned obsessively! Imagine that! I thought I'd love not being forced to clean, but I couldn't help myself, the messiness freaked me out. Yep, those penguins got inside.

Although Tia cleaned every week, she was still messy. She hated being in her American Express and would rip off that girdle and all her clothes the minute she walked in, throwing them about in exchange for her *bata*. Too tired to clean after dinner, she would let the dishes pile high. And as a result, at night you would have a cut-off broomstick by your bed to bang on the floor two, three times so that the mice would scurry away when you needed to go to the bathroom—not kidding.

I'd save up my $2.50 weekly allowance from her and buy mouse poison or traps without her knowledge so I wouldn't embarrass her. I'd clean every inch of the apartment, then report to Tia, waiting for her inspection and approval—weirdo—but would receive an appreciative yet troubling smile instead. And I kept asking permission to do everything, from cooking an egg to taking a bath, to going to the corner store for a Snickers bar. I felt lost without a regimented schedule and someone to report to.

I had a lot of bad nightmares too—of Sister Renata trying to kill me, of the Home, of my half-brother trying to molest me, and of my mother punching me or at times trying to kill me too. I would wake up in the middle of the night breathing heavily.

"Rosie! Rosie! Rosamarie!!! You having a bad dream again. Come on here. Please!"

"I'm okay, Tia. Go back to sleep."

Lorraine, Cookie, and Millie acted as if it wasn't a big deal that I was back, despite my weirdness. That was a good thing, whether it was a concerted effort or not. The block acted in the same vein. No one brought up my time in the Home. I didn't know if they knew about the Home or assumed that I was living with my mother and began living with Tia for some private reason. I thought they were being respectful, but later I found out that years before, Tia made my cousins swear not to tell anyone my business about being in an institution. It was private family stuff and that was that.

And it didn't only apply to my situation. We were just as private about the rest of the clan. Yeah, we would talk shit about each other. I mean, there was a lot of *bochinche* that even went five generations back, but we kept all that in house.

Everyone on the block knew not to gossip about my family. And I mean everyone. Titi, Millie, and Lourdes/Cookie didn't play. Even Lorraine would get at you. Well, never physically, but she had skills to tell you off in a hot second. But Cookie, you knew not to mess with her. She feared no one.

I remember one time when one of the boys who always hung out on our stoop began to talk about a family member of ours. I was so shocked and upset. I'd never, ever heard anyone talk shit about us, or the rest of Daddy's family. I ran upstairs to find Cookie and told her what the kid had said. Cookie ran down and then slapped the shit out of the kid in the face in front of everyone. She told him to never speak of any member of our family again or she would beat the living hell out of him and call his mother to tell her that she did it. Not another word was ever spoken about it. And that was that.

I don't know when it exactly happened, but after a while, being home with Tia, it happened, not just like that, but eventually— happiness.

It was still summer, and it started with dinner. Lorraine was out hanging with Joanne. I stayed in to wait for Tia. She was working late, until after ten. I knew she would be exhausted, so I decided that I'd cook dinner for her. I made one of our favorites: boiled eggplant with sautéed ground beef in *sofrito* over white rice. I also prepared a red onion and tomato salad. Tia didn't eat enough veggies, but at least she would eat that.

"Look, Tia! I cooked!"

"*Ay*, my goodness! Why?"

"So you don't have to."

"That is not why you're here. You know that, right?"

We ate and talked for hours about this and that. I did it the next night and the next. It became the norm, me cooking about three nights a week. Sometimes Don Luis, Tia's good friend, would come by. That's when I would cook something special, like a *bacaloa* salad or *bisteak con sequoias* over *arroz blanco*. I'd make coffee and lay out the *gallettas* for Doña Gladys, our downstairs neighbor, if she came up after she had finished the dishes.

This got me out of the house and acquainted with Bushwick, shopping for food. I would be so shy handing the local butcher or fruit-stand owner food stamps to pay for the groceries. They would make me feel better by not making a big deal out of it, casually asking me how Tia was, offering a free slice of something, telling me they'd see me next Tuesday. Soon I'd find myself stopping to hang out on the stoop with Luis, Anthony, Vinnie, and Jeanette on my way back. Then things took off.

I started to become a part of the neighborhood, going to house jams with Lorraine and her best friend Joanne—Jeanette's sister. We loved getting ready too, doing our hair and makeup for hours—just like Titi, Millie, and Cookie used to do! We'd take just as long getting all pretty just to go to Coney and flirt with the Italian and Russian boys on the boardwalk, taking the subway down, listening to the different boom boxes that would tune in to the same station if Teena Marie's summer hit song "Square Biz" came on. I loved hanging up at Car Barns Hill (now known as Grover Cleveland Track and Field), hanging on the cement bleachers with my friends, looking over the East River at the Chrysler Building, having my own *Saturday Night Fever* daydreams. And talk about *Saturday Night Fever* moments! My favorite thing to do was walk all the way down to and over the Brooklyn Bridge by myself, just to have time for my own thoughts, discovering the beautiful neighborhoods like Clinton Hill along the way, saying to myself that I would own one of those beautiful brownstones one day.

I got a job at Wyckoff Hospital, first as a candy striper pushing the book cart to patients' rooms, then as a typist in the medical-records department. I would still make the rounds to the elderly patients, making jokes, singing show tunes with them to cheer them up—I know, nerd. But I liked it. I even began to venture into the city on my own, taking in the Museum of Natural History fifty times over—super-nerd! Taking trips, back and forth to Puerto Rico, to Dad's, to Tio Monserrate, or up to Tia Aya's became the norm. And . . . wait for it . . . I started to lose all of my emotional weight and my figure was in full bloom—holla! Looking cute was top priority in Bushwick, especially for a Puerto Rican.

I still kind of hated going over to my mother's house, but there were times when it was enjoyable. Lydia could be so entertaining, so funny and quick. And my half-siblings were fun at times too. I loved dancing with them in the living room till holes were burned through my socks, playing cards, having long, intelligent, captivating debates over politics or social issues. I even loved hanging in the basement with one of my half-brothers—not the molester, of course—as I'd help him train for the Golden Gloves that he never made it to.

But the bad things overshadowed everything. Lydia wasn't the tidiest, but once her husband left her for another woman—a couple of years before I came home—she didn't keep things as clean as she used to. By the time I did come back, she had moved again, and the filth in the already run-down apartment was way beyond imagination: rodent droppings, an unbelievable amount of cockroaches and roach sheddings, unnecessary clutter, hundreds of empty shopping bags stuffed into needed closet space, bills stacked here and there, etc. The kitchen walls held on to old grease and nicotine residue, which made them look grayish and muddy. There was a huge hole in the ceiling over the tub where rats would run back and forth on the exposed two-by-four. The building was eventually condemned, but my mother didn't move because she didn't have to pay rent anymore. The weirdest thing I hated the most was the nails hammered into the living room walls that my half-brothers hung their clothes on. It all drove me crazy, but I couldn't clean too much or my mother would get suspicious and paranoid that I thought I was better than she was.

There were also the relentless and spontaneous explosions. A physical fight could spark up in seconds flat over nothing, literally. Like a game of cards with my half-brothers. "Why did you play that spade?! *You fucked up the whole fucking game!*" Then a card could be flipped in your face or the table shoved into your stomach. Another classic was how one sibling or another would gang up on you through mental and emotional torture for days, turning everyone against you. Like talking about how horrible a degenerate you were over some minor incident, all day, every day, as if you weren't in the room. The taunting would get to the point where you were wishing for your death because that would be the honorable thing to do for being such a piece of shit. And the constant threat of getting molested was a good one too. Oh, and let's not forget about Mom's occasional hard-ass slaps to the face and constant insulting jabs. Those were strong deterrents as well.

One time, it was around 6:00 AM or so. My siblings were asleep. I had gotten up early enough so that I could sneak out to Tia's. Unfortunately, my mother was already up, sitting at the small kitchen table and preparing to put on a full face of makeup while having one of her conversations with the wall. I stepped back, trying not to embarrass her during her "chat," while still stealing a peek at her natural beauty. It was the first time I'd seen her completely clean-faced.

"Who's there?" she quietly screamed out.

Shit! Panic!

"Me. Rosie. I have to use the bathroom."

I cautiously made my way toward the bathroom that was inside the kitchen. She put her hands over her face, hiding, embarrassed not that I caught her talking to the wall, but that I saw her without her makeup.

From inside the bathroom, I could hear her softly singing in Spanish like a beautiful songbird. When I gently crept back out, she asked me to sit with her.

"You know I used to sing in nightclubs in Puerto Rico? Oh yes," she said with pride. "But then my husband made me stop. He was jealous—of my talent. Men are like that. They get scared of your confidence. Everyone came to see me. But. . . ."

She trailed off without finishing. She looked so sad. It was the second time I'd felt sympathy for her. The first time was when one of my half-brothers, after getting hit with a wire hanger and belt numerous times by her, grabbed the belt and started swinging back. It was horrifying to witness. My mother cried a river the entire night, hurt and shocked, as the neighbors surrounded her, wiping witch hazel on her face to calm her down. I remember the rest of us kids hovering in a corner, watching, crying. Horrific scene.

But I digress.

My mind drifted, wondering how she had looked singing in a nightclub. Was she dressed in a cocktail dress or a long tight-fitting gown? Was the place a café or a large ballroom at some tourist hotel? How did she wear her hair? Could she have made it big if her husband hadn't forced her to quit?

I was startled by the snapping sound of her compact and found Lydia staring at me.

"God, you're ugly, just like your father," she said, all disgusted and shit.

"I know. You say that all the time."

Why the hell did I say that? She looked up at me with one of her sly smirks.

"You know your father left me when I was eight months pregnant? Oh yes. Left me and my children and went back to his wife. But everyone made me the bad guy."

The familiar uncomfortable silence hung over us for a moment.

"I have to go to help Tia with the Saturday laundry."

I kissed her extended cheek and left.

. . .

After we finished Saturday's early supper, I sat on the edge of Tia's bed as she got under the covers.

"Tia, what happened to your husband?"

"He left me, for another woman," she said defensively, with a slight grin.

"Oh. Sorry."

"Don't be." She laughed for a moment in reflection. "You know what *hap'pined?* I came home early from work and found him in bed with my friend. Oh *jes.* I went to *de* bureau and started packing a *maleta.* 'Minguita, please don't leave,' he says. I said, 'I'm not leaving, I'm packing your stuff!' Ga, ga, ga!"

I forced a slight laugh, trying to hide how sad that story made me feel for her.

"And you never wanted to get married again?"

"What for? *Ay,* men can be so exhausting, even. I don't need *de* headache."

I nodded, trying to make sense of it all.

"Tia, why did you take me in?"

"Because I had to."

"You had to? No, you didn't."

"*Jes,* I did. I love you, so I had to."

She smiled softly. I smiled back and started to cry.

"*Ay,* Rosamarie. Don't cry. You're here now, and I love you, okay?"

I wiped the snot and smiled.

That was the moment I got it in my head that Tia had to get full custody of me. If I wanted to maintain any sanity that was still in me, I had to do it. The problem was that my mother had to give consent, and we would have to go to court. Or she could sign her rights over and just Tia and I would have to go, which I knew would fail because my mother was too smart and her paranoia would make her think we were plotting an evil scheme against her and she would lose it. Well, I was kind of plotting, but there was no malice behind it, sincerely. I spoke with Tia about it, suggesting that she do the asking—thinking that would be easier since Lydia liked her so much.

"Oowie, I don't know. That makes me nervous. You know how she is."

"But, Tia, I just can't keep going over there."

"But why? That's your mother. She loves you."

"No, she doesn't. She doesn't even like me."

"But why you say that? That's not true. She's your mother."

I still didn't and couldn't tell Tia about the abuse. So I brought the idea up to my mother, kind of. I told her it was only because Tia needed me. Her life was so hard and pathetic since she didn't have a man and she was so lonely—that was a big Latin issue back then, not having a man around. And she was so fat and had arthritis and diabetes—she needed me to cook, clean, and shop for her. Also, it would be for school reasons too, since Grover Cleveland High School was closer to Tia's house.

"Oh, you want everyone to think I'm the bad guy, right?" she said in that calm, angry tone of hers. "You think I'm stupid, Rosie?" She wasn't looking at me but at the potato she was peeling with a paring knife.

"No, Ma. I just—"

"I am not signing a fucking thing. And for your information, Minguita already told me everything. Oh yes, I know everything. I know the entire plot. You want a war, Rosie? Is that what you want?"

I was flabbergasted! Tia betrayed me? And on top of that, the weirdest thing happened. I saw through my mother's paranoia. Her feelings were hurt. To see that hurt on such a proud woman broke something inside of me. I felt it in my stomach, like an ache that was old and bad. I walked back to my house stunned and filled with regret. What the hell do I do now? She looked so wounded. And now I am caught as well.

In a non-accusatory way, so as not to tip her off that something bad went down, I asked Tia if she had talked to my mother about the "papers."

"No, I haven't seen your mother for a month. Why? You didn't say nothing about the papers?"

"No . . . kind of."

"*Ay*, Rosie! Why?"

"I don't know! Sorry."

I was in a daze. I couldn't get over it, how I fucked it up and how my mother lied and I fell for it. Well, I lied too, but she lied about Tia betraying me—that pissed me off. How could she do that to her! I kept an even greater distance from my mother after that. I barely went over, maybe once a month for a night or two.

Lydia didn't protest in the slightest. Maybe it was her pride—maybe not. She never came to check up on me, not even for a visit. Matter of fact, she never came to Tia's to visit me, ever. Besides Carmen and Tito, none of my half-siblings ever came to see me—well, except my oldest sister, Amy, who came twice. I guess it never occurred to the rest of them to return the courtesy.

Then the final blow finally happened.

It was the weekend, and I was at Lydia's house. She was going off about me not watching after my little sister, Kathy, who was always hanging out on the street a lot. "You didn't ask me to watch her, Ma."

Smack! I didn't flinch. I grabbed a pack of cigarettes that were on the kitchen table, lit one, and blew the smoke in her face as if I were Barbara Stanwyck in Double Indemnity. (I don't know why the hell I did that. I didn't even smoke! I guess I watched too many film noirs.) I thought she was going to smack me again, but to my surprise, she calmly tried to defend her assault.

"No, you see, I have to fix you, because you have to look out for each other. Like I tell everyone."

"Really? No one in this house ever looks out for me."

Smack!

"I fucking hate you!" I screamed. "I swear to God I fucking hate you!"

She punched me in the face. For the first time, in a knee-jerk reaction, I grabbed her arm with one hand and pulled back my other hand in a fist ready to punch her back—bad move. She quickly grabbed my fist on some kung fu shit, wiggled her arm free, and proceeded to punch me repeatedly to the floor. I managed to scramble away and ran to my house as if my life depended on it.

I came busting through the door with blood running down my nose, panicked as shit as I rushed to the bathroom. Tia, on the toilet, looked up at me and freaked out.

"What happened? *Ay Dios mio!* Your face! Who did that?" she shrieked as she quickly gathered up her underpants.

"My mother!"

"What? No! How could she hit you?!"

"With her fist, Tia! She does it all the damn time!"

The truth just shot out. I guess I was too hysterical to lie at that point.

Then the front door swung open, slamming against the wall. I froze for a moment, then peeked out the bathroom door. It was Lydia! She had followed me! I had rushed in so quickly I forgot to lock the damn door!

"You think you're slick! Get over here!"

"Ma. I'm sorry, Ma. I swear! I'm sorry! Pleeeeaaassse, Ma! Please don't hit me! I'm fucking tired of you hitting me all the time!"

Just as she was about to charge at me, flinging the kitchen chairs out of her way, Tia came screaming out of the bathroom and jumped in front of me.

"Lydia! Please! No! Please don't hit the child! Please! Don't hit my baby!"

Her baby? Major bad move. My mother lost it.

"Your baby? She's my daughter! Not yours! Mine! I gave birth to her, not you!" she said, pounding on her chest and then on the kitchen table with hurt and pain.

The commotion made some of the *doñas* in the building rush upstairs. Their mouths dropped as they saw my aunt on her knees in front of me, pleading on my behalf as the blood continued to flow out of my nose.

"Lydia, please. *Por favor!* [Please!]"

My mother, taking in the neighbors, cleverly got calm in an instant.

"No, you see, she tried to hit me. Yes. (*Sniffles*) I try so hard with this girl, but you don't know her. She lies all the time. She says things about you all the time. How you're pathetic and fat and slow and how she pities you. You see? And then she hits me! It has to stop."

Doña Gladys and even Doña Ponchi didn't buy it. My mother's volatile reputation was too legendary and trumped her calculated response.

Unfortunately, Tia saw the bit of truth. She turned to me, questioning with her eyes. I couldn't lie to her—I mean about the lies, even though my mother was twisting the situation. I looked at my aunt and couldn't say a thing. I loved her too much to keep it going.

Humiliated. Caught. Panicked. I ran to the back window, climbed out and up the fire escape, and ran over the rooftop to the next building, into the apartment of my friend Guy, and then out onto the street. I continued to run to nowhere.

Tia found me the next day at my best friend Jeanette's house across the street. She looked as haggard and bleary-eyed as I did. She kindly asked me to come home; she had cooked one of my favorite meals, *pollo guisado y arroz con gandules*. That was all that was said. It took a few awkward weeks, but things got back to normal between us, and she never brought it up. Lydia never brought it up either. When I eventually started to go over there again after a month or so—I know, I know, but she was still my mother—she was different with me. She offered me a bit of respect and a more grown-up relationship—more like distant friends. It was a relief, but also left me with the disenchanted reality that I was never going to have that mother-daughter relationship I secretly wanted.

CHAPTER 22

DEPRESSION SUCKS. And I was really depressed for a while after the big fight. My grades at Grover Cleveland High School began to drop. Tia would try to encourage me to study. "Why don't you put on music? You study better with it on. Want me to play your 'Bac-ka-rrrack' for you?" I got into a lot of trouble at school, was sent to the dean's office many times. Most of the time it was my fault, but sometimes it wasn't. Still, I took things too far. Like the time I kept correcting my English teacher's use of grammar during class. She told me to stop, and I wouldn't and was very impertinent about it. To make matters worse, I had cursed out my guidance counselor after she told me to reconsider applying to a university since my grades were slipping: "You shouldn't set yourself up for potential failure."

I would cut class early for the first time, ever, and wander off for long periods of time by myself, going to Clinton Hill, sometimes to Fort Greene Park, even though no one dared to go into the park for fear of gangs or getting robbed. Clinton Hill brought me peace. It was the Brooklyn I had seen in the old movies. Those beautiful houses that I longed to own someday snapped me out of it somewhat and refocused my dreams, my goals. I began to try again at school. I had to. I had to be as determined as ever. I had to believe I was immune to the emotional and mental blows of my life thus far. I had to believe that I was above it. If I didn't, how could I win?

. . .

It was the '80s. I was obsessed with boxing (Willie Benítez, Sugar Ray Leonard, and Tommy Hearns especially), hip-hop and new wave music and MTV—even though we couldn't afford it. Life with Tia was my world, my happiness, but I knew I had to leave. Reaganomics and the beginnings of the crack epidemic were hitting Bushwick hard. The lack of job opportunities increased limitations and produced a negativity and an apathy that were trying. There were good, smart, honest, and hardworking people in my neighborhood, but the opposite was also prevalent and now increasing. I was lucky to still be working as a typist at Wyckoff Hospital, transcribing doctors' recorded medical notes from a Dictaphone, but I'd soon be laid off due to budget cuts.

Tia had slowed down too. Her arthritis and diabetes prevented her from working her two extra jobs on the side in addition to her regular work. To see her struggle because for days at a time she could only provide cereal, rice and beans, chicken gizzards, Wonder bread, fried eggs, and leftover *pego* was tough. I helped out as best I could with the money I had saved from my job, told her I was too old for an allowance, and bought meat that I sneaked into the refrigerator on the sly. (Tia never would accept money from me.) Sometimes I'd stuff myself with slices of pizza from Mario's Pizzeria so I wouldn't seem hungry after dinner.

I liked Grover Cleveland High. I loved the old beautiful building, but didn't feel the same way about the majority of the student body. There were a lot of nerdy smart kids, but the rest—*oy vey*, hoodlums in the making.

I was about sixteen years old. Walking home, I had gotten jumped by three girls because of their Five Percenter boyfriend. The Nation of Islam, whose members were African American Muslims, was gaining popularity with young black kids. They made up their own sect and referred to themselves as Five Percenters, from the Nation of Gods: they believed that only the Asiatic black man is God, and only 5 percent of the world possess true knowledge.

So anyway, this Five Percenter in school wanted me to become his main Earth—meaning his main woman. Me not being black and the fact that those girls were only his Flowers—meaning his subset—set them off on a mission to kick my ass. They followed me after school. I fronted, walking casual, while inside my heart was beating.

Please, oh please, God, don't let them kick my ass.

I turned into Car Barns Hill; they made their move, surrounding me. I was terrified!

"You think you cute," said one of the Flowers.

"I don't think, I know," I sassily replied.

"This bitch is crazy," the Flower exclaimed.

"I know you are, but what am I?"

I know, a cornball comeback. Bitch whipped out a razor blade and tried to cut my dimple out—not kidding, shit hurt like hell, screamed like a bitch. I started swinging and popped her in the mouth. She stumbled back. One of the other girls grabbed me from behind while the third kicked me in the stomach. As I was buckling over to the ground, the girl I popped punched the side of my head with a power right hook, repeatedly. Curled up in a fetal position to protect myself as they stomped, punched, and kicked, praying I wouldn't die, I grabbed one girl's pinky and held on so hard that I heard it snap. She screamed for me to let go, I screamed back, telling them I would let go if they stopped. Friends and neighbors from my block finally arrived and broke it up.

Next day at school I walked in, ribs bandaged, busted lip, and a closed fat black eye. The "cool" crowd greeted me with respect. I've gotta get the fuck outta here.

I started to think about the benefits of being in the Home. Seriously. A moral code was instilled in me as well as a motivation to do well in life. Okay, maybe that was who I was all along; but maybe the nuns helped bring it out in me. Whichever the case, they definitely had a hand in making me an ethical and hardworking person.

I watched a few kids my age and a bit older, upstate and down in Brooklyn, get pregnant. Upstate, it was something to be ashamed of, kept secret. Parents would hide their kid's belly, and adoptions were considered, even early marriages, to save face. But in Brooklyn kids were moving in with their baby's daddy or momma as if this was something to aspire to, to be envied even. To me, teen pregnancy was selfish and immature, let alone limiting in your chances for success, regardless if you were rich or poor. Especially if you had issues with neglect and/or abuse you were still experiencing yourself or hadn't dealt with—why subject an innocent child to your growing pains? Forget that. Plus, I had plans. Most of my friends did, like Luis, Vinnie, Anthony, and Jeanette. We all wanted more and were willing to put in the necessary work to get more. I still had a light in me, an optimism that anything was possible if I tried hard enough.

My cousin Titi, Tia's oldest daughter, the heroin addict, suggested that I come to Los Angeles, where she'd moved about four years before. She was stressed out with the kids, and since I used to babysit them all the time, she asked me to come help her out while I went to school. I was wary at first. Besides the fact that I really wanted to go to Stony Brook University, I wondered if she was still an addict. "No, no. I'm done with all that shit." She also told me life in La-La Land was laid-back and fly, and provided opportunities way beyond what I could find in Brooklyn. I decided to give it a shot.

I called Dad. He was upset, didn't like the idea of me being so far away from him and Tia, but supported my decision.

I went over and told my mother. There wasn't a big reaction. She just blessed my trip and told me to call.

Tia cried for weeks! She begged me not to go. I tried hard to explain why I wanted to leave.

"I want to have a career. I want to see Paris and go to Brazil and listen to Astrud Gilberto live."

"Who?"

"It doesn't matter, Tia. I want all that life can offer and more."

"You sound like a Hallmark commercial."

We both laughed a bit. Then she started to sob.

"But I'll miss you so much. I'll worry so much. I can't stand it."

"Me too. So much. Mommie, I want to be able to support myself and not have to depend on anyone, especially you. You've done enough, and I thank you for it."

"*Ay*, you're so stupid, even. You don't have to thank me—for what? Loving you? . . . You promise to go to college?"

"Yes."

My last day—all packed and ready to go—I walked out of the apartment. It seemed like half the block was waiting to send me off. Tears. By the time everyone got in the gypsy cab, Cookie, Millie, Tia, and a couple of grandkids, the body weight made the muffler drag and spark all the way to JFK. Tears and kisses at the terminal, nonstop. Every time I went to hand in my ticket, Tia would start wailing.

As the plane took off, my desire to leave Brooklyn instantly began to fade. I thought of all the loving moments I'd had with Tia and my cousins. All the fun I'd had with Jeanette and the rest of our nerdy clan. I thought of summers in Coney Island, the trips to the Museum of Natural History, walks to Clinton Hill and over the Brooklyn Bridge. I felt a panic inside, questioning if I was making the right choice.

. . .

Titi had never kicked the shit, in fact it had gotten worse. And the neighborhood was not "fly." She lived on the edge of the Crenshaw/Adams District. Her broken-down, cheap apartment was always dimly lit, filled with questionable characters, either dropping off drugs or getting high with her, and muscle men coming by looking for late payments on drugs purchased. Her sweet kids who used to listen to me had become brats. Didn't blame them, though. I understood they were acting out.

They tested my nerves to the limits, but I had learned patience from babysitting Millie's and Cookie's kids. One afternoon, while watching Millie's three kids, one of them had kicked me in the shin. My hand acted on instinct, popping her in the mouth hard to the point of blood, just like my mother would do with me. I couldn't believe I did that, and shame and regret instantly flushed out of every pore, along with immediate empathy. I held her begging for forgiveness as I tried to erase the pain and humiliation. I told Tia when she got home. She just nodded in a grave and slow manner. I fell into an instant depression—I couldn't speak the rest of the night, woke up silent, and couldn't look Tia in the eye when she smiled good-morning. Two days later, as we were watching WABC's Saturday 4:30 movie, Tia said I reacted that way because that was what I'd been taught, but that I didn't have to be like that. I never hit a child ever again.

. . .

I hated Los Angeles—hated it to its core. I hated the pretentious people there. I hated that it was always the same temperature outside. The musical taste and mostly everything else was limited and segregated. I hated the suffocating smog. I hated the fact that you needed a car to get anywhere. The transportation system sucked. I walked back and forth to high school, which was about three miles, to the point where my three cheap-ass pairs of Knickerbocker Avenue shoes had holes in them by the end of the first month.

And walking in Titi's neighborhood was very dangerous. I was on constant high alert every day. At school, which sucked, kids made fun of me, and they weren't just mocking my attire. Los Angeles was the first place other than upstate New York where my accent was pointed out and ridiculed. I had not realized how much Tia's accent had become a part of my own. Even Titi commented on how Brooklyn I sounded and how much I sounded like Mommie. I didn't care, kind of. I was used to people pointing at me, gossiping about me. I did my best to disregard most of it and stayed focused on my goals of going to college, having a career, and finding my own apartment.

Going to school, applying to colleges, filling out financial-aid forms, working part-time at an insurance company as a secretary and file clerk and at McDonald's as a cashier, and caring for two bratty kids was nothing compared to dealing with a heroin addict. The strain of that alone got to me. Although my GPA was fairly decent, I kept scoring low on the SATs. The emotional stress didn't make room for any concentration, and I would blank out during the exam. I didn't understand why I kept blanking out at the time; all I understood was that I kept scoring low, and as a result I kept feeling like I was a failure. But I pressed on.

I never ratted on Titi about the drugs and stuff that were going on, but Tia knew something was wrong, she could hear it in my voice over the phone. She convinced me to come home for a visit. I saved up enough money to go back to Brooklyn to spend Christmas with her and Dad, who was coming a day after . . . and to see my mother and half-siblings. I know. What can I say—I missed them.

Touching down at JFK, I got all choked up seeing the New York skyline. The smell of roasted pork permeating the building as I rushed upstairs made my heart pound. Even though I had stopped eating it since Miguel was butchered, the aroma was too synonymous with Tia and Suydam Street. Homemade *pasteles* tightly wrapped in wax paper with string boiled on the stove while the *pernil* roasted below in the oven. "Don't worry, Rosie. I made *de* turkey too. You won't have to eat Miguel tonight, ga, ga, ga, ga, ga, ga!"

Arroz y gandules, boiled yucca with *mojo de ajo*, candied *yamas*, *platanos maduro*—the works just flowed everywhere! Heaven!

I felt all grown-up and proud when I gave Tia a hundred dollars, cash. She refused it. I was heartbroken. "Why? I worked so hard to give you this money!"

"No, you work hard for yourself and save your money. I have my life. I've made my decisions. It's not your job to worry about me."

I hid part of the money in her purse and the rest in the jar above the stove where she kept her emergency fund.

The next morning I headed to my mother's house. I had three hundred dollars and bags filled with Christmas presents. Lydia's extended cheek was replaced with open arms. Say what? It felt awkward, scary, and good. I gave her eighty dollars, leaving me two hundred and twenty. A part of me felt guilty that I didn't give her the same amount I gave Tia. Was I still angry about everything that went down? Whatever it was, it bothered me like crazy. "Oh, Ma, here. I thought I gave you an even hundred. Sorry."

One of my younger half-siblings, Kathy, had moved upstairs into her own apartment. She had just given birth to a son and was living there with the baby's daddy. It was exciting and weird to me how easily we were clicking since we were never close, I'd never really known her as a person. I saw Terry too, who everyone was calling Tiara now, her birth name, and her little son, Eddie Albert. He was a couple of years old now. I loved Eddie. Loved him the moment I met him at a couple of months old. And he loved me. Tiara always said that Eddie took to me like no one else.

My half-brother, the one who tried to molest me, came upstairs along with Tiara's new boyfriend, this asshole, to say hello. I acted like I was happy to see him because he seemed so guilt-ridden. Jokes were told, along with crazy funny stories that had me dying with laughter. I kept thinking to myself, *Are these the same people I left just a little under a year ago?*

Kathy asked me if I wanted to go up on the roof while she

smoked a joint. We went up, and after we came back down my half-brother and Tiara's boyfriend were gone. So was my money, all of it—and my return plane ticket. Shocked and upset, I went off. So did Kathy. "Fucking drug addicts! I know they took your money!" She bolted downstairs to our mother's apartment and returned with both in tow.

"What? Oh my God! I didn't take it," my brother said, feigning shock and dismay.

"Me either!" said the stupid asshole coke/heroin addict boyfriend.

"Who do you think took it?" my brother continued, shooting accusatory looks at Kathy.

She exploded. "What, motherfucker? Don't even be looking at me! I'm not the fucking cokehead/heroin addict over here!"

My mother came to the defense of both my brother and the asshole boyfriend, of course, feigning shock as well. "He wouldn't do something like that. You shouldn't have left your money lying around like that anyway. That's what you get." Pop went my balloon.

Back at Tia's, I quietly went into the bathroom and sat on top of the toilet seat for over thirty minutes. I felt so stupid. Tia knocked on the door. I told her I was robbed on the subway, all my money and my plane ticket back to Los Angeles.

"Oh my goodness. I'm calling your father."

"No! Why?"

" 'Cause he's your father," she angrily snapped back, "so let him start acting like he is!"

Whoa! Where did that come from? Tia went into her emergency fund.

"Lemme give you some money until your father gets here tomorrow."

Oh snap! Busted.

"Ay, Rosie. I told you. This is for you, not for me!"

She gave me back the forty dollars and told me my father would give me the rest when he arrived. I kept hoping she didn't see the other sixty in her purse and try to give me back that as well. When she went across the hall to Doña Ponchi's house to use the phone to call Dad, I sneaked into her purse, retrieved the sixty, and put it in the emergency jar.

My father bought me a new ticket back to Los Angeles and gave me a fifty in addition to the many Christmas presents he brought for everyone. I hadn't seen him in months, since he'd been away on a ship, and thought I'd need the usual minute to get reacquainted, but no. We simply picked up where we'd left off, sitting in the living room all day listening to jazz records while he told stories of his womanizing adventures during World War II. I know, weird father-and-daughter bonding tactics, but it worked. In fact, I felt so wounded from the incident that it was the first time my body, my being, unconsciously slumped against his for emotional support as we listened to Nat King Cole and Tony Bennett. I remember my dad not making a big deal out of it as he gently held my hand while the record played out.

CHAPTER 23

I WENT back and worked like crazy. I studied like hell for the SATs. I think I got a half-decent score after my third attempt, but not good enough for a full scholarship like I was banking on. It bothered me tremendously, especially since I knew I only had a shot at community colleges now. But whatever, I couldn't afford to dwell on it.

Conversations on the phone with Tia were less frequent and even shorter. She became so worried that she came out to Los Angeles with Millie, Cookie, and Lorraine to visit "temporarily" after I graduated from high school to stay close to me. I pleaded with her to go home, told her it wouldn't be good for any of them to live there. She wasn't having it. She worried day and night about me, and now that she saw with her own eyes what was going on with Titi, she wasn't going back until I finished college.

Millie had found a place in South Central Los Angeles in Watts because the rent was so low and it seemed like a nice neighborhood with its ranch-style houses and palm tree–lined blocks—she didn't know about the Nickerson Garden projects nearby. We had no idea about the gang culture out there; it was a horrible discovery. I decided to stay with my heroin-addicted cousin because it was a much shorter trek to West Los Angeles and Los Angeles Community Colleges (I was going to both at the same time because LACC had better science classes), and to my new job at a law firm as a file clerk, and sadly, it was safer than South Central.

I came home from school one day to find Titi's apartment completely emptied out. She had left without telling me. She owed some dangerous drug dealers a lot of money, and she just jetted, leaving me behind with nothing more than my suitcase and a mattress on the floor with a note on top: "Go over to Millie's if you need a place to stay." All of my money that I had saved up to move into my own apartment was gone too.

I didn't freak out, I couldn't afford to. I had gotten used to drama, and I felt that I had to stay on course and not get distracted. I continued to walk to my jobs, coming home to an empty apartment, scared out of my wits, thinking one of the hoodlums would come looking for Titi and kill me instead. It was stupid to stay there, but the alternative, living in Watts, seemed much worse to me. At night I was in constant fear of the drug dealers coming back. I eventually went to Millie's.

I continued to go to college, started working again—two jobs, plus doing hair on the side—saved my money, and found my own apartment, unfortunately in the Crenshaw area again. One of my jobs was working part-time at the main office of Golden Bird Fried Chicken—an African American family-run business—as the vice president's assistant, who was the president's youngest son, Michael Stennis. I also worked part-time as a waitress at Sizzler's, but was fired. Only later did I find out that the manager did so because he liked me and there was a policy against management dating employees. At first I was pissed, but I got over it after he took me to Lake Tahoe for a week—I know, but Tahoe was off the hook!

The Stennises looked out for me and got me a one-bedroom apartment in one of the apartment buildings they owned in the "Jungle" for only $300 a month. It was still in the Crenshaw district but far away from Watts! It was lovely, with all of the palm trees sprouting out of its courtyards, but to my surprise I discovered that the Jungle was the Bloods' territory. First day, this kid comes up to me: "What set you from, cuz?"

"Oh? Excuse me, are we related?"

"No! Fool! What set? You a Blood or a Crip?"

Great.

I had to get out, so I took another part-time job at a record store near the Jungle, just blocks from my apartment. The assistant manager, who I knew liked me and who knew I didn't like him, offered me a ride home after we did inventory till one in the morning. "Oh, come on, Rosie, don't flatter yourself. I can't have you walk home by yourself through the damn Jungle!"

We pulled up. He asked if he could use the bathroom, he'd be quick. I went into my small kitchen to get a glass of water. When I turned around, he was lying on the ugly dark-colored living room carpet butt naked, stroking his erect penis up and down—no lie!

"What the fuck!" I screamed.

"Calm down, Rosie! Shh! Come here. It's okay!"

Then this ass sits up and makes the mistake of pulling me down on top of his naked disgusting body. I jumped up so fast, like on some Bruce Lee shit, screaming my head off. He grabbed my foot. "Shh! It's okay." Okay? Oh hell no! I quickly wiggled it loose and started stomping the shit out of this motherfucker. While he was curling up trying to avoid my blows, my next-door neighbor, Eric, from Chicago, who always looked after me, ran into my apartment and started to beat the crap out of the pervert. He grabbed his clothes and rushed out before the cops came (which didn't happen until twenty minutes later).

I couldn't sleep that night. I put a butcher knife under my pillow, scared out of my wits. It took me forever to decide to go into work the next day. When I did, this fucker acted like nothing had happened. Just as I was about to tell the head manager what went down and that I was quitting, he told me the asshole had suggested that he give me a raise—a big fat raise—for being such a good worker. I didn't know what to do. I needed that money so badly. I decided to take the money and keep quiet. I quit a week later, though, because I couldn't stand looking at the piece of shit.

I asked Michael Stennis if I could have a couple of extra hours until I found more employment. I really liked working for Michael and his entire family. So much so that when there wasn't a lot of work left for me to do, I used to watch their grandkids and their little friends, one of whom grew up to be the famous street artist Retna. (Can you believe that? I didn't realize it until my husband, Haze, took me to Retna's big opening in New York in 2011. "You used to babysit me and my friend Paris, Kevin Stennis's son.")

The Christmas holiday was approaching. After I came home one night beat and tired from work and school, the phone rang. It was my mother. I had not seen or spoken to her in probably six months, not since my last trip to New York. My mother never called or wrote to me, ever. Her explanation was that she hated talking on the phone and wasn't into writing letters. Funny thing, I don't like being on the phone either, but I still called her once in a while. I answered the phone.

"Ma?"

"Yes, Rosie . . . I. How are you?"

Her voice started to crackle. I could hear her trying to swallow her emotions, but she couldn't.

"What's wrong, Ma? Are you all right?"

"I . . . How are you?"

"I'm okay, Ma. How are you?"

"I love you," she blurted.

"I love you too, Ma."

"Okay. . . . So anyway, Merry Christmas. Bye."

And she hung up, leaving me confused, excited, resentful, and depressed once again . . . but I kept it moving.

. . .

I began to enjoy Los Angeles. Well, its nightlife. I was having fun, like a lot of fun. Thursday night was my three-hour biology lab class, seven to ten o'clock. I'd always sneak out ten minutes early because Thursday night was also ladies' night at Florentine Gardens nightclub in east Hollywood—free before ten. My three girlfriends—Carol, a bubbly, intelligent Mexican American; Nia, a smart, sexy, crazy Filipino; and sweet Tracy, who was Latino and black—and I always went clubbing together. We all wore tight clothes, high heels, lots of makeup . . . like, tons of mascara and black eye liner . . . and, of course, hair spray—love it! The club was close by, and we knew the doorman—if we were under ten minutes late, he would let us in free. The girls would be waiting outside my class in Nia's or Carol's car—there was not a minute to waste. I would bring my club clothes to school, change out of my normal everyday school attire during our dinner break, and come back dressed in a tight-ass hoochie-mama minidress and a gang of makeup. First time I did it, my professor's mouth dropped and the whole class went silent as I clicked my way back to my seat. It'd happen again when I'd be the first to leave a couple minutes early—hilarious.

A talent scout from *Soul Train* saw us dancing at the club one night. He came up and asked me to come on the show. "For real? *Soul Train?!*" Yay!!!! I told him I would go if my girlfriends could come too. "Well, I've gotta see if they look as good and dance as good as you do." One look and of course we were all in! I couldn't believe my luck! That's when my life started to change again.

We arrived at the studio on time, but were made to wait outside the studio gate for over an hour with the rest of the *Soul Train* regulars and newbies. Finally the talent scout came out and approached the gate. It turned into a frenzy, like piranhas at feeding time. He proceeded to point out his preferred picks. The pushing and shoving and desperateness were heartbreaking. "Come on, girls. This is bullshit," I said. As we began to turn away, the talent scout shouted at me, "Hey, where are you going? You can come in."

"Can my friends come too?"

He nodded yes. That made a few of the dancers crazy jealous, which wasn't very nice, but understandable. *Soul Train* created that circus of jealousy. Only the best-looking, sexiest, and most charismatic got in and got to be on the risers, the Scramble Board, or the main platform and received the most camera time.

Even I got caught up in it. There was this one beautiful girl with short red hair who got a lot of camera time, but that wasn't the reason I was jealous of her. This stupid boy I liked, liked her, and blah, blah, blah. Of course my pride wouldn't allow me to admit that—instead, I was a complete ass toward her. "She's stealing my moves!" You know, all that stupid young shit. I remember complaining to Tia about it. "*Ay*, you sound so stupid, even. You don't even know her, what her life is about, it might be hell—and over a boy? *Ay*, please. Don't be like that. It makes you look ugly." I got over it quick after that lecturing.

When the camera came on, my body shook like crazy. All I kept thinking about was my hair getting all sweaty. This *Soul Train* regular, Ricky, kind of took me under his wing and partnered with me. We got picked for the Scramble Board! My first day! When I started to speak on the first take, Don Cornelius gave me an incredulous look regarding my accent. I lessened it; he gave a nod of approval. Instantly, I felt ashamed. I had made my first conscious effort not to sound ethnic. Ricky made me feel better, later telling me he thought that my accent was cute, that it set me apart, and to ignore Don.

My mind was spinning the first time I stood on the *Soul Train* line. I didn't know what to do. Don Cornelius didn't like hip-hop or house dancing. He kept telling me to dance like the other girls, meaning like a vixen. In fact, after my first day he suggested that I dress more appropriately—you know, tight-ass minis and high heels. I was cool with the minis, but three-inch heels? Yikes! I could wear one- to two-inch heels. Three was a whole other thing.

I couldn't do more than stand there and gyrate. All the regulars had routines; all the girls had their signature sexy moves. I didn't have shit. When it was my turn, I started nervously pumping my body back and forth, trying to look like the other ladies, praying I wouldn't fall off those damn heels. While pumping, I kept thinking to myself, *I look like a fucking idiot!* To my surprise, everyone started cheering me on! Even Don Cornelius told me to go down a second time!

We didn't get paid, just a Kentucky Fried Chicken two-piece lunch box—not kidding. I didn't complain, I was happy to be there, and my ass was always hungry anyway, living on cans of tuna fish. But I left the show after only being on it for maybe a year or a year and a half. I say "only" because most of the regulars were there five, ten years plus! All waiting for their big break into the entertainment industry, like Jodi Watley and Shalamar. ("Make that move, right now, baby"—love them!)

Dad finally saw me on the show, freaked out, and told me it embarrassed him to see me dancing like that. I honestly didn't realize that I was dancing that provocatively. I was brought up so Catholic, I had no clue about my sexuality. (I was a virgin until I was twenty—true.) However, my decision wasn't solely based on that. I had gotten into a fight with Don Cornelius during a taping. He didn't like Keith Sweat coming over during his performance and dancing with me. But that wasn't the real reason why he went at me.

Don was trying to form a new singing group and asked me to be a member. I was excited, even though I told him I couldn't sing that good—"Your inability to sing is insignificant. It's how you fill that dress and how the camera loves you." Wow. Okay. But I declined the offer after he wouldn't let me take the recording/ management contract asking for 60 percent to a lawyer. I wasn't anyone's fool. Things were tense after that, but shit really hit the fan when an A&R executive from MCA Records, Louil Silas Jr.— who unfortunately passed away in 2001—had brought an act on the show and saw me rehearsing some hip-hop moves with Ricky and his older brother on the side. Louil was African American and medium height and had a potbelly, scruffy aftershave; he was well dressed, arrogant, confident, and funny as shit. He waved me over.

"That's hip-hop, right?"

"Yes, sir. But Don doesn't like the girls doing it on the show."

"Really? That's weird. I want you to teach it to my new artist, Bobby Brown, from New Edition. He's going solo. But don't tell anyone yet."

My heart went up into my throat!

"Here's my card. Come up to the record label on Monday."

"But I'm not a choreographer."

"I'll pay you fifteen hundred."

"I'll be there Monday morning."

Of course news got back to Don. How dare I not sign with him and go off and make money elsewhere? That's when he started to pick on me during the tapings.

So Keith kept humping, Don kept yelling "Cut!" and I was getting heated. By the time I went down the Soul Train line things were going from bad to worse. Excited that Louil liked and saw the future in hip-hop, I went down the line doing the Pee-wee Herman.

"Cut! Rosie, do it again."

I went down doing the Roger Rabbit.

"Cut! Come here."

I walked over. He pulled me in close and whispered sternly.

"You walk back down that line nice and sexy like you're supposed to."

I walked back to the head of the line, paused, then strutted down as if I were Naomi Campbell on the runway, continued walking past Don to my seat, grabbed my things, and told him I was out. Don grabbed my arm, pulling me back.

"You don't quit until I tell you you can quit!"

Wrong move. I grabbed the first thing I could get my free arm around, which happened to be one of the two-piece KFC chicken lunch boxes, and threw it at him. A chicken wing smacked him dead in his forehead. I was escorted out by security.

I was fuming, sitting in my broken-down Datsun B-210 that I had bought from a base head at college—ha! I was hurt too. This was *Soul Train*! Don was an idol to me, and this was how it went down? I wanted to go back inside to make amends—I *did* hit the man with a greasy chicken wing. And he *was* Don Cornelius! He was still a legend to be respected. Unfortunately, I was too angry, too filled with pride, and too embarrassed to go back.

CHAPTER 24

THE BIGNESS of it all started to kick in when I pulled into the MCA Records parking lot. I was on time, but had to wait over half an hour for Louil, which made me even more nervous. I kept looking down at my outfit, wondering if I had made the right choice, constantly checking my hair. Louil finally came out of his office. He played "Don't Be Cruel" and "My Prerogative." As we listened I got excited. I instantly knew these were going to be hits!

"That's dope! Especially 'My Prerogative'!"

"Really? Well, we're going with 'Don't Be Cruel' first. It's gonna be a bigger hit."

"Nah, I think the other is gonna hit bigger."

"Look at you," he chuckled. "Lemme see what you got."

"What?"

"Your ideas for the routines."

"Um. Okay."

I didn't have anything. How was I to know? I made it up on the spot—fake it until you make it! Thank goodness I already knew how to formulate routines from upstate and hanging in clubs. Upstate I was the manager of the cheerleading squad, so I understood form. And, let's not forget the nuns! They did teach me tap and how to perform on a stage. Down in the city, I was a club head, especially a hip-hop head. I would go to jams, sneak into hip-hop clubs—the Roxy, the World, Latin Quarters—and go to Afrika Bambaataa shows, watching break-dancers like Crazy Legs, Fable, and Mr. Wiggles of Rock Steady Crew in awe. I loved to see dancers

Cliff Love and Doctor Ice—who later became a member of the hip-hop group UTFO ("Roxanne, Roxanne! I wanna be your man!")—tear it up behind Whodini or Scoob and Scrap behind Big Daddy Kane, all doing James Brown, Bill "Bojangles" Robinson, and the fabulous Nicholas Brothers moves, making them their own while coming up with original steps that are still used today.

Hip-hop moved me in a way like never before. I never was a "street" kid, but I was part of the post-Vietnam generation who grew up with the residue of inflation, parents' broken dreams, poverty, and heroin-cluttered streets; who watched Reaganomics and crack tear at souls; who had something new and more innovative to offer than the prejudiced world around us predicted for us. Hip-hop was so incredible—mostly poor, West Indian, African American, and Puerto Rican kids from the Bronx created it, but white people and other various racial, social, and economic backgrounds throughout the city also contributed. (It always bothers me when people in the industry state that it was solely a black thing.) With other types of fun either unavailable or unaffordable to them, they all craved something new and found it in creating hip-hop.

The routine wasn't great but Louil liked it, and liked the style because it was New York. He made some tweaks, told me that Bobby wasn't up on hip-hop but was a quick study. He also wanted sexiness in the routine. "We've got *Soul Train* and a music video. I need two routines. On each, I want him to fuck the air, like this." Louil pumped his pelvis back and forth. I died laughing. "Fuck you, Perez," he said playfully. "I want him to pump his shit hard. I want him to be sex, want every girl to think he wants to fuck her. And I want him to have background dancers like the rap groups. I want Bobby to be the first R&B guy to do that shit." "Okay! Got it. And please don't pump your stuff like that again. You look hilarious." "Fuck you, Perez!" We clicked instantly.

He also told me that before they made their final decision to hire me, Bobby would come over to my place to check out the routine and the dancers. My place?

"Uh, I live in the Jungle. It's not really safe for Bobby Brown to come there."

"You live in the damn Jungle?" He laughed.

"Yes! What's so damn funny?" I asked defensively.

"Calm down. Damn. Look at you, all ghetto."

Ghetto? You can live in a ghetto, but that didn't mean you were *ghetto*. Back home, "ghetto" didn't mean that you were poor or used a certain vernacular or even had a temper. "Ghetto" meant possessing a certain ignorant mentality—it meant thinking that type of ignorance was cute: lacking empathy and doing stupid, malicious things because you just didn't care about the human cost. No, I was not ghetto. I wanted to correct his error in judgment, but didn't. I thought of Sister Renata's warning about my temper and didn't want to blow this. Can you believe that? I took a deep breath and calmed down. "Whatever," I simply replied.

"Yeah, okay, miss thang. Bobby will come by in three days," Louil continued.

"Okay. And thank you for this opportunity. I appreciate it. I won't let you down."

"You better not. Don't make me hire someone else, Little Miss Attitude."

Three days! Holy crapola! I hired this dance group that I loved watching in the local nightclubs called Heart and Soul—Arthur, Willie, Derrick, Bruce, and Kaylan were five guys from Watts. They were original and tight in their routines and looked clean as hell. Kaylan couldn't make it. I offered the rest of them $200 each out of my fee of $1,500—MCA was not going to give me a separate fee for the dancers. I told them that, to save time, we would combine some of their existing routines and some of my stuff and tailor the choreography to Bobby.

We practiced and rehearsed hard as hell. It was kind of easy for me to edit both of our styles. I could see the entire dance number in my head. It unfortunately wasn't easy for Heart and Soul to accept their routines being cut up, and it took them a minute to get the New York style down. There was a lot of arguing, to the point where it began to get ugly, on both sides. I finally told them that if they couldn't see the bigger picture and compromise, I would have to hire another group instead. I had little time for bickering and no room to lose this job. Arthur, who spoke with a slow southern Los Angeles drawl, stepped in and set things straight.

"Hey look, man. I didn't bring my ass all the way down from Watts to blow this shit. She gonna get the Soul Brothers [another local dance crew], and our asses will be assed out back on the bus to damn Watts! So let's do this shit or take our asses the fuck on home."

From then on, Arthur and I were a team—although he didn't know it yet.

I went to work hard. I knew this was going to be big. Hip-hop artists didn't get prime-time camera action back then. Break-dancing and popping were featured here and there, but hip-hop, no. I knew that with Bobby it was going to blow up! And the boys hated my ass over those three days, but I was on a mission. They weren't used to structure. I made them do the routines over and over again until everything was perfect. I broke down the routine by each eight-count. If an arm or foot wasn't where it was supposed to be, I'd stop everything and make them do it again. I was a taskmaster, as strict as Sister Renata and the nuns. I was surprised by how embedded it was to be that way, and how easily it came out—scary, right?

We were all nervous as hell. Bobby came in with only his brother Tommy, dressed in sweats and a T-shirt. We were expecting bodyguards, limos, designer clothes, and whatnot. We didn't know at the time how little money he made with New Edition.

Bobby shook everyone's hand, was very sweet, and spoke low and soft. Tommy was gangster and kept it real. We did the routine, me acting as Bobby. We could all see from Bobby's reaction as he sat on my piece-of-shit couch that he was hyped! This was so different from New Edition, and Bobby knew what I already knew—this was going to take him to another level. He hired us on the spot! The fellas and I started screaming, jumping up and down and hugging each other! Then the bad news came.

Tommy asked to speak with me alone. I sent the boys outside. He told me they only needed two dancers, like the rappers. He picked Derrick because he thought he was the best-looking and Willie because he liked his charm. Great. They already thought I was a bitch, and now they were really gonna think so. Bobby and Tommy left. Heart and Soul came back into my apartment. I put my game face on. "Derrick, Willie, you two are gonna dance behind Bobby, okay. The rest of you, I would love it if you stayed for support. I'll still pay you what I promised. Cool?" No one moved. The silence was killing me. Then Arthur stepped up again.

"Fuck it, man. At least two of my homies will be representing Heart and Soul. Come on, let's do this shit."

. . .

Bobby casually strutted into rehearsals with a facade of calm and confidence. Derrick and Willie may have been puffing up, but they were scared as hell. I wasn't nervous at all. I was excited, happy, and focused. So focused that I understood how they were feeling, saw right through them and knew how to handle them, especially Bobby. Bobby was acting similarly to the way I had with some of the kids in "outside" school, acting as if being in the Home had no effect on me, creating an aloof facade to hide my true feelings behind. The only difference was that I never strutted. I didn't have that skill set or the nerve.

It surprised me that choreographing was so easy and so much fun, that it felt so right to me—not just coming up with routines, but guiding artists to become their best. My empathy allowed me to connect with Bobby, to make him feel good about himself as an artist by reaffirming his talent, and to provide a safe environment for mistakes without embarrassment, ensuring nothing would go down at his emotional expense. I would take Bobby aside to whisper minor corrections, never making his errors a big deal; I'd praise his improvement without false adoration and champion him when he organically did something that was on some superstar shit. It was the same feeling Tia provided me. The same feeling Miss Connie, Beth, Nigel, and especially Grace offered me.

Heart and Soul and the routine didn't make the "Don't Be Cruel" video. The dancers and I were disappointed. We had busted our asses in preparation and were not told until after the video was shot. Louil thought Bobby and the dancers weren't ready. But we were ready enough to perform on *Soul Train* a couple of weeks later! Showing up on *Soul Train* not as a dancer but as a choreographer, for none other than Bobby Brown, was something else. Half of the *Soul Train* dancers were happy for me, and the rest were jealous as hell. And the few dance crews that were on the show were jealous of Heart and Soul. I understood. I didn't take it personally.

Don, though, forget about it. He was so angry. "What is she doing here?!" Louil smoothed things over with him. I had told him what went down, and he instructed me not to utter a word, just to act professional, and he would take care of the rest. I desperately wanted to apologize to Don, but didn't push it. I had bigger fish to fry.

Bobby took the stage and killed it! Not the entire routine, but it didn't matter. He was so dynamic, he had the crowd in the palm of his hands. Even though Derrick and Willie showed their nervousness, they stayed in the pocket and the crowd loved them too. It sounds corny, but when Big Lou, one of the most popular *Soul Train* dancers to date, enthusiastically high-fived Bobby during the number, I jumped for joy. It meant a lot, seriously.

Even before the episode was aired, Louil Silas Jr. made sure everyone in the music business knew that I had choreographed Bobby. By the time Derrick, Willie, and Bobby performed on *The Arsenio Hall Show*, I was a name in the record and music video industry. Motown asked me to choreograph "Dial My Heart," a new single by its boys group, called the Boys, produced by L. A. Reid and Babyface for their *Soul Train* appearance and later multiple videos. I also staged and went on the Boys' first major tour.

I brought the rest of Heart and Soul along. I hired Arthur as my assistant choreographer on every job. Derrick, Willie, Kaylan, and Bruce tagged along to help out for some spot dates too. We were having a blast, hanging out, making up routines, rehearsing, telling stupid jokes. It was fun. My life was fun, and I was making some money—God bless America three times!

One of those dates was where I met Mike Tyson. Actually, I had met him before in Brooklyn, but he didn't remember. In Brooklyn he was the champ even before he was the Champ. I'd run into him all the time in the clubs. When the Boys tour pulled into Chicago, Mike Tyson was there to meet them. Mike was a big fan of the Boys and met up with everyone backstage, hanging with us for a couple of tour dates. I loved him. He was a dented can too: smart, damaged, silly, and still on the make. As the Boys were about to go on, we went over the numbers, and Mike was on the side watching. I was wearing spandex and a tank top. I went to sit next to Mike, and he whispered, "Damn, Wosie. You got a biscuit booty."

"Mike, shut up."

"Okay. Sorry."

We both laughed. He never hit on me again.

. . .

A little under a year had passed. All was good, and then sadly, Derrick and Willie fell out with me. They had decided to do Bobby's new video, "Every Little Step I Take," without us and didn't tell us we were axed out. We had already spent hours choreographing most of the song—teaching it to Derrick and Willie! They finished the routine on their own, filling in the empty spaces with some really fly steps, I must admit. I was upset, not that they moved on, but that they pulled a fast one. They told Arthur they felt justified because they had thought I gypped them on the initial fee from our first job together.

From what I had heard, Bobby and his "people" told Willie and Derrick that they should have gotten more money because the routine was theirs—not true. It was a sleazy tactic to sidestep me since I had asked for more money for the video. I had done my homework—other choreographers, like Paula Abdul (who I loved), were making close to $10,000 a video. And they were trying to pay my ass only $1,500, on a hit artist that we helped become a hit, with a huge video budget to boot? Fuck that. I had never gypped anyone. We shared steps, but "shared" is the operative word. Plus, the concept and the structure were all mine. And had I fed them out of my fee every day—four guys—and paid for gas to and from the rehearsal studio and jobs, dropping them off in Watts.

Derrick and Willie ended up making less money after all, because in the end they were only hired as dancers, not as choreographers. Thank goodness Bobby took them on tour or they really wouldn't have made anything. I do have to admit that "Every Little Step I Take" was great—an R&B video classic. I would have to be a real hater not to admit it. They really did a great job.

. . .

Believe it or not, I was still going to school during this time. It was a joke. I was failing my classes, spending too much time taking choreographing jobs, lying to myself that it was only for financial reasons to help pay for college expenses. And since the music industry in Los Angeles—with its misogyny and Derrick and Willie's backstabbing—was making me depressed, I decided it was time to go home, try to apply to Stony Brook University in Long Island, and get my priorities in order. I needed to go back to the place I had thought I needed to move away from, the place that had brought me the most happiness and a sense of home. I had to go back to Brooklyn.

My friends took me out for my last week in L.A. to a club called Funky Reggae, where Matt Robinson, Holly Robinson's brother, was spinning. Spike Lee was having a "butt" contest to see which black chick had the biggest ass—no lie—as a device to promote his latest movie, *School Daze*. Disgusted by it, I jumped on the stage, okay, so it was a speaker, and bent over shaking my ass, making a mockery of the whole thing. Bouncers came over with this little skinny guy and told me to get down. My bravado vanished. In fact, I got a bit teary, thinking they were going to throw my ass out. Instead, one of them told me that Spike Lee, the little skinny thing, wanted to meet me. Who? Honestly, I didn't know who the hell he was. I loved *She's Gotta Have It*, but didn't recognize his name.

He was kind of laughing, looking at me, amused, and I started to get pissed. He held out his hand. "Sup. I'm Spike. What the hell were you doing up on that speaker?" he says, still kind of laughing. I rolled my eyes at him and said something, I don't remember what, because I was still kind of shook, but it made him laugh again. His hand was still extended. I gave him a half-ass handshake. "Tonight is fate," he said. I was like, "Oh you wish." He bent over with laughter. Who the hell was this guy?

"Where you from?"

"I'm from Brooklyn."

"Aah, shit! Where?!"

"Well, from Bushwick, but I'm staying with my sister in Bed-Stuy."

"Bed-Stuy?! Aaahhhh, shit! This is fate! Fate! Hey, Monty, give her our number!"

My friends and I left quickly after that. As we were walking outside to our cars, I went to throw the card away, but my girlfriend Marion grabbed it, screaming, "Nooo! Do you know who that is?" Thank goodness she did. I was too nervous to get on the phone, so Marion called first. Spike wanted to speak only with the girl with the accent. I got on the phone. He told me he wanted to meet with me about a movie project. I told him I wasn't an actress.

"Oh yes you are!"

I told him I couldn't meet with him anyway because I was traveling with Marion to Washington, D.C.—she was transferring to Howard University—and then I was making my way by train to Brooklyn. "I'm staying with my sister Carmen in Bed-Stuy."

"Bed-Stuy! Ah, shit! This is fate! We're gonna be in Maryland tomorrow and heading back to Brooklyn afterwards too! Let's ride up together."

I made Marion go with me. Well, actually she wanted to go because she wanted to see this dear friend of ours, Robbie, who had just moved to Brooklyn. I'll get into Robbie later. Anyway, I don't know why I trusted him enough to go with him and his producing partner, Monty, but I did. I think it was Monty's kindness. I think it was curiosity from the hype by Marion. Or maybe it was all of the above—duh! I kept thinking to myself, *Could this be? Am I going to be like Lana Turner who was discovered at a drugstore in Hollywood but wasn't really?* (Imitation of Life—love!) I don't know why, but I believed it to be so, but was kind of freaked out about it too.

For the majority of the ride Spike was quiet, but he would burst out laughing in the middle of one of my stories about Suydam Street and Soul Train, writing down things that I had said, like, "And his shit was to the curb." A few days later, back in Brooklyn, he asked me to audition for a part in his new flick, Do the Right Thing.

CHAPTER 25

I HAD planned to move in with Carmen and her "common-law" husband, Wilfredo, who everyone called Chavo, who unfortunately recently passed—God rest his soul. Chavo was half Italian and half Puerto Rican, medium height, white skin, light green-brown eyes, and light brown wavy hair. He was Carmen's first love, since the age of fourteen. She used to get beat-downs from her mother for going out with him because he was a "bad boy," and the gossip was that she lost her virginity to him. They in fact got caught their first time doing it behind a rock at Crash Boat Beach—scandalous! When Chavo moved to New York to work for his father's "business" acquaintances, Carmen, at the age of eighteen, did everything in her power to follow him a year later. The whole family, except me, was upset because they all knew of Chavo's activities. I had no clue, but quickly found out when I moved in.

Spike dropped us off somewhere, I don't remember, but it wasn't near my sister's house. Marion and I took the subway and got off the A train at Utica Avenue in Bed-Stuy with our suitcases. We couldn't find the place for anything. We kept buzzing and knocking on doors to no avail. Our bags were getting heavy as hell, and we were scared off our asses. Then I remembered it was above Casablanca's.

Carmen lived above Casablanca's, a bar that had seen better days. The lettering on its sign was faded, and the front door creaked each time it swung back and forth as old Southern rhythm-and-blues blasted through the darkness onto the street. Stumbling out were drunken fifty-something black men and women dressed as if they were in a 1970s time warp, wearing double-breasted gabardine suits and gators. The only entrance I could see was the one that led inside the bar. And I wasn't trying to go in there. I went to the corner pay phone.

"Where are you?" Carmen excitedly asked.

"At the corner pay phone."

Carmen looked out her window.

"I only see some skinny bitch in tacky peppermint-striped hot shorts."

I looked down at what I thought was a cute outfit and then at my reflection coming from the pay phone. I had lost a lot of weight from dancing and starving but never took notice.

"That's me, stupid!"

"Oh! I'm so sorry. I thought you was some crackhead." She laughed.

"Could you just tell me where to go?"

We approached a wooden/steel door on the side of the bar. It creaked open. It was pitch-black inside. A crackhead with three missing front teeth jumped out.

"Aahhhh!" Marion and I screamed bloody murder!

"Who dat?! What the fuck you want?" yelled the toothless crackhead.

"I'm sorry. I thought this was my sister Carmen's building," I said, trying not to look scared.

"Oh shit! You mean Chavo's wife?"

He looked spooked as hell. Then another crackhead came out of the darkness holding a gun—no lie.

"Who dat?"

"Chill, man! That's Chavo's wife's sister!" the first crackhead answered.

Inside was a dingy, small kitchen that had a small bedroom off to the side. Carmen greeted me with hugs and kisses, with her one-year-old, Angela, the cutest baby ever, in her arms. "I'm so happy you're here! Say hi to your Titi Rosie, Angela!"

Angela looked like a white version of Carmen. She balled up her tiny fist and swung it at me. "Angela! Don't do that! That's your Titi Rosie!" "Carmen, this is Marion, my best friend that I told you about." "Hi, Marion! Welcome. Come on, let me take you guys to your room. I hope you like it." I turned my head toward the small bedroom. Carmen cracked up. "Not there. It's past this hidden door. We just have that part as a front for welfare and the cops." Say what?

The wall/door opened up to a long hallway, the length of the entire building, with rooms shooting off to the right. My bedroom was huge! Unfortunately, like the rest of the house, it was tacky and ostentatious as hell. It had a painted rug on the wood-side paneling wall and a spotted leopard bedspread to boot. The rest of the house was decorated in blue, white, and gold, with mirrors everywhere.

"Chavo likes the Marie Antanette period."

"You mean Marie Antoinette?"

"Whatever." She cracked up. "Please don't start with that 'I know it all' shit. You get high?"

"Uh, no! You do?" I asked, all shocked and nerdy and shit.

"Hell yeah. You drink?"

"Uh, a glass of wine now and then, but not really."

"Oh my God, you're still a freakin' nerd."

She lit up a joint and poured herself a Scotch, Dewar's on the rocks, and raised her glass in a toast. "I'm so glad my sister's here! *Salut!*" I know Marion, who is a churchgoing person, was shocked to shit!

Then Chavo walked in, carrying a milk crate filled with used handguns. He had gotten so fat and wore so many gold chains around his neck and gold rings on almost every finger that he looked like the Puerto Rican–Italian version of Mr. T.

"Rosie! Hey! How're you? Sorry 'bout my men downstairs.

None of them fucked with you, right? 'Cause I'll fuck them up! Oh shit! What the fuck you got on?" He laughed. "You look like Peppermint Patty. Carmen, help me put away the guns. Rosie, can you get me un *café*?"

Stunned, I quickly went to the kitchen to make coffee while Carmen helped her "husband" hide the handguns underneath the wooden floorboards. Welcome back to the BK!

Carmen and I hung out thick as thieves. We never got along better, laughing for hours at each other's stories, being our true selves, and accepting each other without effort. The change in her did bug me out, though. It was weird hearing her use the latest slang and gestures, like a Brooklynite. And she had gotten so fat . . . I mean, really big.

"It's from the baby. And I'm so bored all alone all the time. I just eat. Plus, Chavo makes me eat with him when he has the munchies too. He gets high to forget what he has to do for the 'company' every night."

That made me so upset, to see her accepting this life. But she loved Chavo and wanted to keep her family together. I must say, Chavo did treat me well. He always made me feel like family instead of just a guest. He never asked for anything from me except to make him a cup of coffee. Always asked if I needed cash, which I politely refused. (I would shudder to think where and how that money was made.) Yet, I was still upset that he had helped turn my sister into a gangster's stay-at-home wife—it was so unbelievable it was hilarious, and so wrong. She was better than this.

. . .

I had to fly back to Los Angeles to audition for Robi Reed, the casting director for *Do the Right Thing*. I thought that was so ironic.

Do the Right Thing was bittersweet. I knew immediately after reading the script that the film was going to have big political ramifications, that it was going to ruffle a few feathers, and that excited me. But there was the nudity issue. Oh, the nudity issue that I wish to this day hadn't become such a big deal. Why? Because I get sick of talking about it, so here's all I will say. And then I'm done with it.

I didn't have a problem showing my body—can you believe that with all that Catholic stuff shoved down my throat? Why? I don't know. However, I also didn't want ice cubes down the crack of my ass, or an ice cube heading south to my vagina. I didn't even want an ice cube on my breasts. It was gratuitous. There had to be a more artistic way, but I had already signed the contract that only stated "nudity" and didn't relate how much or in which way, so production told me there was little I could do about it. I took the contract to another lawyer for a free consultation. He kind of said the same thing, but felt there would probably be room for negotiation. Since I didn't have the money to hire the lawyer, I told Spike that if he had the nerve to ask my "brother-in-law" permission, since my father was in Puerto Rico, I would consider it. He called my bluff. I didn't know the guy was actually going to go and ask Chavo.

Spike came over with Monty, his producer. Carmen only allowed them in the front room, there was no way she was going to reveal her secret living quarters. I wanted to kill Spike. "Monty, Monty! Lookit at the Bustelo can! The Bustelo! Lookit at the plastic flowers and the plastic flowered tablecloth! Love it!" Carmen was mortified and embarrassed . . . me too.

Then Chavo came in from the side bedroom. He was listening the whole time. He walks in with a sly grin, wiping his machete down with a kitchen towel before he set it on the table. Spike started cracking up, "Oh shit!" Chavo, in a calm, scary, joking tone, says, "What's so funny?" Spike shut the fuck up quick fast. Chavo then leaned in close and smiled. "So, you want to ask my sister-in-law to do what?"

A compromise was made: no ass-crack, nothing close to the

vagina. It sounds so silly, right? Spike, by the way, says he doesn't remember any of this.

The first day of rehearsal was crazy. Although the cast and crew greeted me kindly, there was this one girl who wasn't so nice. The role was originally for a black girl, and I could understand her being upset; but every time I tried to break the ice, I would get the sucking of the teeth and the rolling of eyes. Oh boy. I was already terrified to be there so I subconsciously retreated inside and kept my distance from her, which of course worked against me, just as it had done many times before. She thought I was stuck up and a bitch. When the real seasoned actors came in, I came off as aloof and moody. And when I did speak, I masked my intimidation and shyness by whipping out my smart aleck side. That didn't work out too good either. I didn't realize my behavior until years later, truly. Spike never reprimanded me either. Maybe he should have, maybe not. Maybe he knew that it would have shut me down, since I was so new to this, or maybe he got a kick out of it. Who knows? Monty would smooth things over, telling everyone that I was "special" and "intensely artistic."

Good thing I clicked instantly with Martin Lawrence and Robin Harris. Both of them were funny as hell, I loved hanging with them. I remember the day Monty took them to an apartment that production had rented for them around the corner from 40 Acres' offices. Robin had asked me to come along. It was a shithole. I don't know if it was Martin or Robin, but when we all stuck our heads inside, one of them, with perfect timing, quoted the line from Coming to America: "It's a shame what they did to that dog." We died laughing. They couldn't stop killing that one joke for hours.

I was so very anxious my first day of shooting. But I have to say, I felt very confident about how to play this character. I've been acting all my life, hiding, creating different realities, and suppressing true emotional responses. I easily took on the persona of Tina— taking it from the few girls I would watch from my window on

Suydam Street in Bushwick, who undeservingly expected so little from their frustrated lives. I took from the hard-core girls who later came to the GH and who got pregnant too early as an escape. And I took my own frustration and anger from being born into a situation that felt contrary to who I was.

The sweet side of filming was the personal interactions and connections. Robi Reed, the casting director, couldn't have been more supportive. Ruth Carter, the costume designer, made me feel sexy and safe on set, especially when it came to the love scenes. Gosh, I was so nervous for those days! Dan Aiello, a sweetheart. He saw me one day wandering off on my own on set looking scared and confused. "Hey, darling. Nervous? Come sit with me. See, this is how this thing goes. . . ." John Turturro and Richard Edson were great too. Almost all the girls on set had a crush on Turturro, but he was clueless. Ernie Dickerson, the cinematographer, and his assistant, Darnell Martin, were fabulous and kind, especially during the nude scenes as well. Even with Spike, we had our moments on set that were hilarious. And Carmen, and at times my half-sister Kathy, came to the set to hang with me, making me feel secure. Filming all day and then clubbing with Kathy all night was mad fun. It was a great summer.

Kathy liked this Puerto Rican guy on set, Angel, and wanted me to double-date with his friend, Sixto. "Wait. I know that name, Sixto," I said. She pointed him out. One look and I told her I didn't want to go. Something felt weird about it. I called Tia up. "Sixto? Jes, he's your cousin. We call him Yunior. He's Rachel's son. You used to take baths with him and his brothers and sisters when you was a baby." Holy crapola! I almost went out with my cousin!

Sixto and I didn't click immediately, we are both stubborn as hell, but thanks in part to this film, he has become one of my best friends and relatives.

And despite shit that went down with Spike and me—which will remain as private as possible as far as I am concerned—I was and will be forever grateful for the entire experience. I am so appreciative that I went up to him and his lovely wife, Tonya, years ago and asked, "Can we start over?" We shook hands and that was that. I'm really happy that we're cool now. He saw something in me, and it changed my life, again, but in a much bigger way. And let's not forget about the gift he gave me by way of that opening-credits scene! Feel me, people? That whole experience was off the hook!

. . .

I couldn't get seen for another film. *Do the Right Thing* had not come out yet, I didn't have an agent, and Tia was so worried, and worried about the inconsistent choreography work too. I would go back to Los Angeles for a few video gigs from time to time. Arthur and I began to get work again, but now everyone was doing what we did, so the jobs were tight. Tia would beg me over and over to go back to school and find work in an office. I didn't want to break her heart, so I did. I didn't apply to Stony Brook like I had planned on; I went back to working as an office manager, but as soon as I got a call for the Diana Ross video *Workin' Overtime*, produced by Nile Rodgers of Chic, I quit.

My choreography was beginning to repeat itself. Everyone wanted and insisted on the "Bobby Brown" feel. It bored and bothered me. I told Rolando Hudson, the video director, that I wanted to find real New York house dancers from the clubs that I frequented and use them as extras instead of ones from hip-hop central casting. I wanted to bring a new authentic vibe and style of dance that was absent in the music video world. And I wanted to have Ms. Ross's hair blowing during the video, like it was in her Central Park concert. He gave me carte blanche—holla!

I flew Arthur and Willie in to do the job with me. Willie and I had made up. He had gotten arrested for some stupid shit right before he was scheduled to leave on tour with Bobby. Willie called Arthur in a panic, asking him to ask me to bail him out after Bobby refused. What can I say? Under the tough act, I was still a softy. I paid the bond. Willie got released too late and cried like a bitch when I had to tell him that Bobby called me (can you believe that?), asking me if I'd ask Kaylan to take Willie's place, which he did. So Arthur and I took him along.

I knew exactly which dancers I was going to hire, a group of kids popular in the clubs for developing a new style that combined house, hip-hop, jazz, soul, and African dance—Stretch, Henry (aka Link), Jamal (aka Loose Joint), Trini (who danced for Salt-N-Pepa), Peter Paul, Frankie, Tron, Casper, Rubberband, Peekaboo, Asia, Marjorie, Voodoo Ray, Caleaf, and Caleaf's younger brother, Ramier, to name a few. Not only were they among the most popular in the club scene, but I especially took notice of them because I had fallen in love, at first sight, with Ramier a couple of years earlier, but was too shy to act on it.

Ramier was from East New York—a nice kid from the projects with strong, hardworking parents, a tough loving mother and a sweet stepfather who did their best with four kids. He was sweet, sexy, loving, patient, hood, and could dance his ass off. Once he found out that I was in love with him, he became my man.

I couldn't handle being so in love. I'd had only two real boyfriends before Ramier: Louis Padilla's brother, Freddie, who quit me after a week because he said I couldn't kiss (it was really because I wouldn't put out, but who's counting) and Alan Stewart, who I dated in college. I turned every minor incident into a dramatic novela scene, subconsciously trying to make Ramier prove his love for me. But he was wonderful. He offered me true love and security, which empowered me to share my childhood with him, especially stories about my mother. He was the only person since my friend Eileen and her mom, Gene, that I told. For some ungodly reason, Ramier wanted to meet her. I refused. I told him that I hardly visit and since she wasn't of sound mind it wasn't a good idea. He insisted. I gave in.

We walked into Lydia's apartment. Ramier was surprised to see how cluttered and messy it was since I had become such a neat freak.

"Ma, this is my boyfriend, Ramier."

"Nice to meet you, Ms. Perez."

Ramier held out his hand. Lydia offered a limp handshake without saying anything in return. Oh jeez.

We sat down in the living room where a couple of my half-brothers were. Ramier introduced himself to them. They were polite but were letting him know, without saying it, that they didn't like the fact that he was black.

Then one of them excuses himself and goes into the kitchen where my mother was. They both started whispering and giggling, thinking that we couldn't hear their conversation, but we could hear it clear as a bell.

"Oh my God. He's so black! Their babies are going to come out with nappy hair!" said Lydia, chuckling.

Oh, why did she have to say that?! That was enough for Ramier. He got up, grabbed me, and said, "Let's go."

We left without saying good-bye. Outside, Ramier turned to me and started laughing.

"Yo, no wonder you're so weird. Your family's fucking crazy. And I'm sorry, but your mother is fucking nuts!"

Oh my goodness! That was music to my ears! I wasn't the complete asshole I'd judged myself to be for feeling the same way! I burst out laughing.

Roland Rolando loved the dancers, and the video was a hit. Diana was a hoot too. She never came to the three weeks of rehearsal, showed up late to set, learned a few steps, and still killed it. And that hair was blowing, honey! That video, because of the dancers, changed the game, and most of the guys went on to their own successful dance careers, dancing and choreographing various artists from Mariah Carey to Michael Jackson.

Andre Harrell of Uptown Records came over to the Mayflower Hotel on Central Park West to see me about choreographing one of his groups, Heavy D & the Boyz, for their new video, *We Got Our Own Thang*. He wanted that club feel from the Diana Ross video. Andre had put me up at the hotel—just for an interview, mind you. He wasn't trying to see me in Brooklyn, and more important, I had developed a reputation for being late. It was pure PTSD. I would get so freaked out about being late, like back in the Home with Sister Renata, that I would end up being late.

I had invited Kathy to stay with me. We began to get close. She would hang with me a lot—clubbing, eating, and sleeping were our favorite things to do. I feared being alone in a space that wasn't familiar, a result of staying in Titi's abandoned apartment by myself with the constant threat of someone breaking in. Kathy had fallen on hard times financially, so it worked out to both of our benefit. Also, I was tired of getting hit on by music company executives and managers, and I wasn't trying to be alone in a hotel with Mr. Harrell.

Our appointment was for 4:00 PM. By 9:00 PM, I had given up on Mr. Harrell, so I took a shower and got into my granny nightgown and satin cap. (Yes, a granny nightgown and satin hair cap, just like Sister Renata! Can you believe it? Not for nothing, a satin cap does wonders for the hair.) Ten o'clock, the front desk called, said that Mr. Harrell was on his way up! Kathy just sat there finishing her Mississippi Mud Pie, laughing at me scrambling about trying to find my bra. Too late, Andre was knocking. Kathy opened the door and flopped back down on one of the twin beds. I quickly ripped off the satin hair cap, trying to smooth out my hair.

"Hi, Mr. Harrell. Please come in. Sorry about my attire. I didn't think you were still coming."

"It's all good, Money. Call me Andre. Let me see what you got."

"Oh! Now? Okay."

I turned on my boom box and started dancing, barefoot, in my freaking granny nightgown. Kathy was quietly cracking up behind Andre's back. I was so nervous that I did a jump too high and fast and my freaking tit fell out! I kid you not! Mortified!

"Oh my goodness! I'm so sorry, Mr. Harrell!"

Andre was smiling, trying not to laugh.

"It's all good, Money. It's just a tittie. Ain't like I never saw one. I mean, I never saw your shit, but it's all good, Money. I like it. Let's do this! Make some money! I'll send my boy Puffy around to pick you up and take you to Hev's in Mt. Vernon. He'll be your driver to take you back and forth. We start tomorrow with rehearsals."

"Wait, Puffy? You mean Sean Combs, the club dancer?"

"Yeah. He works for me at Uptown. Him and Hev are tight. He'll pick you up in the morning. Don't be late. And watch them titties, Money!"

He left. I turned to Kathy and jumped up and down screaming with excitement.

"Yo, Puffy's a dick," my sister interjected.

"That's all you can say?"

"Uh, okay—happy for you—did a great job. And Puffy's still a dick. You better watch your back with him."

Puffy was well known in the club scenes, and not everyone liked him. The dislike came from him always being on different kinds of hustles, sometimes at the expense of others, and because most of the dancers in the clubs felt he didn't have an original style of his own and "bit" off of everyone. It may have been true to an extent—about his various hustles—but Puffy did have something of his own vibe. Okay, so he did bite off a lot of dancers. But, every dancer bit off of someone—half of the *original* hip-hop moves were taken directly from James Brown. I was cool with him and didn't know him well enough to make that sort of judgment based mostly on gossip. I had hated when the "outside" kids and their parents made judgments about me, so I tried not to go there.

Puffy was on time, serious, and all business—I respected that. Almost every day for a straight month, as we drove up the West Side Highway to do *Money Earnin' Mt. Vernon*, I listened to him spin his tales of how large he was going to be. He kept talking about how grateful he was to Andre and in the same breath how he was going to become a millionaire, take over shit, and one day become Andre's boss. Most would have written it off as bullshit talking, but there was a bit of me that believed he was going to do it—he was too committed and always on time. "Yo, you should do this shit with me, Rosie. When I take over, shit's gonna blow the fuck up!"

I loved Heavy D & the Boyz from the first hello, especially Hev—God rest his soul. They were so funny and fun, and never once did any of them try to hit on me. We worked well together— two videos and a tour. And being on a hip-hop tour was no joke. Touring with The Boys—four little brothers accompanied by their mother—was one thing. Being the only girl with a rap group on a hip-hop tour was a whole other bag of tricks.

First day loading up the bus, Heavy told me that I couldn't be down with the tour unless I rubbed clean the golden eagle's wings that were molded into the wood-side panel of the bus. I refused. I thought they were trying to pull a fast one. "I'm dead up. Every-one's done it already. Rosie, if you don't do it, then you're gonna jinx the whole tour. Come on, dammit, rub!" I still refused. Heavy got off the bus, saying that he couldn't get back on until I did it. All the guys, the dancers—G-Whiz and Trouble-T-Roy—God rest his soul too—Black, Black Damien, Deejay Eddie-F, Jeff, came down on me too. I gave in and rubbed the eagle's wings. "Nah, harder," said G-Whiz. "Harder. You gotta mean that shit." I rubbed harder. "Hev! Rosie's jerking off the eagle!"

That night they put water in my bunk. I had to sleep on the narrow, tiny sofa up front. The next night, wondering why my bed stunk so badly, I found half-eaten chicken bones under my pillow that they had hid. Another night they locked me in my hotel room by jamming the lock, making me late for roll-out, laughing at my ass running after the tour bus. They'd ask me to watch a comedy with them, and it would turn out to be a porno. They were constantly making fun of my accent and my obsession with my hair, and had spontaneous play-fights where it would be me against five to seven guys—all this young boys' club shit was never ending, and I loved every minute of it. Fun. Fun. Fun.

Although I had a great time with Hev and the guys, I hated being on a rap tour. The high level of misogyny resulted in a lot of frustration, and the loneliness got to me. There was, and probably still is, an unspoken rule in hip-hop: a guy can be the biggest ho on the planet, but a girl is a slut, a dumb bitch—degraded and scorned in a hot second—if she bats an eyelash at a guy. And every woman in hip-hop was fair game, especially when we toured with groups like 2 Live Crew, who had dates on the tour as well. (Not for nothing, they would rock their set every freaking night.) Almost every guy on all the tours I worked on hooked up and had a little black book of groupies sorted by the various area codes. The guys were never frowned upon, but the groupies were. Groupies ran high, and the disrespect for them on the road ran higher. They would have girls give blow jobs for free tickets, bang them out on the empty tour bus before rolling to the next gig, make them show their tits just for a laugh, all that shit went down. Good thing was, Heavy D & the Boyz never stooped that low, and if they did, they never did it in front of me like other groups did.

This type of juvenile behavior made women who were serious about their careers very cautious, secretive, and bitchy. You had to be. Heavy had sat me down one night after I innocently waved back hello to MC Hammer.

"You can't be like that. You can't be waving at niggas like that!"

"I was just waving hello. And please stop using the N-word. Besides, Hammer is a nice guy but not my cup of tea, and I have a boyfriend."

"And? I'm telling you. No one will take you seriously—your career will be done. It's fucked up, but that's the way niggas are, and that's the way shit is. I love you, Rose. You need to stop acting all naive and shit and wise up. I'm just looking out, 'cause you're my little sis."

Digital Underground had joined the tour for a few dates. That's when I first met Tupac. He was a dancer/roadie/guest rapper for the group. He had this wide-toothed, shiny bright smile that was infectious and inviting. "Hey! What's up, Rose? I'm Tupac." He was sweet, shy, funny, very intelligent, extremely charismatic, and another dented can.

God bless America two times that he showed up, it was fun to have another sensitive goofball around. We hung out a lot, cracking corny jokes, discussing literature and film, hearing his poetry, hearing his dreams of success. He would also share his tales of neglect during his childhood, share his pain in an honest way. His ability to be so open was impressive yet haunting. I didn't have his courage at the time to share mine with him. That took a while. Weird thing was, Heavy and the rest of the guys never said anything about our budding connection. Tupac had that effect on people. Everyone just respected him. Yeah, he hooked up with females, smoked weed, and got drunk too much, but he also had this integrity that few questioned. Gosh, I really miss that guy. God rest his soul.

Russell Simmons and Lyor Cohen hired me to choreograph and stage Slick Rick's show. He was booked on the July 1989 LL Cool J Nitro tour, along with Eazy-E, N.W.A, Too $hort, and my favorite, De La Soul. (Now, De La Soul probably had their hook-ups, but I never saw them act disrespectfully toward women, ever. Plus, most of the time we would hang out, all four of us, and do stupid fun shit. I loved hanging with this bunch of nerds.)

I liked Ricky, he was very sweet with me, but back then I knew not to cross him or his crew. They had a volatile rep. His dancers hated me too. They were insulted that I was hired to "fix" their show that they had put together. I got it. Plus, I was making more money than they were—that pissed them off too. Most people understand that the choreographers naturally make more money than the dancers, but they didn't get it. The attitudes, the sucking of the teeth and rolling of the eyes at every suggestion, just slowed shit. And when things would escalate, Rick's mother would step in on their behalf and nothing would get done. It was exhausting.

Lyor came into rehearsals one day, told me he needed to speak with me alone. I found Russell and LL Cool J waiting outside. LL Cool J! Next to RUN DMC, he was the biggest thing in rap, especially on tour. Lyor and Russell knew of the problems with Rick and the dancers. They told me that Todd (meaning LL) liked my style and work ethic and wanted me to do his show instead. In fact, they wanted me to leave at that very moment and start working with LL at his rehearsal space.

"Um, now? Like now now? What about Ricky?"

"Don't worry 'bout Ricky," said Lyor. "We'll handle that. And give you a raise of an extra five hundred a week. Cool?"

I hesitated. Regardless of the money, it was crazy and wrong to just up and leave. Right?

"Rosie, they hate you. Ricky's mother told me the dancers can't wait to jump your ass after every rehearsal," Russell added.

"Can you make that an even thousand?"

Working with LL was on a whole other level. First thing, he ensured his crew and staff were in sync with him by having us all move into his Queens apartment for a month's preparation. (Although he had female dancers, I, again, was the only female on staff, and we all got along.) He demanded a relaxed yet professional work environment and expected everyone to work as hard as he did. He woke up early, worked out every morning, ate healthy—most of the time, when he didn't have a yearning for White Castle—and was on time every single day. He was involved in the tiniest of details but still listened to your ideas, challenged them, pushing you to do better. I loved it! He even made the dancers, three girls and one guy, step up their look. They were representing him, and he wasn't having anyone looking busted, especially the chicks.

"Rosie. We gotta get these girls to the OTB salon."

"Off-track betting?"

"No, off-track bitches. Girls need some hair on their heads, and some makeup tips too."

"I can't tell them that!"

"Yes, you can. And you will. You're in charge, right? Trust me, they'll scream their heads off for some hair."

And they did. I was shocked at the time that anyone would be so excited about getting a weave! Now? Well, I'm not mad at a few snap-ons.

Only two out of the four dancers I got along with, but at this point I paid it no mind. This was my job, and my job was to do it well, not get all caught up. One thing for sure, these dancers worked hard—very hard. Pettiness aside, we got down to business. The numbers were really good, and the dancers did their thang!

Busy Bee joined the show as LL's hype man and brought the fun! Sometimes we had more fun on the bus with his constant joking than we did onstage. That's saying a lot, because LL was great fun and amazing onstage, always in the moment, always in command. It was a great gig. Well, except dealing with LL's father. He was rude, mean, was always hitting on all of us girls. I never brought it up to Todd because that's how it was—you just dealt with it. The tour did okay. Todd was trying new things, but his audience wanted "Rock the Bells." Still, our show was amazing—and the tour, shit was crazy.

On the first show date, I ran into none other than Slick Rick—I froze up like a deer in headlights. "Yo, Rosie. How you gonna play me like that?" Then he pulled out his gun! Yes, folks! Everyone started pushing and shoving. I ran like a bitch into a corner, sunk down, covering my head, hoping I wouldn't get shot. Thankfully, the bodyguards rushed in quick. Ricky calmly put his gun away and acted like everyone was making a big deal out of nothing. He asked to speak with me. One of the bodyguards picked me up and brought me over. Rick smiled bashfully.

"Sorry. We cool. Right?"

"Yeah, Rick. We cool. Sorry 'bout that too."

He gave me a pound like I was one of his boys, and that was that—crazy world of hip-hop.

While on tour, I was notified that *Do the Right Thing* was finally premiering. And the timing worked out, we had dates in New York. I got excited and in a split-second panicked. All I kept thinking was that all these rappers, everyone, was going to see those damn ice cubes on my big-ass breasts. I told Todd about the premiere during dinner at this Creole restaurant in New Orleans. (He would take all of us out to dinner from time to time to really nice restaurants.) I also told him about the nude scene. He just started laughing.

"Oh shit. Your man knows about them ice cubes?"

"Oh my goodness, I never told Ramier!"

"He's gonna know now! Hey, I'm just playing with you. That's a good look. I'm happy for you."

. . .

When I got back to New York for the premiere, I was shocked to find out that Ramier had gotten locked up for selling narcotics. Say what? I had no idea that he was involved in drug dealing, honestly. I was devastated. Puffy heard the news.

"Yo, Money, lemme go with you. We could both dress in white and blow that red carpet up!"

"I couldn't do that to Ramier."

"Nah, nah, nothing like that. Ramier's my boy. I just want to go to the premiere. It's a good look."

So I had four tickets, and I went to my very first premiere with

Puffy along with two of my half-sisters, Kathy and Amy—and no, I didn't wear white.

Carmen didn't want to go. Dad couldn't go, and Tia was in L.A. I invited my mother. She didn't want to go either. My brother, the one who tried to molest me, the one who stole my money and plane ticket, wanted to go. He didn't even ask me if he could go. When I went to Lydia's to pick up my sisters, he just jumped into the limo the day of, all dressed to the nines—can you believe it? I told him I didn't have an extra ticket, which was true, but he and everyone else didn't believe me, made me feel like I was fucked up when I told him he couldn't come. Leaving my mother's house in the limo with my two sisters, I started to get upset. I felt so bad and guilty.

Sitting in the dark theater, I was blown away by the magic of filmmaking. I knew that this was my new path, and I wanted to give it my all. I didn't want to give up on choreographing either, I did love it, but my new focus was movies. I told Tia, who was still concerned about my schooling. My father was happy, but concerned too. Not about me wanting to become an actor—he was over the moon about that—but about my breasts being splattered on the big screen for all to see.

I had never told him. How are you going to tell your father something like that? What was worse is that he had invited the entire town of Aguadilla, all his friends and our family pastor, to the local theater to watch the film! When the ice-cube scene came on, my father gasped, jumped up, grabbed his heart, and fell out cold—no lie! He was taken away in an ambulance. I felt horrible. I flew down immediately.

God bless America three times that it really wasn't a heart attack but a panic attack. He still milked it for days! While lying helpless on the couch, he told me, "Let's make a deal. Next time you do something like that, do it with class and let me know by saying you're in an . . . 'artistic' film."

CHAPTER 26

I GOT rave reviews!

Everything changed. Everything. I found myself very uncomfortable and conflicted about the attention and the fame that came with it. I love my fans, and it's great when I hear them say that they appreciate my work, truly! I mean, without an audience loving what you do, what's the point? But I wasn't prepared to deal with all of the new "friends." I wasn't prepared for how those I knew and those I didn't began to treat me differently too. Most important, I didn't like being stared at, pointed out, and talked about as if I weren't standing in front of the person or group that was doing any or all of this. It drove me crazy. I acted as if I was handling it, but inside I was a bundle of nerves.

The strangest reaction to everything was Lydia's. Boy, did she jump on the bandwagon. When I saw her after all of the hoopla of Do the Right Thing, she was so kind and nice with me and I fell for it. I still kept somewhat of a distance, but when I did go over to see her, I relished in her attention. When I would slip her cash, she acted so humble about it, telling me she loved me so much and that I was a great daughter. Okay. I didn't fall for all of that stuff, but still I liked the fact that she was liking me a whole lot more than before.

And on top of everything else, there was dealing with the press. *Oy vey!*

A lot of the media jumped on the image I had portrayed in *Do the Right Thing*, labeling me as street and tough. Their racism pissed me off. Attention, all racists! Not all people who are poor are street and tough! We are many things, just like everyone else! Not an interview was done with me that they didn't perpetuate that persona immediately.

"How does it feel to come from the hard-core, dirty streets and now be part of Hollywood?"

"Don't you think it's a fluke, someone like you, to be in the movies?"

"You really went to college to study bio-chem? That's unbelievable!"

It was so disrespectful. And when I would get upset over their lack of respect, they had a field day confirming their opinions.

This hurt me career-wise tremendously. Yes, my accent was strong, yes, I was Brooklyn, yes, I was poor, but did that mean I should be limited to only playing unintelligent, downtrodden, and humiliating stereotypes?

I wasn't going to let them win either. I told one of my representatives at the time that we had to fight this: she needed to get me a shot at those Jessica Lange–type roles—love her! She patronizingly told me I was far from Ms. Lange—okay, probably true—and that I shouldn't expect too much. Well, forget that. She further suggested that I try to sound less ethnic. "Yes, that, and, well, if you change your hair color, maybe a little nip."

"You mean look less ethnic too?"

She shrugged her shoulders, "Everyone does it." Now, I have no problems with plastic surgery—it's the new mascara—but for these reasons? Come on, people!

Turning down work was tough. But I stayed strong. The only other role I could even consider after *Do the Right Thing* was playing a crackhead ho for HBO's *Criminal Justice*, also starring Anthony LaPaglia, Jennifer Grey, and Forest Whitaker. I agreed to it since my character was a co-lead, and more important, the story was politically and socially worthwhile.

Jennifer Grey couldn't believe what I had to deal with. She

introduced me to her agent, Jane Berliner, at CAA, over the phone. I simply told Jane I wanted access to the same opportunities that everyone else had. *Get me a shot and I'll do beyond my very best to get the work.* She signed me immediately, over the damn phone! Being with CAA gave me a new power and entrée into the rooms I needed to be in—the momentum was building. Yay!

Criminal Justice debuted on HBO. I got rave reviews once again—holla! And my popularity increased. That was good and bad. The press started in again asking a million personal questions. I never lied about being poor, being on welfare, being from Brooklyn, being a love child, and not being raised by my mother but by my aunt. Yes, I did leave out any mention of the Home and the Group Home. I wasn't ready to go there. I knew that if and when the press found out, they would descend like vultures and further perpetuate this uneducated-street-urchin image they had conjured up. But honestly, I held back because I didn't have the emotional strength yet to lay out years of abuse for the entire world to see. Who does in their early twenties? Shit, who does even after thirty?

Since I had left the system, I had made a new start. I was having great fun and on my way to the type of life I've always worked for. I wasn't the girl from the Home who was to be pitied, who was less than because her parents gave her up. I had a sense of self that wasn't so wounded and was getting stronger. I didn't want to lose that. It would break my spirit. Plus, it was my right to keep that information private. And don't give me that crap about being in front of the camera—that it comes with the job. Bullshit. That's some Jedi mind trick invented by yellow journalism.

It was an effort to fight for those good roles and to keep the press at bay by telling humorous stories and staying on topic in all the interviews about the work. And it was working. The press stopped asking about my past and I got the attention of the major studios and independent industries. They started to see more than just my ethnicity—yay!

Then I made a really bad decision. As I've said, Lydia came a-calling, acting like she was the best mother ever, and I fell for it hook, line, and sinker. So much so that when a television show celebrating Latin celebrities wanted to do a profile on my mother and me, I jumped at the chance. I subconsciously wanted to be perceived as someone who'd always had that supportive mom like normal people did—the same bullshit I had worried about in the Home and the Group Home.

The interview was done in Carmen's house. When the cameras began rolling, Lydia went on a tirade about herself and how her dreams of being a singer were squashed, how my father was a piece of shit to her, and blah, blah, blah. Nothing was said about her support for me—or about me at all for that matter. How could she? The interviewer, who was also the main producer, Rosanna Rosario, who is now head of El Diario newspaper, kept trying to guide the discussion back to me, asking Lydia if she had brought any pictures of me throughout the years. There weren't any pictures to be shown; there weren't any wonderful stories about our mother-daughter bond since there wasn't any such bond whatsoever.

Making it even worse, when the interviewer tried to steer the conversation back to my budding new career, Lydia started talking incoherently to the walls. I wasn't in the room—Carmen came running and told me what was going on. The interviewer, the whole crew, felt so embarrassed for me that they called it a wrap. Hurt? Yes. Embarrassed? Beyond. But defeated? No.

The great thing is that the producers never aired my mother's interview—God bless America two times. They just aired the stuff they recorded with me. Rosanna Rosario told me that it wasn't their agenda to exploit what had happened that day, it was about the bigger picture of promoting Latinos who were making it in the industry without compromise. "We have to look out for each other," she said. The scandalous story had no place in their news special—cool! Ooh, Lydia was steaming mad that she didn't make the cut. That's when the tension between her and me kicked in all over again. But, I was still happy that they didn't abuse the situation. I did have some friends—people in the press, even a few paparazzi, who did have integrity and wanted to make the world better.

. . .

After numerous red carpet appearances, I began to get bored with it all. Seriously. Okay, not so much bored, but anxious. Yes, I loved going to movie premieres and openings of plays, but getting all done up, worrying about what to wear, was too much—it wasn't fun anymore. Then it hit me. The red carpet could be a gift, not just an anxiety attack or an entity to be wary of. It wasn't just about my career and me. I had to see beyond the glitz and see how I could use the press for good.

The rewards were immediate. Outside of feeling good in my soul, a blessing came my way while I was choreographing a charity event for Arsenio Hall for AIDS. It was held at a high school gym. I went down to the locker room in the basement after the halftime performance to change. Who do I run into? Don freaking Cornelius! He was walking straight to me. I froze. Then I started to turn the other way. "Hold on, Rosie. Come here . . . Please." I turn back around. "Look," he said, "I once said you didn't have any talent. And you proved me wrong. Seriously. You really did a great job in *Do the Right Thing*, and I'm sorry." "Ah, that's okay, Don. I'm sorry too, for the chicken thing." He laughed and then held out his arms to hug me! Can you believe it? It was the best! We saw each other every now and then, and I was very sad when he passed. I'm so glad we made peace.

It was the early '90s. I began to dive into the charity scene really hard now. I began volunteering for the Gay Men's Health Crisis Center and advocating for better education in the public school system. Things were going well with me, career wise, and in the relationship department.

After Ramier, I began dating Robbie, Marion's friend. The first day we met, which led to our first spontaneous date, I knew Robbie was gay. After that date, we just stayed friends, but eventually became a couple . . . that never had sex. I know. But he was gay. Being African American and from a well-to-do family from the South, he was beyond closeted and lived the life of a straight man. He never admitted it, never mentioned being gay, and I never asked. Why? I don't know. Maybe I felt that it was his business to share with me. Maybe I fell too deeply for his kind, considerate, gentlemanly ways. Maybe I needed someone that felt safe, that I felt respected and loved by. I moved in with him. We never did it, honestly. But we were intimate in a way that was very loving. Eventually, he gave me my own room so that I could sleep better—he snored. Okay, it was because he was homosexual but who's counting. I knew he couldn't last like this. His clandestine late-night escapades got in the way of our trusting bond, and I finally let go, but we remained close friends.

A few years later, Robbie was dying of AIDS. Man that killed me. Why him? Why anyone? I'd really dedicated myself to the fight against AIDS and became a so-called AIDS activist while still working with kids and education. Why AIDS? I don't know. I just felt this heavy compulsion in my heart to do so. Laurie Fabiano, who was head of the Gay Men's Health Crisis, asked me to attend an AIDS dance-a-thon, and Robbie saw me on the press line from his bed. He rang me up.

"Hey. Listen, I appreciate all you're doing, but make sure you're not doing it to promote your career, don't do us any favors."

"Excuse me?"

"I know you! I know you spent hours on your hair!"

"True. But what does that have to do with the price of eggs?"

"I just don't want you to be like those other celebrities. If you're going to fight for us, do it for the cause, not for the cameras."

Wow. Besides being thrown by what he said, I was worried by how different he sounded, so weak and upset. I went to see him to make sure he was okay. I had not seen him in about a year. I tried to conceal my shock and heartbreak when I saw the devastating toll that AIDS had taken on his body. You hear about it, we talk about it, but when you see AIDS up close and personal, it's a whole other thing. I promised him I would fight, hard and honestly.

I put all my energy into it. I wore the red ribbon at every event, on every step and repeat, and used the microphone to spread the word. I showed up at almost every dance-a-thon, every walk-a-thon, and countless rallies and protest. I wrote editorials. I visited hospitals, hugged AIDS patients, told them jokes to make their day brighter, and gave speeches at high schools, ranting on about safe sex. I volunteered for days and hours at the GMHC headquarters, following Laurie Fabiano around at the GMHC learning everything I could about advocacy and the politics surrounding HIV/AIDS.

I went up to Albany with her and screamed at lobbyists, always with the haunting visual of dear Robbie pushing me on. I listened to Laurie when she chastised me for making mistakes now and then—like the time I put my foot in my mouth when we stormed city hall. The sound bite that all activists were told to say was, "If Mayor Giuliani cuts DAS [Division of AIDS Services], he'll be cutting off his nose to spite his face." I was so hyped up and nervous, especially since Susan Sarandon (love) was standing right next to me, that when the camera got into my face I yelled, "If Giuliani cuts DAS, he'll cut his face!" Or something stupid like that. Boy, that didn't go over well. And NY1 played it over and over. But it made headlines, and DAS wasn't cut.

On and on I went, never stopping, even when I wanted to. Odd to say, all this activism gave back to me. It brought a light to my soul that I cannot describe. I was always made fun of for my need to be nice, to be a do-gooder, for wanting to make the world a nicer place, and here was that opportunity, through Robbie's simple challenge. It made me appreciate Nigel, Beth, Miss Connie, Grace, and many others who had given back to me, making my life better. This opened me up to many different causes that spoke to my heart as well—like stopping violence against women. AIDS activism unknowingly began another career for me—a career of advocacy and activism that has stayed with me to this day.

Sadly, Robbie passed away from the disease. My heart hurt like never before. And I will always keep fighting until there is a cure.

. . .

From all of the choreographing jobs, especially LL Cool J's tour, I had enough money to finally move out of the damn Jungle and was ready to buy my very first house! Yay! I wanted to make sure there was enough room for Tia and me. I told her I wanted her to live with me, and when I made more money, I'd buy her a house of her own. She refused! I kept begging and begging until she exploded, "*Ay*, don't keep being irritating, please! I keep telling you, that's your money. I'm okay. Plus, I don't want to leave my grandkids. You know how their mothers are."

I was hurt. I wanted to take care of that stubborn woman. I got the house for myself and got her a nice apartment but had her believing it was Titi's—yes, Titi, the heroin addict. We had made peace. After she contracted hepatitis from dirty needles, she got sober and became a different person. Titi told Tia that the apartment was only $200 and she could afford it. Tia bought the lie and I kept paying for it on the sly. Unfortunately, Titi's hepatitis worsened and eventually she died from the disease. It was so sad. Everyone took it hard, especially Tia. I really wanted to take care of her better, even more now. Still, she refused to move in with me. "Why?" She left the apartment and moved into an assisted living building that Millie, who was on disability, had moved into. Jeez! Of course I took care of her, but I still had to lie about it.

CHAPTER 27

BACK ON tour with LL, I had gotten a call from Keenen Ivory Wayans. I had met him at Eddie Murphy's house parties in New Jersey at his mini-mansion he called Bubble Hill. Keenen had his own show in development on the Fox Network, *In Living Color*, and wanted me to be the show's choreographer. Yay! There would be five beautiful girls opening the show with him, à la *The Jackie Gleason Show*. They would be referred to as the Fly Girls, and he wanted them to dance like real New York dancers. A producer from the show would be calling me in the next few days to work out the deal.

I never got the call. I kept calling Fox Studios, asking to speak with Keenen, but kept getting derailed to the show's line producer, Kevin, instead. "We're looking at other choices, and we'll let you know." Kevin called on a Tuesday and told me they'd found some-one else. The show debuted without me. I was disappointed, but I moved on. I still had a tour to deal with.

LL's tour pulled into the Universal Amphitheater in Studio City, California. Hanging backstage, supervising the performance, I saw two of the Wayans brothers wandering around. Then I saw Keenen with his new girl, Daphne, who later became his babies' mama, standing in the wings. They were so hot and horny for each other. She was standing in front of him while he was grinding the shit out of her booty, thinking no one was noticing.

Keenen had called over someone on the crew asking him who choreographed the show. When he told Keenen it was me, Keenen immediately asked to speak with me. I told the crew guy to tell Keenen I was too busy. I didn't want to endure further humiliation. I don't remember if it was Marlon or the other brother, but one of them finally came over and asked why I didn't take the job. Huh? I told him what happened. Keenen came over.

"I dissed you? You dissed me!" he said.

"What? I talked to that Kevin guy, and he told me, blah, blah, blah!"

"You messin' with me, Rosie?"

"Nope."

"Listen, come to my office tomorrow and we'll fix this shit."

"I can't just break out on the tour like that!"

"How much is LL paying you?"

"Fifteen hundred a week."

"I'll pay you three thousand a week, and if you do well, I'll double it after three months."

"Hmm, let me ask Todd. I don't want to dis him like that."

During a quick changeover, Todd came toward us, stage left, said hi to Keenen. Keenen explained the situation. Todd looked at me and cracked up in my face, telling me, "You better get that TV money." He gave Keenen a pound, gave me a hug, and jetted back onstage.

. . .

First day. I arrived extra early. Rehearsed for two hours alone, nervous yet ready! Keenen called me into his office. "First thing, about Kevin. You're here, so let it go. Now, we need three numbers per show—an opening, a middle, and an end, each twenty-eight seconds long, and an assist in picking the music. You are in charge of the girls. Make sure they stay looking good—no fat, busted chicks allowed. Work with hair, makeup, and wardrobe. And I want them to dance like MC Hammer's girls too. If you don't deliver, bullets will be flying, homie." He laughed. "That goes for all of the staff, so I hope you don't catch one. Welcome."

"Thank you so much for this opportunity. I won't let you down. Oh, I usually work with my assistant, Arthur Rainer. That's cool?"

"Ask Tamara, the co-executive producer. See if it fits in the budget."

"Okay. Oh, another thing. I need to pick the music. And I don't do 'Hammer.'"

"What's wrong with Hammer?"

"Nothing. If you want Hammer, hire him."

He laughed his ass off.

The girls were pretty cool, though a few resented that I took the other choreographer's place and that I used street vernacular (". . . And then you spin all around, and boom, stop on the down beat . . ."). These were technically trained dancers and were thrown by me. Their eyes would discreetly roll, some would chuckle. "You mean pirouette, and stop on the last four count of the second bar." Here we go again. I understood, but whatever. I liked these girls and I liked their work ethic even more.

Their hip-hop skills were severely lacking. I was tough with them, making them do the numbers over and over until it seemed second nature to them. I remember making all of them stand in front of the mirror and just bop their heads to the drummer's beat until their necks were sprained. I wanted everything to come off as innate. The worst thing I hated most about hip-hop dancers was that forced "street" vibe, looking like a satirical portrayal of a low-level corner drug dealer. Hated it. They never fully got it. The girls just couldn't get that swag down like I needed them to. I decided to combine their technique with hip-hop and precision dancing from cheerleading, and threw in a lot of Ann-Margret (love) via Viva Las Vegas. And the Fly Girls were born!

After a few weeks of completely exhausting work, I knew I had to get Arthur in there with me. I had to have someone take some of the pressure off and to have my back. I was hesitant to ask the co-executive producer after what happened with Kevin, so I just brought him in on my own, paying him out of my salary, promising him that I'd get him the job soon enough. After the first week with Arthur, being ahead of schedule and not all stressed out, Keenen came down to rehearsals one day to praise me for a job well done.

"This is Arthur, my assistant I told you about. He's been helping out tremendously. But he's not on pay yet."

"Cool. Arthur, welcome, you're hired." Yay!

Arthur and I put in approximately ten hours a day—me, sometimes more. We would always come in two hours before the Fly Girls' call time, working on new routines. Man, those were the best times, so much fun dancing, messing up, figuring it out, taking five and telling stories, cracking jokes in between, getting back into it—arguing over steps, and then cracking some more jokes. By the time the girls got there, we were spent but hyped—the freedom and opportunity Keenen gave us was so exciting that we would get recharged in an instant!

When I was choreographing, I wasn't thinking about my mother. I wasn't thinking about what had happened in the past. Working all hours into the night after the girls had gone home, meticulously deciding on what songs to pick, editing them down perfectly, brought me so much joy that there wasn't time for dwelling on things.

Things started to ease up between the girls and me, mostly because of Arthur. I was too shy to engage in chitchat, honestly, and Arthur was an easy icebreaker. During our lunch breaks we would sometimes sit in a circle, and Arthur would start telling jokes, softening the room. He allowed me to feel comfortable enough to join in the fun. Unfortunately, I couldn't participate too much. I still had to deal with the music too.

The show was pretaped in advance of some of the artists' release dates. I had to be ahead of radio, ahead of *Billboard*, and ahead of the dance trends. The show would tape for two weeks and be off the third, then back the following two weeks, and so on. That third week, I'd fly myself back to New York (on my own dime, thank you) and go deep inside the hip-hop club scenes—clubs like Carwash, MK's, the Tunnel, the Building—to scope out who or what was hot or not. I'd meet with Russell Simmons, Lyor Cohen, Tommy of Tommy Boy Records, Tommy Mottola, Andre Harrell, Puffy (now head of A&R for Uptown Records—believe that!), to name a few, and figure out momentum in the business. The best help I got was from Rhonda Cowan, who worked for Russell Simmons at Def Jam.

Rhonda doesn't remember the first time I met her, but I surely do. Rhonda was at one of Eddie Murphy's house parties in New Jersey. She was messin' with Eddie's brother, Charlie, at the time and was in the middle of a heated argument with him, yelling, "I know this motherfucker is not trying to tell me what to do! He better stay in his lane and shut the fuck up and buy me some new shoes." I died laughing. She turned around, looked at me, and said, laughing, "I can buy my own damn shoes, but you know what I'm saying. Motherfucker better act like he knows." Hilarious. I loved her the moment she opened her trash-talking, intelligent, and opinionated mouth—crazy as a loon and fly as shit. Without Rhonda's help and friendship, I would have had a more difficult time getting what I needed to do my job well. And she made hanging out fun—crazy fun.

Rhonda Cowan, Tracy Waples, and April Walker—that was my hang-out crew in New York City. These were my girls! We went everywhere: pop clubs, ghetto clubs, lounges, Rucker playgrounds, house parties, premieres, dinner parties, you name it. Shit was mad fun.

I was hanging out at this pop-up club, Carwash, where I saw this new group called Leaders of the New School and was totally blown away. This gave me the idea of featuring acts on the show. I thought to myself, *If I book these guys, this is going to blow up like crazy, and In Living Color is going to look hip as shit.* Keenen wasn't with it at first. The producers were worried about the cost. I wouldn't stop asking, I was a pest. Then Keenen finally gave in, told me I had one shot. I couldn't get Leaders on because the ink wasn't yet dry on their recording contract. And the record companies weren't biting with their established acts—too much of a risk on a new show was their thinking. I went with Def Jef, a rapper, who was only known locally in Los Angeles. That didn't go so well with the response from the viewers. I begged Keenen for another try.

Rhonda introduced me to Shakim of Flavor Unit, who managed Queen Latifah—love! Keenen loved her too and let me put her on the show. After her performance at the top of the second season, every hip-hop act wanted to be booked. I mostly had carte blanche, but Shawn Wayans, who had a very different musical taste from mine, wanted a say-so. So I booked most of the acts, but there were a few I didn't, which bothered me like hell, but it was a Wayans production, and they were very good to me, so I fell back out of respect. Kind of.

. . .

Wait for it . . . I got nominated for my first Emmy for my choreography—holla! The cast and crew got nominations too! Everyone was excited, kind of. Keenen called me up to his office. Oh snap. What the hell did I do now?

"Close the door."

"Am I fired?"

"No. (laughs) Just wanted to tell you that the girls come up here almost every day asking me to fire you. Saying that you curse all the time, are too strict, and push them to their physical limit. What the fuck are you doing to them?"

"Huh?" I eked out, tearing up. I thought we were getting along.

Keenen laughed in my face. Now, I wasn't choking up because I was hurt—trust me—okay, I was a little bit, but who's counting.

"It's not funny. Yes, I'm strict! Yes, I push them! Do you see how everyone's talking about these girls? Everyone! We got the damn nomination, for Christmas' sakes! And the music guests that I have picked—forget about it!"

"Calm down. You're not fired. I'll take care of the girls. Get back to work, silly."

"Thank you, Keenen. Oh, one more thing. Can I talk to the director? I hate how the numbers are cut. They don't show off the dancing or the girls properly."

"Tell you what, you direct the segments yourself. You can work with the editor too. Now, if you fuck it up, bullets will be flying, homie."

Keenen and the show won big that year. But I lost to Paula Abdul—so I wasn't too disappointed. I love Paula.

I started to ease up a bit on the girls and not take everything so seriously. Carrie-Ann Inaba and Deidre Lang were the first of the Fly Girls to come around. Cari French, I never had a problem with, no one ever did. She was hilarious too—made me laugh almost every day with her dry wit. Lisa-Marie Todd started to soften a bit too, but kept her distance. Michelle Whitney-Morrison, she was pretty cool, she was always respectful.

This was good because I started to see them differently. I started to see who they were as people and as dancers. I was so impressed with Deidre's technique that she gave me the idea of giving the girls solo numbers. Carrie-Ann was a great dancer with great poise and a goofy sense of humor. When she would do her own thing, her lyrical, sexy moves were original and so freaking cool. She introduced me to the up-and-coming choreographers and dance groups in Los Angeles and the different dance styles that were emerging. She may not know this, but she gave me the idea to feature different dance crews on the show, like the Soul Brothers and Two for Two, who later became the recording artists the Pharcyde. Lisa-Marie had style and inspired me to ask Michelle Cole, the wardrobe designer, to dress them even sexier. Gosh, she was so amazingly beautiful.

Michelle Whitney-Morrison was different. I liked her a lot, but she and Arthur would go at it. She had been antagonizing Arthur while I was away filming this television series that I desperately wanted off of. When I came back, tensions were thick. One day, while I was in the editing room working on the dance numbers, one of the girls came rushing in: "Arthur and Michelle are fighting!" We bolted to the rehearsal room. As I whipped open the door I saw Michelle fall backwards, like timber!

"Arthur!" I screamed.

"Bitch called me a nigga! Then tried to slap me! So I popped her ass!" Arthur shouted back.

Jeez. Out of pure shock, I let out an inappropriate nervous laugh. Michelle, pissed, ran up to Keenen's office, demanding that he fire Arthur and me instantly. When Keenen found out the whole story, she was the one who got fired. Was it completely fair? No— not at all. I was very upset with Arthur. I told him violence toward women was not acceptable on any level and if he ever did it again we couldn't work together.

Gosh, it was difficult watching Michelle pack her things. The whole situation was messed up. I truly felt bad for her. Dra-ma . . . on the high seas!

So we had to find a new girl. I hated every one of Keenen's picks. He hated every one of mine, said they were not sexy enough for prime time.

"What the hell does that have to do with their talent, Keenen?"

"We're not doing some ghetto show, Rosie. We're doing national television," he snidely answered.

"And? The Fly Girls' number-one audience is prison inmates!"

"Exactly. What fuckin' prisoner wants to sit there looking at some busted-looking chick?"

The search for a new Fly Girl was on. By the time we pulled into New York for our first round of auditions, it had turned into a media frenzy! Thousands and thousands of girls were wrapped around the block. Keenen, worried that it would take forever to see each one, decided that I should cancel out the "busted"-looking ones on sight. I told him that wasn't a good idea—this was New York, and these girls were not professional dancers and would not, probably did not, understand the concept of typecasting. We'd get our asses beat in a hot second. Keenen wrote my warning off and decided to take charge. He got started: "Next, next, you stay, next. . . ." He got to this one girl:

"Next."

"What, motherfucker?" she said, with her hand on her hip.

Keenen replied, "Girl, take that hand off your hip," laughing in her face.

In quick, rapid ghetto-style punches, the girl started swinging. Bodyguards came rushing in. I cracked the fuck up in Keenen's face. He couldn't do anything but laugh with me—hilarious.

Second day, we still had nothing. Then I saw this curvy, heavy-set, big-ass, beautiful girl. She wasn't the best dancer, but definitely had an immense amount of star quality and a stunning face. Keenen said no, said she couldn't dance as well as the other girls, called her chubby and corny. We started to argue. I lost.

We went back to Los Angeles empty-handed and held more auditions. I gave in to Marlon and Shawn's pick: this girl named Carla, a very nice, good technical dancer, but too virginal in her expression to stir the likes of prison inmates. Keenen knew it too.

After a few episodes, Keenen finally told me to fire her. Man, that was hard to do—she took it hard too, but was classy and dignified about it.

"Keenen, I say we call that Puerto Rican girl from the Bronx and offer her the job."

"Who?"

"The one with that big ass and the star smile. We'll hit gold, Keenen. I promise. . . . Please?"

"I don't know. Girl needs to drop at least twenty pounds."

"I'll make sure she does."

"And we've gotta cut her hair, give her some edge."

"Are you crazy? I can't ask a Puerto Rican girl to cut her hair! You ask her!"

"Fine. But you take care of the rest, and if she doesn't deliver . . ."

"I know, I know, 'bullets will be flying, homie.' "

Jennifer Lopez was hired. Keenen took all the credit—I didn't care. Unfortunately, he did make her cut her hair! I was devastated for her. At first she charmed everyone—the girls, the talent, the producers, and me. I was very happy. But within less than two weeks, every day almost, all of the girls were coming into my office complaining how she was manipulating wardrobe, makeup, and me, all to her advantage. And they didn't appreciate all the attention I was giving her. Huh? I had to give her attention so she could catch up—technically she wasn't up to their level.

When I asked Jennifer about it, she told me the girls were cold, ostracizing, and jealous of her. Oh boy. I decided to let them work it out themselves. After a while, other departments started to chime in with their own complaints about her being pushy and opinionated. Hmm. Still, I didn't do anything.

I saw how the constant pressure I was applying was taking its toll on her and didn't want to add to it. Keenen was hard on Jennifer too, although she didn't have a clue. He would always call me on the red phone reserved for producers during live and pre-tapings, telling me to take her out of a certain number if he thought she looked fat that week or too clunky in her moves—true story, folks. And of course, I couldn't tell her it was Keenen's decision. I was the choreographer, he was my boss, and that was that. Boy, the hurt I saw on her face was hard to dismiss. She sucked it up like a pro for a while—then she finally broke.

One day during rehearsal I took her out of a number that was too technically difficult for her to execute, but she didn't see it that way. She came into my office during break and went off on me, screaming, pounding on her chest!

"You pick on me, me and only me, every fucking day! Every fucking day! I work my ass off, deliver, and you keep pushing me aside, treating me like I'm shit! I know I'm good! I'm better than any of these girls and you know it!"

Wow. She had put forth this sweet-girl act, and all this attitude was hilarious. I thought about the complaints against her. But, I took a deep breath, thinking about the fan mail from inmates that had increased because of her and how Keenen loved her as well, even with all his complaints.

"Look, I'm sorry if I'm too harsh, but I'm hard on you because I see your star quality, and I'm just trying to bring it to its fullness."

She immediately calmed down, with a twinkle in her eyes. "I've got star quality?"

"Yes. Look, I'm just trying to help. Just keep doing what you're doing, and I promise you, you will be rewarded for it."

She worked harder than anyone after that. Came in early. Stayed late. Dropped about ten pounds in two weeks. Took a new subtle approach in working with others. I was impressed with her te-nacity and ambition. And I delivered, rewarding her with more camera time.

Unfortunately, that didn't make things easier with a few of the other girls—not everyone saw her efforts in the same light. Some of the staff even told me they thought her intentions were truly self-serving and thought she had me under her thumb. Even so, I began to take a sincere liking to this girl.

"Why don't you come over to my house for dinner?"

My roommate Tamla hated her. My sister Carmen hated her. Even my father, who liked practically everyone he ever met, hated her. I was so confused. Honestly. I thought she was funny, charming, and polite the whole evening. Carmen told me, "She's a bitch. She'll stab you in the back in a fucking second." So confused.

Keenen wanted to turn the Fly Girls into a recording group. He positioned me as their co-manager. I didn't want the job. I had too much on my plate: working on the show, still meeting and auditioning for movie roles, continuing the fight against HIV/AIDS. I was beyond tired. But I had such gratitude toward him that I accepted.

I hated the job. Especially when Keenen asked me to figure out who should be the lead singers. Man, I knew that, whoever I picked, the rest would resent me even more. I was right. Without any agenda, I told Keenen that Carrie-Ann had a voice but was too pageant-sounding. Deidre did too, but sounded too Broadway. Jennifer was very pitchy but had a commercial tone that the other two didn't have. I also told him that these were just my opinions and felt he should pick the lead. Word got back to the girls through office gossip that I thought none of them could sing. Jeez. They were pissed, all of them. I didn't take it too personally. Okay, I did a bit. Keenen decided that the three girls would share lead vocals.

The songs chosen were kind of good. But there were constant delays. The girls were not in agreement with their contract and would stall in the recording studio as a bargaining tactic. I didn't know this at the time and thought they were taking this opportunity for granted. When I would report back to Keenen, he'd be pissed, telling me to fix it. Ugh! I felt so much pressure!

One day in the studio, after hours of bullshitting, I said something that I still regret to this day:

"Come on, girls! You've gotta try harder. If this record fails, what are you going to do? Keenen will fire your ass, and you'll be known as the girl who used to be a Fly Girl."

Stupid. Stupid. Stupid. Jennifer, to my surprise, was the first to fire back.

"No. That's not true. I'm more than this."

A few others followed. Embarrassed, I backpedaled and offered a wimpy apology, trying to smooth things over. Jennifer changed a bit with me after that, attitude up the butt, but let it go after a while. Whew! In the end, Keenen was so fed up with them that he canceled the whole thing. Even though I was so relieved, I felt bad too. But I had gotten a role in Jim Jarmusch's *Night on Earth,* and I had to set my focus elsewhere. I left Arthur to deal with the fallout until I got back.

CHAPTER 28

Night on Earth was crazy fun. Working with Jim Jarmusch was something I had really wanted to do since I began acting. It was beyond low budget but I didn't care. All of the actors had to share a tiny hotel room in place of a trailer and also for hair, makeup, and wardrobe. Mad fun. But it did get to me when I went to lie down in my "dressing room" on location, which was in the basement of a piece-of-shit tenement building in Brooklyn. I looked up and saw a dead rat stuck on a pipe that ran across the ceiling. When I got up to run out, a live rat ran across my foot. Still, the whole experience was great!

After that film, I fought like hell to be seen for *White Men Can't Jump*. They wanted an Italian American or Irish American girl. It was tough, even for CAA, to get me an audition, but they pulled it off!

I was the only girl of color in the waiting room. Four A-list actresses sat there, artificially confident. I, on the other hand, was so nervous that my hair started to sweat and frizz! Holy crapola! I rushed to the ladies' room and splashed water on my face. Then I looked down and noticed that I had gotten my period all over my jeans! I took them off and washed and dried them with the hand dryer quick before it was my turn to go in.

"Rosie? You're next."

I walked into the casting office. A middle-aged man, who I assumed was the casting director, walked in and sat behind the desk.

"How are ya today?"

"Not too good. Nervous. Just got my period, and. . . . God, why did I say that? I'm sorry. Embarrassing."

He laughed. I nervously laughed back. Then a woman walked in and introduced herself as the casting director and introduced the man sitting behind the desk, Ron Shelton, as the director of the damn film!

"Oh my goodness! I thought you were . . . I didn't mean to tell you. . . . Well, I'll just leave now."

"What? I loved it! Sit down. Let's start reading."

We did so. He stopped me midway and turned to the casting director.

"Hey, call in Woody, would ya? Do you know Woody Harrelson from *Cheers*?"

Woody walked in just as cool as a cucumber and cute as hell.

"Oh my goodness! You're so cute. You look better in person," I shrieked gleefully.

"Why, thank you, darling. I think? (*laughs*) And you're not too shabby yourself, if I may say so myself . . . which I just did."

We both laughed.

"Okay, you two, we haven't started filming yet. Let's read."

We did so. And when it came to the part of the kiss, we—well, I should say, Woody—went for it, tongue and all. And yes, I didn't resist, but when the kiss went on too long, I got embarrassed and pushed him off of me, giggling and blushing.

I went through several more callbacks. The studio, as I was told, had a problem that I was Puerto Rican; they were worried about the interracial aspect. Here we go. Woody and Ron fought for me, as did the producers. And I finally got the part! I am so grateful that they put themselves out there like that. That's the only way things change—when everyone joins the fight and you're not the only one rushing up the hill.

One of the first scenes we shot for *White Men Can't Jump* was inside the freakin' Jungle! Woody couldn't believe I had actually lived there. He told me that Wesley Snipes cracked up when he heard. I got pissed. Wesley, I thought he was cocky and arrogant, and I told Woody how I felt, and he fucking told Wes! Wesley comes over to me.

"Yo, I don't care if you like me or not, and you don't do it for me either, so we good. All we gotta do is our job."

"Woody!!"

"What? He's my boy, and I want you two to get along."

I apologized to Wesley, and we shook on it after I punched Woody in the arm. Being on team sports and having more male friends than female friends, I had that male understanding that a handshake carries a lot of weight—it was dropped and we were cool. Actually, we were so cool that the three of us instantly acted as if we had known each other for years.

As we jumped into the car and began shooting a wide shot of us driving off out of the Jungle, Wesley turned to the both of us and said, "You know this shit's going to be big, right? Gonna blow the numbers off the fucking charts!"

The first sex scene was up. Ron Shelton assured me that everything would be done tastefully, and if I wasn't comfortable with anything, he would stop and change whatever to my liking. Yay!

It was a completely different experience from Do the Right Thing, yet I was still nervous. Naked, in just a towel, I couldn't come out of the fake bathroom on set. I was wasting time, but Ron and Woody and the crew waited respectfully. After an hour—not kidding—Woody asked me if I wanted to smoke a joint to calm down.

"No, fool!"

Then Stephanie Cozart Burton, makeup—who also was makeup at In Living Color—knocked and handed me a shot of whiskey. I never drank hard liquor, only wine. I guzzled that bitch fast—and I still couldn't come out.

Then Woody knocked. "Rose? Darling? Can I come in?"

"No!"

"Why?"

"I don't want you to see me naked."

I know, but I was shy and I kind of had a crush on him.

"Rose, you're beautiful, and there is nothing shameful about the human body. And it's not about your body. It's about this scene and the love our characters have for each other. Come out, please. Everyone respects you here, especially me, and everything will be done respectfully. Hey, I'll tell everyone to go away, and it'll just be me and you."

". . . Okay."

I took a deep breath and opened the door. My towel slipped a bit, revealing my breasts.

"Oh my God! Your tits are huge," screamed Woody with glee!

"You pig!"

I slammed the door in his face. All I could hear was Woody cracking up and Ron cursing him out. I couldn't help it and started laughing too. I opened the door. Woody was still laughing, now on his knees trying to apologize.

"All right, all right, let's just get this over with!"

Boy, did we have fun. And chemistry. I had a blast on set. To date, this was the most fun I've ever had filming. To date, these two, Woody and Wesley, are among the few actors I have a real friendship with too. And yes, I had a crush on Woody—a big one. But I knew his personal assistant, Laura, was madly in love with him, so I fell back. I liked and had instant respect for Laura, thought Woody couldn't move two steps without her, and realized that he didn't know how much he was in love with her either. Thank goodness he finally figured it out and married the woman!

White Men Can't Jump was a huge success, just like Wesley predicted. Doors were opening and the roles were less stereotypical! Yay for me! And the money increased as well, which was badly needed. No, I never got over a million—they weren't handing out big checks like that for us Ricans back then—but I came close to it, partly because I started demanding more. Well, I got just a bit more, to be honest, with *Untamed Heart*. And the money from *In Living Color* was still coming in. Keenen had doubled my salary by now too.

I went to Tia and told her I wanted to make a down payment on a house for her. She refused! I insisted and got the house anyway, brought her over, and she still refused. I let the house go.

I couldn't go anywhere without being stopped after *White Men Can't Jump*. I loved the fans. At times, I'd be brought to tears when they told me how much I made their day brighter by my work. But some of the fans frightened me. Ninety-five percent of the fan mail I received through CAA, my management, and at *In Living Color* was positive. The remaining 5 percent were sickos, writing how they hated me because I was Puerto Rican, how they wanted to rape me, stick their penis in my ass till I bled. One guy wrote me over and over in his blood, praying for my death, telling me he wanted to strip my brown ass naked, rape me, and then paint me red and nail me to a telephone pole until I slowly died!

PTSD hit an all-time high—paranoia to its fullest. I was scared to be alone with anyone on an elevator. I was scared to walk to my car at night, even though it was on the Fox Studio lot. I double-locked my doors at home, hoping no one had followed me. My representatives and coworkers at the show told me this was par for the course—easy for them to say. They didn't understand the depths of a real threat.

I couldn't shake the fear for a very long time. I started to subconsciously turn down really smart and good offers. My subconscious knew that the bigger I got, the bigger the threats would be.

Then *Fearless* came along.

. . .

Fearless was a long shot too, especially since they wanted an Italian American for the role even though the real-life person the character was based on was Asian American, a survivor who lost her baby in a major plane crash they both were on. I loved this script. CAA agents Jane Berliner, Carol Bodie, and especially Kevin Huvane fought like hell to get me seen. I was number eighty-something, sitting in the hotel lobby among a handful of ladies, all white. I have never been great at auditions—seriously. My nerves get the best of me. This time, the sweat started, the frizz began, and I thought I was going to pass out. I ordered an espresso, and then another one. By the time I was called, my stomach was fizzing and my head was boiling hot.

I walked into the hotel room, pasty and sweaty. Peter Weir, the film director, and Howard Feuer, the casting director, greeted me warmly. I asked to use the restroom. Montezuma's revenge hit hard. I was so embarrassed, sure that they heard everything since the bathroom was fifteen feet away! I was so freaked that I splashed cold water on my face to calm down. Oh no! My hair! Oh no! My mascara! I took a washcloth and patted the black streaks off my face. I tried my best to dry my hair, but it wasn't working.

"Rosie," asked Howard as he knocked. "You okay in there?"

I came out looking even pastier. They both paused, and then Peter smiled and softly asked me to begin. We read some scenes, and in the middle of one Peter asked me to pray.

"Pray? Like I'm at Mass or like at home or in the booth?"

"Excuse me? What booth?"

"The confessional."

"Oh, right. Just pray like you're home praying."

I did. He nodded. Then he asked me to lie down on the couch in a catatonic state, a state where I was in the depths of depression, beyond tears. Well, hell, that was easy as pie for me! I did so.

"Thank you, Rosie. Where are you from, what background are you?"

Oh shit, here we go. I told him I was from Brooklyn, spent some years in upstate New York in a Group Home—I couldn't believe that slipped out! Then I said, "I'm Puerto Rican."

"Ahh. I see. Well, thank you for coming in. You did very well."

I didn't believe him. I mean, I did think I read well, but I didn't believe that he liked me, because he asked about my nationality and background.

A few days passed. In Living Color was on hiatus, and I was back in Brooklyn, living down the block from Rhonda Cowan in a duplex apartment. My half-sister Kathy had been living with me for the past three years with her four-year-old son. She wasn't working and had gotten pregnant again by her new boyfriend. I helped her out by letting her stay in the apartment until she got back on her feet, and she helped out by apartment-sitting while I was gone.

The waiting was driving me nuts. I couldn't keep my mind off of the film. In the grip of a severe panic attack, I went on a shopping spree and spent $2,000 on clothes. I know that doesn't seem like a lot of money to most actors, but I did mention that I was frugal . . . okay, cheap. I came home with shopping bags galore. Kathy asked what I had bought her. I told her I didn't get anything for her, sorry. She was upset, told me that I was selfish. Say what? She's been living rent-free for the past three years and I'm selfish? Okay. I didn't want to deal, told her I was going over to Rhonda's to hang. She asked me to bring her back some food. Sure.

Several hours passed. I stopped by the corner bodega and got Kathy tons of Hostess treats. She went off because I didn't get her a real meal. We got into an ugly fight. Well, she fought with me mostly. I didn't want to hit back because of her pregnancy but finally had to because she was kicking my ass! And, I fell down the staircase trying to get away from her, banging my head against the banister.

I had to get my ass out of there quick fast. I ran to Rhonda's. My feet were bleeding, and so was my head. It was swelling up like a grapefruit. We rushed to the hospital. I had stitches in my foot from broken glass and was treated for a hairline fracture on my skull.

I planned on going home the next day to collect my things. My dear friend Wendel Haskins, who was my boyfriend at the time, came over to Rhonda's.

"Don't go home, Rosie."

"Why?"

"I think your mother and the rest of your brothers and sisters are in front of your apartment selling all of your shit on the sidewalk."

It was true. Wow. Humiliated and hurt, I asked Rhonda if I could stay with her for the night until I got Kathy out. That lasted for weeks. Yep, I slept on her couch for the entire time. I was done. Done! I didn't want anything to do with my mother or her children anymore. Finally, *finally*, I realized that I'd been chasing a dream that would never become reality.

A week after the fight, Jane, Carol, and Kevin Huvane called. "They want to see you again. This time with the lead, Jeff Bridges!"

Dammit! I was still bruised, beaten, and on crutches. How the hell was I going to walk into the audition room like this? Fuck it. I wasn't going to let this stop me. I got on a plane and took my hobbling ass into that audition room. "What happened to you?"

"I got into a car accident. Sorry, don't want to go into it. Depressing."

"Look on the bright side," Peter said, "it works for the character."

I smiled. I felt he didn't buy my lie. Good thing Jeff and I clicked—what a sweetheart he was, and such a generous actor.

Back at work, Keenen took me into his office and asked about my "car accident." I started crying and, in confidence, told him the truth. Motherfucker laughed in my face! "Damn, she kicked the shit outta your ass!"

"Keenen! It's not funny!"

"Yes, it is! And why are you crying? You're here, right? You're back working, doing what you love, and you're keeping it moving, right? Fuck that ghetto shit, okay?"

"Yeah."

He then hugged me. "Go back to work and come over the house later. We'll watch the game. . . . Damn, she kicked your ass!" Hilarious.

After four more callbacks, I got the part! Peter was right. The depression worked in my favor. But I was scared out of my wits taking on this big role.

We were shooting up in northern California. It was around eleven at night, the night before my first shoot day. I was a nervous wreck, pacing, convincing myself that I couldn't pull this role off. I called Peter's room and told him I wanted to quit. I didn't want to mess up his film. "I'm coming up!" he shouted.

When he showed up, he asked, "Why do you feel this way? Why do you feel like you don't deserve this role?"

Did this man just read my ass? It was the first time I had realized that I had issues with my success, that I felt guilty that I had made it, that I had made it out of the system, got to live with Tia and not my mentally ill mother, and had reconnected with Dad and could revel in his unconditional love. What I also realized—and I knew this deep inside—was that I could play this part with ease. I understood loss, depression, betrayal, and how to pull yourself back together. I clearly knew I could kick ass—no question about it. I was just scared to explore that vulnerability.

"I'm not hiring anyone else. We're going to do this together, and you're going to be great. Open up your script."

We rehearsed until one in the morning. My call time was at five.

This film was the most challenging project I've ever worked on, yet also the easiest. Peter tapped into the vulnerability that I had been hiding for so many years. And because of the trust we had established in the wee hours of the morning, I gave everything to the part.

Peter gave me all of his trust as well, never telling me how to play the character, trusting my instincts, tweaking me and guiding me when needed and whenever I felt lost. Jeff Bridges, Isabella Rossellini, and John Turturro were supportive as well—most notably Jeff. We had great fun together. I watched him, asked him why he made certain choices and how he did things, yet he never came off as superior or condescending.

. . .

Back home, after filming was completed, I had found a new tiny, inexpensive apartment, still in Fort Greene. Although I had gotten a decent check from *Fearless*, I was counting every penny. I had to pay out on a potential lawsuit from the landlord of the duplex I was staying in with Kathy. She had destroyed the place and racked up a bill of over $10,000. The payoff to the landlord was nothing compared to the lawyer fees. They were in the hundreds of thousands and had drained my pocket substantially. Thankfully I was frugal and had some savings left.

. . .

Forest Whitaker, whom I starred with in HBO's *Criminal Justice*, had directed a film for the network called *Strapped*. There was a promotional screening at the Public Theater for young people. I went to support it and was really moved by the film.

During the Q&A, they asked me to say a few words. Not thinking about the repercussions, I spoke honestly about being in a Group Home, about being a nice, shy girl with a bad temper, about frontin' like I was a badass, which wasn't who I was, about holding a knife to the Group Home parent's neck so her husband would get off of my half-sister. I talked about choices—how this stupid act could've changed my life. If the Group Home parent didn't find my actions ridiculous because she knew I was a cornball who was scared for her sister, I could've been brought up on charges and things would've been very different.

Why oh why did I tell the truth? Those comments made headlines, and the press went on the attack. The only bad press or negative comments I'd ever received up to this point was about how irritating my voice was. I know, but it was my real voice, change and growth takes time, people—can we move on?

My biggest fear came to fruition. My time at the Home and everything else was revealed. My mother and some of my half-siblings, and my half-sister Tiara, called the tabloids and told them that I was a big fat liar. They told the press that my aunt did not raise me, that I was in foster care, and that the incident with the knife never happened. Say what? Then Sharon, one of the Group Home parents—who was not the GH parent I was speaking about—was interviewed by said tabloid and backed their story up against me.

First of all, neither Lydia nor Tiara was there—Tiara had already been transferred back to the Home before she went to live with Lydia full-time. Secondly, neither was Sharon. And lastly, how dare any of them sell me out like that—especially my mother!

I refused to dignify any of it with a response. I was so boiling mad. Fans thought I was cold, a liar, and a bitch.

My new world that I'd fought so hard to obtain was closing in on me. The tabloids, the fact that I was still depressed over that fight with Kathy, the way my mother and the rest of the clan acted—it was all way too much for me to handle. Also, *Fearless* had stayed with me longer and affected me more deeply than any other film. I kept having nightmares about my mother trying to kill me, about babies dying and planes crashing. I stayed in a lot, became antisocial and grouchy, stopped going to clubs and whatnot.

Carmen was great—she came by or called every day. So were

Rhonda, April Walker, and Julie Shannon, my best friend who I had met at In Living Color. Julie in fact came to stay with me for a while. Dad had come up to visit a lot as well. He was worried about me too. He was staying with Carmen and Chavo in their new two-story house in Jamaica, Queens. Chavo was still doing his "thing," and they were pulling in close to twenty thousand a week. You wouldn't have known it by the way they dressed—still ghetto as hell, especially Chavo.

It was such a joyful feeling to know that I had so much support from my family and friends. It was as if I was in a slugfest, in the tenth round, and they were all in my corner letting me know that I could get past this and still win the round. And I did.

CHAPTER 29

I GOT the part of playing Nicolas Cage's wife in *It Could Happen to You*. Yay for me! Nick Cage is fine as hell and a stand-up guy, by the way. So excited. I almost didn't get it, though. When I met with the director, Andy Bergman, he thought I was too nice for the role, he couldn't see me as an annoying bitch.

"Really?"

I was so flattered—ha! I think he was referring to my shyness. Like I've said, I don't always do well at auditions or meetings. Meetings are easier, and most of the time I do great in a room, but sometimes I get anxious.

I told Andy about a particular person who I wanted to base the character on. Said person lived in the hood but wore Chanel and pronounced it "channel," like on the television, wasn't that bright, thought her shit didn't stink, and was a bitch on wheels—that person still holds it against me.

So anyway, I got the part and was able to climb out of debt and make a down payment on a beautiful home in . . . wait for it . . . Clinton Hill! My childhood dream of having one of those gorgeous homes had become a reality. Yay! I asked Tia to come back and live with me. She didn't want to leave her grandkids in California. Okay! I get it! I stopped trying. Well, not really. I still paid for this nice ranch-style house I had leased in my cousin Millie's name that she and Tia were living in.

. . .

A coup went down at In Living Color. I don't know all of the details, but Keenen was out, fired as executive producer of his own show. I felt such loyalty to him that I decided, if he was out, I was out. They didn't want me to quit, but I had to go. I pushed really hard that they keep Arthur too. He added so much and had taken over for me on various occasions when I was away filming—I knew the Fly Girls would be left in great hands. And he did a wonderful job. That was the last time Arthur and I worked together. I felt that loss for a long time. We had such great fun just doing what we both loved and getting paid for it! He was so dear, always had my back, always made me laugh, and inspired me to greatness. My choreography was never the same.

Four years I was at In Living Color. Four years, fifty-nine episodes, and three—*three*, thank you—Emmy nominations for choreography. I loved every moment of it. Loved the work ethic and challenge that Keenen brought my way. Loved booking artists and introducing real hip-hop to middle America—groups like Leaders of the New School (who produced Busta Rhymes), Nice & Smooth, Tupac, Heavy D & the Boyz, Public Enemy, the Pharcyde, Jodeci (K-Ci and Jo-Jo), Black Sheep, MC Lyte, and so on. I even booked Slick Rick on the show! I bonded with Jim Carrey, who would stay late like I did, trying to come up with original skits. Loved to listen to Paul Mooney's "I hate white people" jokes, Tommy Davidson's erratic antics, David Alan Grier's corny repartee, Damon's and Marlon's constant silliness, Jennifer Lewis's audacity, and Jamie Foxx's razor-sharp comedic timing that no one could touch.

Speaking of Jamie, he was special, still is. I remember Keenen asking me to go with him to some comedy club on Sunset Boulevard to check out this raw and original comic he was thinking about hiring. Jamie was on fire! His material was great, and he had the audience in the palm of his hand. Keenen and I couldn't stop cracking up. He was hired soon after.

Jamie recently told me the story of our first encounter at In Living

Color that I'd forgotten. The executive producer hated that I played the music so loud in my office when I was working on song choices and placed me down in the basement by myself. Anyway, I was in my office timing out a piece of music. Everyone knew not to bother me when I was working. I had so much to do and little time for interruptions, especially while I was editing music.

It was Jamie's first day. He came down to meet me. He opened my office door without knocking. I was right in the middle of counting the seconds where I needed a piece of music to be edited. I didn't even see who it was and I started screaming.

"Close the fucking door!"

"I'm sorry!"

He quickly slammed the door shut. I went back to work. Two seconds later, he creaked open my door again!

"I just wanted to say hello and—"

"What the fuck!"

Slam! I finally realized it was Jamie and started laughing to myself—especially when I heard him speaking to himself.

"Damn! Just wanted to say hello. Bitch is no joke."

Hilarious. Love Jamie. Great solid guy too. I'm so happy for all the well-deserved success he has had.

I was sad to leave the Fly Girls too. They had become a big part of my life and career. And I was very happy how most of them went on to bigger and better things. Deidre Lang became a successful dancer on Broadway. Cari French married her long-time sweetheart. Carrie-Ann Inaba had a small role in one of the Austin Powers movies and was the featured dancer on Madonna's tour—where she tore shit up sliding slowly down a pole half naked with a shaved head—fierce! And she is now a cohost and judge on the hit *Dancing with the Stars*. Jennifer became a major movie star and worldwide pop artist. Despite all the malicious gossip and the previous hurt feelings, I'm very happy for her success despite popular belief.

We weren't close but we had stayed in touch after *In Living Color*.

After Jennifer's first big movie, she made some disparaging comments about me. I was blindsided. I'd thought we were cool. I called her up, she wouldn't pick up. Frustrated, I left her an irate message on her answering machine. Instead of calling me back and hashing it out like friends do, she went on a major talk show and reiterated my lashing. Wow—whether wrong or right, not on national television, people! Afterwards, everywhere I went I heard that she was telling everyone how I treated her like shit during the show. How I was jealous of her success and that's why I went off on her. Say what?

Oh snap, Carmen was right!

A couple of months after the whole talk-show thing, we saw each other in a nightclub. I was with two of my best friends, Eric Johnson and Julie Shannon, and some other girl. It felt like everyone in the club was watching, waiting, salivating.

A few minutes later, Jennifer came over to me, smiling, saying hello as if nothing had happened. I should've let it go, played it off too. Instead, I killed her with my biting tongue. Andre Harrell broke it up, told me I was acting stupid. She walked away, hurt as well. This *was* stupid. Why were we fighting like this? Then Jennifer came back and apologized. And she wouldn't leave until I accepted, repeatedly asking, "We're okay? We're okay, right?" I accepted her apology and thought that was that.

Leaving the club, Eric kept saying that I looked pathetic for even engaging. She wasn't worth the energy. I was so angry with him, but I knew I should have walked away.

The next few days that followed, I was still upset. The glee and excitement on everyone's face at the club as they watched us fight had sickened me. I kept asking myself, why did she hate me so much over a phone message? And how did it get so public? We ladies of color all know how hard it is for us in the entertainment business. This kind of shit hurts us all and those that will follow in our footsteps.

I quickly found out what was going on. Some of my so-called new friends had jumped on the Jennifer bandwagon and talked mad shit behind my back to her as a tactic to get in good with her, making up shit and distorting stories about my time at In Living Color. Funny thing—they were the same people who used to talk shit about her. One particular so-called friend of mine was so upset that I couldn't get her a decent agent—I tried, but no one wanted to represent her—that she conjured up the whole thing about me being jealous of Jennifer as a way of getting back at me and impressing industry people with power. Petty bullshit. Welcome to Hollywood, folks.

I took a deep look inside and asked myself what my part was in this. Seriously. I still needed to know why I reacted so poorly to this pettiness.

Then it hit me. I was still holding on to some of those old cards, working on old hurt feelings from the past, and using the same weapons that had served me well back then—in this situation and in others. That war was over, and I didn't have to fight back like that anymore. I now had a wonderful life, with wonderful opportunities, and I was better than this. This was young stupid shit. I had to let go. And I did.

Unfortunately, I still hear rumors to this day. And every time I get asked about her in an interview, regardless of what I say, it's twisted into a negative light. Sadly, there are mean, malicious people who get off on talking bad about others and who keep the fight going—them and yellow journalism. It's okay. Like I've said, I've moved on. And I hope she has moved on as well. And hey, not for nothing, girlfriend did apologize.

. . .

The film Fearless was a flop in the States, it lasted three weeks in the theaters. The studio put all of its marketing dollars into another film that year, scared that *Fearless* was too depressing for American audiences. Then Europe came a-calling. It was a humongous hit overseas! The film and cast were getting recognized and nominated all over the place. The Foreign Press nominated me for a Golden Globe for best supporting actress, and at Germany's Berlin International Film Festival I received a nomination for the Golden Bear Award for best newcomer and Isabella Rossellini got best actress. The cast and Peter were flown over to attend the ceremonies. I brought my best friend Julie to travel with me. We got a knock on our hotel room door—it was the producers. "Yes?"

"Rosie! You got nominated for an Oscar!"

"Ha-ha. Very funny."

I slammed the door in their faces. They knocked again. I opened. "We're serious! You got nominated!"

A dag-gone Oscar! Holy crapola! Nicolas Cage was the first to send a telegram. My first call was to Carmen, my second was to Dad, and I saved the very best for last—Tia. She screamed for joy!

Just when things were going great, this asshole wannabe actor-model who I had never met in my entire life went to the press and stated that we had gotten engaged. Why? Because his terrible manager told him it would get him publicity.

Lydia and my half-siblings, who I had not seen or talked to in almost a year, believed the story, went to the press, and told them how horrible a person I was for not inviting them to the supposed wedding or engagement party that never happened. They went so far as to say how ungrateful a daughter and sibling I was for not taking care of them, letting them live a life of poverty. Say what? Despite the fact that I had spent a year and a half pulling myself out of debt in part because of them, last time I checked they were selling my shit on the street while I was recovering from head trauma and not one of them called to see if I was okay—except for the oldest sister, Amy, who had nothing to do with it—or for that matter to apologize. Yes, there was a bit of truth to the scandal—

not the engagement part, but the fact that I was distant from them. But come on, people!

All hell broke loose. I was chased by paparazzi. The tabloids went crazy again. I was scorned and ridiculed, again. Instead of focusing on my nominations, this was the pressing story. I was accused of being a big fat liar, again. Great. God damn it, I was angry! How dare they, all of them? They had no right. But what was done was done. All the horrible memories and pain from the past that I thought I had left behind came back. My publicist at the time, David, who had the best intentions, told me to shake it off, to go out and be seen as if nothing had happened—easy for him to say. I should have. I should have played that stupid game and kept it moving, but I didn't possess that skill set. I felt too much, felt all of it too much.

David was beyond frustrated with how I dealt with the Foreign Press too. I was defensive, at times passive-aggressive. I was sick of the condescension. "We can't believe you pulled this role off! It's amazing! It's such a fluke! How did you do it?"

"I just did what the director told me to do."

Bad move. So much for letting go of those damn cards. I pinned myself into a corner, making myself look like a dummy who was manipulated into an Oscar-worthy performance. And when they asked about my past, I just retreated within and went quiet. I knew it was stupid, but I couldn't stop it. I decided to go back to Brooklyn before the ceremonies.

One night, hanging out with Dad at Carmen's, still angry, still in my bitch-ass mood, Dad told me that I should make peace with Lydia and forgive her. It wasn't her fault that she had mental issues. I should understand. Say what? I just nodded silently, out of respect, which I had a lot of for this man. I mean, I never even cursed around him, ever. Then, another night, he jokingly brought up a recent incident that involved this recording artist I thought I was having a relationship with—he thought we were just messing

around, even though he told me otherwise. For some ungodly reason, this artist wanted to meet my father. I had never introduced
a guy to Dad, ever, not even Ramier. I kept refusing, but later I
gave in.

"Make sure you address him as Señor."

"Is that some Puerto Rican shit?" He fucking chuckled.

"Yes! It is, okay? And it's some simple respect shit too. So please,
don't humiliate me or him."

We walked in. He walked up to my father. "Hey, what's up,
man," . . . and gave my father a freakin' pound! I thought I was
going to die! My father didn't reply, just nodded, with enormous
disgust, and wouldn't even look his way for the rest of the visit. I
was pissed, at both of them. Dad didn't care. "It's your life. Do what
you want, but you should break up with him. Now!" And I did.

So anyway, Dad brings this back up.

"I was right! I know when a man's no good when I see one. He
had no respect for women, for anyone, not even himself. I'm glad
you listened to me and ended it. I hope and pray for your happiness
that next time you pick better."

Ooh, that pissed me off. I unleashed all the anger that had been
building on my poor dad.

"Well, I guess if I had a better example, instead of you, I'd pick
better."

"No, no, no, no. Please, baby. Don't be like that with me. I'm
your father!"

"My father? You can only call yourself a father if you're being a
father! You were never there for me, ever! You left me to rot in the
Home! And don't give me that crap about not being able to bring a
love child home, 'cause you had no problem bringing Carmen. Yes,
I know! I know that she's a love child too! I swear to God I wish I'd
never been born to you or my mother!"

"Please! Rosie!"

He grabbed his heart. I dismissed it, thought he was milking for sympathy. I kept going. Then he slowly got up and went upstairs into Angela's bedroom to lie down on the bottom bunk. I followed, still on the attack. Carmen ran up, yelling for me to stop, telling me to not do this to "her" father. I turned toward her, telling her to stay out of it, this was between "our" father and me, and I was going to have my say!

When I stormed into the room, I saw my father curled up, crying like a little boy, clasping his heart. Carmen sprinted into the bathroom to get a glass of water and a cool washcloth. I knelt down in front of him, stroking his head to calm him.

"Daddy, please stop! I'm sorry! I love you, Daddy. So much!"

And there it was. I finally said it, said what I'd always felt, what I always wanted to say even if I didn't know it. My father turned around and sat up, breathing heavily, then his head fell heavily on my shoulder and he began sobbing. Carmen came back in, handed me the wet cloth. I gently wiped it over his face, helping him to calm down. Carmen excused herself, saying she was going to get a glass of water so that we could have our moment.

Dad eventually caught his breath. He then looked down at the cheap, tacky carpet. (Carmen never had good taste.)

"All these years I thought I would never hear you say it. I know I don't deserve your love, but I thank you."

"Papi, stop. I'm sorry. Please forgive me."

"There's nothing to forgive. I'm so sorry. You have no reason to, but I pray that you find it in your heart to forgive me one day—for everything."

And there it was. The apology I always wanted, even though I didn't know how badly I needed it. His apology calmed me immediately. "I forgave you a long time ago, Pops. I just wanted you to be my dad, you know. And you have been."

He reached for my hand, and we sat there for quite some time, holding hands in a quiet new beginning. We both felt Carmen's presence as she hid respectfully in the hallway. He waved her over. "Come. I have something to show you both."

We went into Carmen's bedroom, and the three of us sat on her bed as he brought over a shoebox from his suitcase. It was filled with pictures of all the women in his life who held a significant meaning for him. He proceeded to pick out only the ones that meant the most.

"This one was my first marriage. She's not good-looking, kind of plain, but a good woman. Bored me to tears."

We all chuckled a bit.

"I thought that's the kind of woman you were supposed to marry. You know, a good woman who cooks and cleans—but I didn't love her. I always regretted how I hurt her. . . . This one, was only for the sex. . . . This one was crazy. . . . This one had style, I loved to show her off. But she was crazy too. This one, that's your mother, Carmen—took me for every cent I had. That's why I lost my house. . . . And this one is my wife. It took years for me to understand how much I love that woman. . . . But your mother, Rosie, she is the only woman I truly loved."

I looked over at Carmen. I grabbed her hand.

"You know, I love you both very much, and I want you to always be there for each other and for your brother. We're family. . . . You know, I don't know why I love crazy women, but I do. Maybe it's the sex."

"Dad!" Carmen and I screamed and laughed in unison.

"What?" he said, laughing, "It's the truth. Crazy women are good in the sack."

"Dad!"

We spent the next several hours going through all the pictures and hearing all of the slightly inappropriate stories attached to them. After a while, Carmen left to start dinner. Dad and I continued to talk. He told me the truth, the whole truth, about meeting my mother, leaving Angel—his wife—and everything behind for her. He told me about her shooting at him and how he left her—and unfortunately me as well—when, too late, he found out about her mental illness. He told me how he wanted to get me but Lydia wouldn't let him—but even if he did get me, he was scared to bring me home for fear of Angel's reaction since he had already begged her to take in Carmen. Most important, he said he was as much at fault as she was in all of this: he shouldn't have left her pregnant like that, and he prayed that one day she and I would forgive each other too.

"You know, I know she wasn't the best mother . . ."

"Uh, yeah, Pops."

He kind of laughed.

"But, you know, not for nothing, I wasn't the best papi either. But you gave me another chance. Everyone deserves another chance."

I wanted to tell him everything—about the emotional and physical and mental abuse I'd endured from Lydia, even what my siblings endured from her, which they all did. I wanted to cry out that even though my half-brother tried to molest me, the real pain came from Lydia when she smacked the shit out of me and accused me of lying. All of it. But I didn't.

I didn't want to spend the rest of the time defending what had happened. I didn't want to lie to him that I had forgiven everything my mother had done, and would agree to excuse all of her bad behavior away because she was crazy. I just wanted to keep spending this precious time with my dad. I wanted to keep holding his hand and listen to the wonderful, ridiculous stories of his adventures.

CHAPTER 30

I FLEW back for the Golden Globes a couple of days before they happened. I went over to see Tia to ask her to come with me to the awards.

"You wanna go to the Golden Globes with me?"

"*Ay*, no. Then you would have to push me around everywhere and everything. No."

Tia's diabetes had gotten worse, and they'd had to amputate part of her leg. Sometimes she would scratch it, thinking that the part removed was still there. I had taken her to the set of *White Men Can't Jump* with me a couple of times. She hated it. Hated having to be pushed around, waiting for long hours.

"It would be my honor to push you around."

"*Ay*, please. Don't be stupid. Plus, then I have to find something to wear and do my hair and it's humid and everything. How is your mother?"

I gave her a look.

"She's your mother. You should still look for her."

I took a deep breath and calmly told her the truth, finally.

"Tia, you don't know this woman. She has fooled everyone. Remember all those times I came home black and blue? Remember how I told you I fell down or whatever? Lydia did that to me. Remember the time she came after me and I ran home to you bloody and bruised? She did that to me. So please forgive me— I love her, but I do not like her, and I do not want a relationship with her either. I'm done."

"*Ay*, Rosamarie, don't say that. She's your mother."

"She's not my mother. You're my mother. You've always been my mother. And I love you for it. So please, respect my feelings on this."

"But you have to understand. She's crazy. You have to forgive her."

"No, Tia. I don't. At least not right now."

Tia looked at me for the longest time without responding, like she was finally putting all the pieces together. She started to well up. I was getting frustrated. I don't know why, but I was. I took another deep breath.

"See, this is why I never told you. I didn't want to see you hurt."

"Oh, Rosie. I keep telling you, that's not your job."

"Yes, it is, Mommie."

Later we watched an old movie and I gave her a manicure. We never brought my mother up again for the rest of our visit.

I went to the Golden Globe awards ceremony with my agent and I think my publicist. As I took my seat, I wondered if all of my peers were looking at me differently because of the scandal in the tabloids. I went to the bar to get a glass of wine. It was just the bartender and myself. Then, of all people, Rodney Dangerfield walked in, eating a hero sandwich in his bathrobe and slippers! He was living at the Beverly Hilton, where the ceremonies were taking place.

"Hey, what's going on? All the commotion woke me up! Look at all the fake boobs. Where am I, Hollywood?"

I died laughing. Two waiters quickly pulled up a small table and chair for him. He looked over at me. "Wanna sit?"

"Me? Oh man, would I! But I'm nominated and I have to get back to my seat."

"Hey! Good for you. Who are you?"

I died again. "Rosie! My name is Rosie Perez, sir. I'm so excited to meet you. I think you're hilarious, Mr. Dangerfield."

"Oh, good. Tell everyone you know, kid. Wait! I know you! Funny girl."

"Thanks, sir."

"Don't mention it, kid. And stop calling me 'sir.' Someone might ask me for money. Good luck tonight."

I didn't get the Golden Globe. Was it because of my asshole behavior, or was it that the better actor won? Who knows? But I got to meet Rodney Dangerfield—yay! And I took the loss like a champ. Seriously. It really surprised me how I was able to shake it off and enjoy the whole event.

. . .

So I call up my father.

"Hello, baby! I'm playing this song by Peggy Lee. Great singer and what a body! You know, I dated a woman in 1972 who looked just like her. What a body she had!"

"Dad. Please. Don't start with one of your long soliloquies about women. Wanna be my date for the Oscars?"

"About time! I was dying waiting for you to ask!"

Why didn't I ask Tia? I did. Figuring that she would say no again, I told her that I asked Dad to be my date and wanted her to come along. She shook her head no with this sad smile.

"What's wrong?"

"Nothing. I'm happy you're bringing him."

"Please! Please come! If you don't come, I'm gonna be so sad!"

"Why you gotta be so dramatic? It's okay. You go with your father. I'm so proud of you."

It made me very upset. Man! I asked Carmen instead.

I felt like everyone wanted me to wear something daring, press-grabbing, but I wanted something that reflected a respectful girl whose father was her date to the Oscars—a black velvet Armani gown with a laced open back and slight train won.

Carmen took forever to find an outfit. She had gained even more weight, and nothing fit except matronly looking gowns. She finally settled on one. It was a tight-fitting black, long, off-the-shoulder kind of—it had straps—gown. The top part was white with large white stripes down each side. She walked out of my guest room dressed in it. Dad and I gasped. Then he blurted out, "You look like Orca, the whale!"

"Dad!" we both screamed.

"What? She looks like Free Willy," he said laughingly. I must admit, it was funny as hell.

Carmen and I felt out of place. I also felt melancholy, thinking about Tia, even thinking about my mother, wishing things were different. Dad, he felt happy as a clam with all of the hoopla. He flirted with every starlet, every woman on the red carpet.

"Dad! You're embarrassing me. It's not cute."

"What? Can't a man live?"

I was mortified and tickled pink. Good thing I chose him to be my date. I knew he would cheer me up. I was really scared that the media on the red carpet were going to ask me about Lydia and not about my nomination—thank goodness no one did!

We walked in, and Carmen spotted Raquel Welch. She pulled out her cheap-ass instant camera she'd picked up at the 7-Eleven. "Ooh, Ms. Welch! I'm Rosie's sister. Can I take your picture? I'm Puerto Rican."

We took our seats. Pops and I were seated in the front row, while Carmen was seated three rows behind. When Nicole Kidman and Tom Cruise walked down the aisle, all heads turned. I could hear only Carmen's voice shrieking with excitement. The couple took their seats . . . wait for it . . . right next to Dad and me—holla! I was so excited—I love both of them! I wanted to say hi, but was too shy. Then Tom reached over and introduced himself, then Nicole said hello to Pop and me, with congratulations—cool!

Then Dad got a diabetic attack! I panicked. I didn't want to leave him, but I had to get him some orange juice or something. Tom leaned over.

"Is your father okay?"

"No! He has diabetes and needs some juice."

"Go. I'll sit with him, make sure he's okay."

"Oh, thank you!" Tom moved over to my seat and held my father's hand! Can you believe it? Love him.

I dashed out, got a cup of OJ, and rushed back in. I then got stopped by security. I didn't have my ticket or anything on me.

"Please," I begged. "My father's sick. Diabetic. I need to get him this!"

They still wouldn't let me in. I exploded! "I'm fucking nominated, you ass! If you don't let me in and something, God forbid, happens to my father, I'll fucking sue your ass and this whole fucking production! I swear to God and the entire fucking universe!" They let me in.

Tom was still holding Dad's hand. Love this guy! Dad drank the juice and calmed down. He and I thanked Tom, then Dad whispered in my ear, "Who's that?"

"That's Tom Cruise, Daddy!" I whispered back.

"Oh! He's Puerto Rican or Cuban?"

"No," I laugh. "It's C-r-u-i-s-e, not C-r-u-z."

"Oh. Wonderful guy."

Then, right before they were about to go live again and announce my category, Whoopi Goldberg—love!—who was that year's host, walked down from the stage and over to me and said, "You're gonna win. You deserve it. I feel it."

I turned toward my father with the biggest grin on my face. He gently grabbed my hand, whispering softly, "You're gonna lose." Huh? How the hell could he just say that to me? "The kid's got it. You can't compete with a kid. But it's okay," he continued. "I'm proud of you. I love you, baby." He squeezed my hand tighter. I leaned over, pulled his face gently toward me, and kissed him tenderly on his cheek. "Thank you, Papi. I love you too."

I looked back at Carmen. She was a nervous wreck. We smiled at each other, I reached my hand back, and she reached hers toward me. Our hands never physically met, but, well, you know—luckiest girl in the world. I turned to Dad.

"I wish Tia was here."

"Me too, baby."

They announced the winner, Anna Paquin, for her wonderful and moving performance in The Piano. Dad patted my hand and then smiled at me. We both started to chuckle. Why, I don't know. Immediately after they went to commercial and the applause stopped, Carmen stood up and screamed, "You were robbed! Fucking little bitch!" Great. Mortified to the millions—not really. Shit was hilarious.

I think I was the happiest loser in that place. We had such a great time at the after-party too. Especially when Antonio Banderas asked us to his table! That was such a nice thing to do. He was so great with my dad, even though Dad kept hitting on every woman in the joint. He even hit on Sidney Poitier's wife. We were graciously asked to come to his table too—so cool, I loved every picture that man ever made! We politely said thank you to Antonio and headed over. Mr. Poitier had not joined us yet. Dad sat next to this beautiful woman, leaned in, and started in with his corny repartee. I kept pinching him under the table to stop.

"What? Why you pinching me?"

"Dad," I tried to discreetly whisper. "That's Ms. Sidney Poitier!"

He chuckled and in the same breath turned his head toward her and said out loud, "And may I say he has impeccable taste." Lady was tickled pink.

. . .

Months later, still in Los Angeles, I crashed.

All the drama with my family and the tabloids, all the hoopla with the Oscars, everything just came crashing down on me. Plus, my manager at the time—who I had fired shortly after the awards—told everyone I had quit the business because I lost! Say what? Not true. Jeez. I couldn't eat. I couldn't sleep. I couldn't even do my hair! Carmen said that I looked like an emaciated Chia Pet.

I kept thinking about the emotional cost of being in the public eye, not just for me, but for my cousins, my sister and brother, and most of all, Dad and Tia. Both Ismael and Ana Dominga were proud Puerto Ricans with impeccable reputations for being honest, humble, and good people. Aguadilla is a small town. And Dad was its unofficial mayor. I know it must have hurt when the whispering started.

Daddy told me to come down to Aguadilla and get away from the entertainment business. I stayed in bed for the first few days, coming out only to sit with him in the living room to listen to old jazz records or watch a boring Western. When his friends would come over, I'd excuse myself politely and go back to bed. He finally convinced me to get out of bed and go into town with him to get a couple of ice cream cones. Later, we went to Crash Boat Beach. We sat on the sand as I listened to him tell his tales of life after the war.

". . . And in 1957 I went to the Village Vanguard to see—"

"Dad," I interrupted. "Would you mind if I stopped acting?"

"No. Why would I mind? It's your life, you can do whatever you like."

"No. What I mean is, what if I quit? So all this craziness could go away."

"Well, like I said, it's your life, you—"

"I know it's my life!" I yelled. "Can you just say what you want and need to say? Man!"

"Don't be like that with me, please. I don't like that. It makes me upset, 'cause I love you too much."

I let out a deep, frustrated, guilt-ridden, but kind of happy and hammy smiling sigh.

"Sorry, Papi. Sorry I've been such a b-i-t-c-h."

"No, no, no. Never call yourself that . . . even though you can get, you know, how you get."

He started chuckling, cautiously at first. Then he couldn't hold it in, and we both started to laugh.

"I'm very proud of you," he said. "I don't care what you do, as long as you love it and keep being my daughter. And don't worry about the craziness. It's not real. You know, in 1939, before the war, I was sitting on this very beach when I made out with this beautiful . . ."

He stopped for a moment and looked at me.

"Baby, you look beautiful with your hair natural like that. You don't look like a Chia Pet."

I smiled. To a Puerto Rican, that's a big compliment.

"Pop," I softly said.

I don't know why, but at that moment the timing felt right. I quietly told him everything—almost everything. I didn't go into detail about what happened in the Home or about the verbal, emotional, and physical abuse from Lydia, and of course I left out the molestation parts: I didn't want to kill the guy. I simply told him there was severe abuse from all parties. Told him that I battled with depression, and that when I came down here just to sit with him, it helped. A lot.

I saw the pain and sorrow in his eyes. I also saw him marveling at me, through this slight curl coming from the side of his mouth. He hugged and kissed me. I gave it right back. We were both smiling. It was weird shit, but it felt good. I still felt sad. There was just no anger attached anymore.

"Come on. Let's go home. You know, in 1945, I went to the Apollo to see Lionel Hampton! Oh yes! Only blacks were allowed in. So I knew if they heard my accent, I wouldn't get in. Oh yes! It was like that. So I acted like I was mute. Went up to the ticket booth and held up one finger. When I got inside, I saw a friend of mine from the ship—black Cuban guy. We started laughing and talking in Spanish, telling each other how we got in. Ah, but nobody cared. Inside, the American black people didn't care. We were all just having a good time! Oh, and there was this beautiful lady. . . ."

. . .

Of course I didn't really want to stop acting! I mean, come on, people!

I felt renewed. Staying strong, I got new representation with one of my former agents, Carol Bodie, and signed with another agency, ICM. I would still be offered stereotyped roles, and I still turned them down. But I could wake up each morning and look at myself in the mirror and get respect. I did independent films that I felt proud of, and became proactive and produced two projects for HBO, *Society's Ride* and *Subway Stories*, along with a movie, *The 24-Hour Woman*.

And Broadway came calling. Yay! Who knew I was such a ham for the stage? Tony Award–winning stage and film director George C. Wolfe did and told me so! He was the artistic director of the Public Theater and wanted to offer me a role in Tony Kushner's play *Angels in America*, which George was directing for Broadway. I stupidly turned it down. I know! Still, he didn't turn his back on me and hired me for my debut at the Public Theater in *References to Salvador Dali Make Me Hot*, pushed me hard with loving hands, and showed me the depths of my talent.

More Broadway theater roles came my way. And I did Eve Ensler's *Vagina Monologues* along with the likes of Jane Fonda, Whoopi Goldberg, Amy Irving, and Mary Alice. I met Oprah Winfrey for the second time when we did the *Vagina Monologues* benefit at Madison Square Garden. When she entered, it was like the oracle entering. Brooke Shields was sitting next to her, and I was sitting next to Brooke. I begged Brooke, who had become a good friend, to switch seats with me. We were like two little kids.

"No!"

"Please, Brooke! I'll cook for you!"

"No!"

Then Eve asked the audience to stand. She then asked them to raise their hands if anyone was a victim of child abuse of any kind—rape, attempted rape, incest, domestic violence, or all of the above. Oprah raised her hand. Okay, we all knew that. Then Brooke raised her hand. Most people kind of knew that, since the malicious tabloids had exploited her issues with her mom. Then I slowly raised mine. Holy crapola! This was the first public admittance I had ever made. Brooke looked my way—we had shared secret stories and bonded years back. She smiled, cried, and hugged me. Then Oprah turns to me—not Brooke, ha!—and says, "Oh, honey. I didn't know. You're a survivor too."

Hold up! "Survivor"? The way she said it was without guilt or shame but with strength and dignity—Oprah's no joke, people! She held out her arms to me. I rushed into them, crying like a little kid.

"Shh, it's okay," she said. "You're okay. You've survived. Take it. Own it. It's yours."

Holy crapola! Then she patted the seat that Brooke was sitting in for me to sit in. I turn to Brooke with a gloating smile, whispering, "Did you see that? Did ya?"

"Oh, shut up, Perez!" We died laughing!

I was a survivor. I'd accomplished a lot. And I had my life that I always wanted too. I had my beautiful home in Clinton Hill. I had my activism and sense of purpose. And most important, I had my family's and friends' love and support: Tia, Daddy, Carmen, Tito, all of my crazy cousins—especially Millie and Sixto—and my very good friends. I even got married, even though I divorced a year and a half later—ha! But that relationship, even with all its problems, served me well and taught me a lot about healing.

Seth and I started dating in 1995. We moved in together I think in 1996. He was the first man I had ever lived with. It was a great relationship, but like I said, we had a lot of problems.

Around the early part of 1997, I believe, I was not in a good place because of my mother, which I'll go into in a minute. Eve Ensler had advised me to seek psychotherapy. I told her I wasn't into it. I had tried going to see someone with Seth, and I hated it. My experiences with Dr. Tisby and the Home had closed me off to it. Eve told me that not all doctors fit; sometimes you need to shop around and find the one who works for you. She shared with me how this one doctor, Dr. Susan Grand, had helped her tremendously. Psychotherapy didn't heal all her pain—there were times it would come back out of nowhere—but she learned how to cope and deal and get past a lot of it, how to find peace.

Peace? That fucking word again, that word Tia and Daddy always kept telling me to find. I thought I had peace, but I guess I didn't. Hell, Eve had some deep issues. If it worked for her, maybe I should give it a shot. I told Seth that I wanted to go but couldn't bring myself to do it. He held my hand on the way to Dr. Grand's office and waited in the lobby for me.

"Hi, Dr. Grand. Yeah, so, I'm only here because my husband wants me to be here. I don't really need this. I really don't believe in this. I'm Puerto Rican, and we don't do this. But everyone thinks I should give it a shot, so I'm here, but I really don't need it."

She nodded, smiled, and then sat silently for what seemed forever.

"Yeah," I continued. "I'm gonna go. This is stupid."

"Okay," she responded. "Before you go, forget what everyone else thinks. I just want you to think, for yourself, if there is any part of you that believes you should be here."

"No . . . not really . . . I just . . . oh my goodness! I'm. . . ."

I started bawling like an ass! And those were the only words I said for the rest of the hour! Every time I tried to say something else, snot and tears would shoot out.

"So, our time is up. Would you like to come in again? Tomorrow?"

"No thank you. This really isn't for me. . . . What time?"

I stayed in therapy for a couple of years. God bless America three times! To be honest, the first six months were a wash. I kept lessening the severity of my past. I kept hiding things from her so I didn't seem a complete mess. What can I say? I do have a lot of pride. And if I did tell her the complete truth about a certain situation from the past, I would always ask if my reaction to it was an indication of mental illness. She suggested that in addition to seeing her, I should see a psychiatrist as well. Say what? Bitch, I'm not crazy!

"You keep asking me if I think you're crazy, which I don't think you are, yet you seem not to believe me. I think if you see a medical doctor, they will tell you the truth. And hopefully you'll believe it and understand the benefits of receiving help . . . And I think medication, which I can't prescribe, might help you with your depression."

Well, I never! The nerve of this woman! I am not depressed! Well, maybe a bit. But I certainly don't need meds! I definitely am not going to see a freaking psychiatrist!

So I go see the psychiatrist. She was more straightforward, not harsh, but to the point. She asked me a bunch of medical questions and a lot of other things pertaining to my behavior. At the end of the session, she told me that I was not crazy on any level, but that I did suffer from post-traumatic stress disorder—all the night terrors, the paranoia, the flashes and thoughts of possible danger, the explosions of anger, and blah, blah, blah. She also told me that I was wasting time in my therapy with Dr. Grand by not being completely honest and open—and that medication could help me get through this difficult time.

"If you are diabetic, you need insulin. If you have cancer, you need chemotherapy. If you have PTSD, you need psychotherapy and sometimes meds."

I took her advice and got on medication for a while and went back to Dr. Grand. Oh my goodness, how great therapy was for me. And how great the pills worked too. It helped me feel normal for the first time in my life. That underlying anxiety was the first thing to go and I was able to tell my story without an agenda in a safe environment without judgment or public scorn. I was able to see how PTSD was limiting me, and I learned ways to cope and deal. I really worked hard on myself even after therapy. It was one of the best things I have ever done for myself. Truly. Especially since this was around the time I was dealing with more drama and heartache from my mother.

CHAPTER 31

I HAD the honor of being asked to be the Madrina in the Puerto Rican Day Parade! I believe it was around early 1995. The drama of the scandal, the nominations, and the ceremonies had passed. I was in a good place.

So, I was in the parade by myself in a small convertible, waving at folks, feeling proud as can be. My youngest half-sister, who I had not seen in years—I hadn't seen any of them since the fight back at the duplex and all that horrible drama—broke from the crowd, ran up to the car, told me that Mom had contracted AIDS, shoved a telephone number in my hand, and then ran back into the sea of people, leaving me dumbfounded.

I knew I had to call, had to go see her. I just sat in my house speechless for the rest of the day. Seth tried his best to console me. I tried to pull it together. I called Carmen, and she came right over. I finally called Lydia. I honestly do not remember a word I said. All I knew was that I had agreed to go see her.

Seth went over with me because I was afraid, I didn't know if I was entering a trap. You never know with my family. I knew I had to suck it up and put all that fear aside. And I was right. All of my half-brothers were there. One of them was trying to videotape the visit, and it wasn't for sentimental reasons—trust me. I refused to come in until he put the camera away.

I expected her to be frail and thin, but she had put on some weight and was embarrassed that her hair wasn't done. Even so, since I had spent so much time around AIDS patients, I could see the beginnings of the terrible disease. I held back the tears. She did too. Weird thing too, she acted as if nothing had happened, no tabloids, no betrayal. I did the same. I told her that I had high connections in the AIDS community and I could get her the help and proper care she needed.

"No, I'm okay. I have the Medicaid, and I'm okay. I'm just happy to see you."

I called my friends in the AIDS community on my cell anyway. They told me that when she was ready, they would make things happen. My mother still refused any extra help.

Seth and I took the whole clan out to lunch to a nearby restaurant. Lydia took forever getting ready—I mean like three hours just to leave the house. I was sitting across from her. Seth was seated next to me. She kept staring at me, it made me very uncomfortable.

"What, Ma?"

"Lòpez was right."

"What?"

"Lòpez. You remember Lòpez. He said you had talent, just like me."

I looked at Seth, confused.

"You don't remember? When you wanted the whistle instead of the doll. I smacked you good, but you didn't care. You wanted that damn whistle. Remember? And you went outside and everyone was watching you perform? . . . Lòpez was right." She started laughing. "You had talent."

I was exploding inside. That shit wasn't funny. I felt like I couldn't breathe. Seth grabbed my hand under the table. I turned to him. He was crying, and then he directed me toward Lydia. She was still staring, but now there were tears streaming down her face. I took a deep breath and grabbed her hand. My heart opened up and began to break for her.

"You had talent, Rosie. Lòpez was right," she kept repeating.

"It's okay, Ma. It's okay."

Later that day, when I gave Lydia money and told her that I would send more through my account, one of my brothers took me aside and asked me for money too—I couldn't believe it. Even though I had money, I didn't have millions like they thought. And even if I did, they had a lot of nerve asking me. They were four grown men who had treated me like shit in the past, who lived off her in that tiny apartment, rent-free—four capable men who could have provided for her as well. I gave him the rest of the cash I had on me. Seth was disgusted and made some excuse for us to leave. As we left, I was scared that two out of the four of them would follow me and hurt me in some way. I know that sounds ridiculous, but they were a violent bunch and they did have great resentment toward me. But then my thoughts quickly turned to Lydia. My goodness, this was horrible. I was so torn up about it. Why her? Why anyone? Man, this really got to me.

I called her, though not frequently, always asking if she needed anything, chatting with her cheerfully to brighten her day. I sent flowers on holidays and her birthday, but I rarely went over. I didn't feel safe there, physically or emotionally. I also made good on my offer: I set it up with my accountant to send money whenever she needed it. Weird thing, it didn't hurt so much that she never called me like it had done in the past. I guess now with her having AIDS, it wasn't that important.

A couple of years later, I finally told Dad that she had contracted the disease. I'd tried to tell him before, but Lydia didn't want me to, didn't want me to tell anyone. Also, I didn't have the nerve. I felt like he was still in love with her on some level. Man, he cried so much. He told me he wanted to go see her.

We brought four bags of groceries. I brought along a bunch of cash too. She was alone, in a small, cheap apartment. I was pissed that she was living like this because she could have moved, with the money I was sending. My four half-brothers had just gone out. (Yes, folks, they were still living there, still not helping her out.)

Her usual makeup-covered face was bare and tired-looking. Her good looks were gone. Still, she held on to an attractiveness that still compelled you to stare. And Dad couldn't stop staring. He clearly hadn't gotten over her—neither had I. I was all grown up, yet I still got nervous just being in her presence, but I wasn't afraid of her anymore. I mean, I was cautious of her actions but no longer fearful. Sad. She wouldn't make eye contact with me and kept fidgeting with an old portable tape player/radio.

"You're still beautiful, Ma."

She gave me that sly smirk and rolled her eyes. This time that look seemed heavy, sad. She popped in a worn cassette tape. An old-school, traditional Spanish ballad played.

"You remember this song, Ismael?"

Dad nodded. She began to sing softly, still a beautiful voice. She looked up at him like a shy schoolgirl, still wounded by their failed love. They both welled up with tears. It was as if I wasn't even there, it didn't matter that I was there. She was locked into him and he into her. Then it came.

"You sure you remember this song? No, you don't. You don't remember anything, but I remember everything. You had so many women. So many."

"Never with you, Lydia. Never."

"Hmph. Really?" She looked at me. "Do you know he left me? Oh yes, with you in my belly."

"Lydia, don't do this. Please. That was so long ago. Hey! Remember Santo? He and Ponchi got together! Oh man, he used to hate her! Hated her. God, that woman was so ugly, but she got him."

He grabbed her hand and smiled warmly. She smiled back. Her bit of pride was hanging on the tears that were welling up.

"I'm gonna go to the store. Want anything, Ma?" I asked.

"No, thank you, baby," she said.

Baby? Okay.

I was gone for like ten minutes. When I returned, they were

singing Spanish love songs to each other. When we left, my mother hugged me, tightly, told me she was going to call and come visit.

"You see, baby, everyone can change. You know, she has a lot of problems, but she loves you in her way. Make sure you look after her."

"Sure, Pop."

She never called, never wrote, never. This time I didn't hold it against her. It was okay.

. . .

Even though I was beginning to let things go, Seth and I would go over, but not often, maybe three, four times a year—I know. I was working a lot, but truth be told, the chaos in that house and the potential of a violent outburst disgusted me.

It was 1999. Seth had proposed. We had been together for years, and I didn't really want to get married. Why? I don't know. I guess I thought, if it ain't broke . . . you know? Or maybe it was because I'd never seen a successful marriage and was scared. Anyway, we got engaged. Less than a year later, we began to plan the wedding.

We set the date for a Friday, then planned everything quickly. We were to marry in four weeks. Thinking about my mother's side of the family, I was worried about exposing Seth and his family to all the possible drama. Seth was worried too. I told him that we should invite them, but that we shouldn't give them too much time to conjure up some type of scheme. What can I say? These people had made me paranoid.

I called Kathy. I had missed her terribly and wanted to make peace. I told her about the engagement and asked her to tell Mom and everyone to come to the wedding in two days. I know. I couldn't trust them, but felt they deserved to be there. Seth, Carmen, and everyone else disagreed. Kathy told me that she and my youngest sibling would be there, but that Mom and everyone else didn't want to go.

It was good to see Kathy and my other little sister. I was glad that at least they came to the wedding. Gosh, I did miss them, especially Kathy. Then the shit hit the fan.

In July 2000, the *Daily News* front page carried this headline: "Rosie, Her Mom, & AIDS . . . Activist Perez Shuns Mom Who's Dying of the Disease."

Say what? Not again! Fuck. When is this going to stop?! The truth about my difficult past also started to seep out again. If I hadn't worked on myself up to that point, I probably would have fallen apart. Poor Seth. All he kept saying was, "I told you so!"

This was the worst kind of yellow journalism. And the piece was written by Juan Gonzalez, who was a former Puerto Rican Young Lord, an activist group from the '60s and '70s that fought for Puerto Rican justice—irony. I was disgusted by his so-called investigation. His defense was that he tried to call and get my side of the story. My side? Why should I have to comment on something that was fiction? Mr. Gonzalez should have done his homework before the newspaper printed the damn story. This should have been dismissed as what it was, tabloid yellow journalism.

The AIDS community and my dear friends Lianni Greaves, Laurie Fabiano, and Larry Adelman—God rest his soul—came to my defense, telling the press that I did in fact try to help my mother but the help was refused. And my accountant told the press that I had been giving her money throughout the years, but it didn't matter. What was done was done and opinions had been formed.

I wanted Tia. I needed my father. They both came to visit and stayed with me at my house. It was great to have them there at the same time. We all just hung out, gossiped, told stories, cracked jokes. I loved being with them. I loved being bored with them. I got to cook with my father. It brought me so much joy, and I got to take care of Tia, which brought even more joy. I'll never forget having to bathe her. She was really sick with complications from her diabetes. I had to climb in the shower with her to help her clean herself and to help hold her up. When she turned around and saw me in my shower cap, she started cracking up. "Ga, ga, ga, ga, gaaaa! You look so stupid in that thing." I laughed with her and told her, "Be quiet, you old woman, and lift up your arms." It was an honor and I will cherish those moments forever.

After the fallout, despite this betrayal, I still went over to see my mother. To say it was a tense scene is an understatement, but Seth was with me most of the time. And sometimes my dad would go with me and I was able to get through it. The first time Dad and I went over to my little sister's apartment, where Lydia was now living, Dad and I heard my half-brothers plotting: "She's coming up! Get the camera! Call the press!"

Dad told me to wait downstairs. He was going in to handle everything. I told him that I wasn't afraid of them anymore. I was sick and tired of their shit.

"Yeah, okay. Just wait there, please," Dad told me.

Dad walked in, very calmly, greeting all of them with a smile. He told them that I wouldn't come in until they put the video camera down. To my surprise, they listened to him. He had that effect on people. He told me to come up. I greeted everyone politely. Then he cooked everyone pigeon stew from the groceries we had brought over. While the food was simmering, I went to the back to be alone with Mom.

My dear Lord, she was so skinny. I knew it would be just a matter of days. She couldn't look at me. Then she started to cry. I sat next to her, and she started to rock back and forth, still crying, holding my hands.

"You have to forgive me, Rosie. You have to! Please! For everything I've done! You have to forgive me!"

My heart sank.

"It's okay, Mom. Please calm down."

"No! You have to say it. Please, Rosie!"

I took a moment that seemed like forever. I was still angry, just being honest, but I didn't want to be. I wanted this to stop, all the hate, all the anger, all the pain and hurt and the horrible past.

"I forgive you, Mom. I forgive you. I hope you can forgive me too."

"I never wanted to hurt you. I love you, Rosie. I always loved you."

A couple of weeks later, Mom was taken to Bellevue Hospital. She was in ICU for a couple of days. Seth and I were exhausted from going back and forth, keeping vigil. Carmen and Sixto came with us too. I stood by Mom's bed with Carmen. She had tubes coming in and out of her, her face was swollen, her body emaciated. Carmen said a prayer over her, then told me to come and pray with her. I held Mommie's hand. She looked up at me, slightly nodded her head, and blinked her eyes twice. "She just forgave you, Rosie. Did you see that?" said Carmen.

"Yes, I did."

Seth wanted to drive out to the Hamptons that night, to the rented home of a friend, to get away. I didn't. I wanted to stay. But I gave in. I felt I had put him through so much already that he deserved a break. As I was sitting out in the backyard by myself, I felt a strong wind pass through me—right through me. Now, I don't believe in shit like that, but I knew that was my mother. I said out loud to myself, "She's gone."

Then the phone rang inside. Seth answered. He came out back. I looked at him and asked, "She's gone, right?" He nodded yes.

There was a pain of regret and a feeling of compassion and empathy for my mother that shocked me. I regretted that I didn't forgive her sooner. I regretted that we never talked about her childhood together. I regretted that I never knew or met her father. I understood her pain as a woman who had God-given talent but couldn't see it come to its full fruition because of her abusive marriage and her mental illness. Yet I felt so disconnected from her. Why? Why did I come to this so late?

. . .

Tia had become gravely ill around that same time. I was flying back and forth soon after Mom had passed to spend time with her. I didn't want to lose her too before telling her everything I ever wanted to tell her and asking her everything about her life, which I did as much as possible. When I told her about feeling that wind rush through me when Lydia died, she smiled and told me that God had come into my heart and that was why I was open to feeling Lydia say good-bye. She told me that I needed to stop torturing myself—it was all over. Lydia was in a better place, and she loved me and forgave me. Then she quietly turned to me and said, "You should've took me to the Oscars. I was the one there for you, not your father."

"But you said—"

"I know."

I gently grabbed her hand. "Tia, I'm so sorry. You're right, I should have insisted."

"*Ay*, it's okay. I just wanted to get that off of *de* chest. Ga, ga, ga, ga, ga!"

"Tia, why didn't you ever let me buy you a house?"

"Really, I don't know. That was stupid, right? Ga, ga, ga, ga, gaaa!"

Tia passed away eight months after Mom did, from diabetes. The grief and sorrow I felt was way more than I'd felt for my mother. As promised, she had a horse-drawn carriage at her funeral while The Beatles' "Penny Lane" played in a loop at the service. I didn't attend. I couldn't. I didn't want to remember her like that. And the pain of her not being here still hurts, every day.

. . .

It was 2006, I think. I was in a really great, happy place. Unfortunately, Dad wasn't doing so well. We were in Puerto Rico to spend time with him. He'd had two strokes and was very ill. Carmen and Tito had gone to the beach with Ramon, my boyfriend at the time. Holding hands, Dad and I were watching back-to-back boring Westerns, which he so loved. He was tired, old, weak, and kept falling asleep. I tried to slip my hand out of his to get some fresh air out on the balcony, but he gripped it back and woke up.

"No. Don't leave me. Please."

I didn't move.

"I miss Minguita."

"I do too, Daddy."

I stayed on that couch from one o'clock in the afternoon until six that night. He passed away four days later. God it hurt, still does.

His service lasted for four days. The wake took three days: the funeral director had to extend it because there were so many people calling and insisting that we wait until they came and paid their respects. One of Dad's final wishes was that we drive around the entire town of Aguadilla on our way to the burial with a truck in front carrying two big woofer speakers blasting a certain song of his choosing. Daddy had given our brother Tito the CD prior to his passing. He refused to let any of us know what song he had chosen.

The whole town came out. When the procession began, Tito popped in the CD. "I did it my way" blasted out in Spanish. Carmen, Tito, and I all looked at each other and cracked up.

. . .

I miss Dad. I miss Tia even more.

I began this process to honor Tia. I wanted to thank her for raising me, for teaching me to love, for teaching me to let go, for everything. She was and still is my greatest inspiration. I wanted to give back to her by telling our story and sharing the wisdom she gave me with the world. But I never imagined that this journey was going to give back to me.

I fell in love all over again with my father. Oh how happy I am that he never gave up trying to win me back. And it began with that stupid drunken confession and was sealed with that apology. I hope he knew how hard I fell for him. I think he did. To this day, I can't hold back the emotions whenever I think about him.

I'm so glad Tia and Dad taught me the importance of family. My sister Carmen and I still have stupid silly fights but forgive each other in an instant. Tito still lives in Puerto Rico but we are in constant contact. And my cousins-sisters, we never lost touch and talk to and try to see one another as often as possible—especially Millie and Lorraine. And cousin Sixto, the one I almost went out with, well, he drives me crazy on a daily basis, but I love the pain in the ass—he is still one of my best friends. We all love each other very much and will forever have each other's backs—even when we're fighting. Ha!

And here's the craziest shit of all. I never thought I'd find even more compassion for my mother. I got to see her in a deeper way than I had before. Gosh I cried for her all throughout this process. I needed that. I needed to release a lot of the pain that I thought was gone.

I also came to understand that I wasn't the only casualty— especially after Tiara passed away from an accidental overdose way too early a couple of years ago and I didn't have the chance to tell her that I loved her and forgave her. And most important, I didn't have a chance to ask her to forgive me. My half-siblings on my mother's side were victims too. They did horrible things, yes, but I'm not without sin. Okay, so you may say that what they did doesn't compare to the mistakes I have made, but I have learned that it isn't a contest. And I don't want to keep score. We were kids that were all abused and didn't know how to articulate all the pain and anger. What happened when we were younger is a wash, forgiven, left in the past, as far as I'm concerned. Now, what happened when we all grew up, well, I'm finding forgiveness every day and hope the same for them. And I hope they are getting the help they need so they can break the cycle of pain, violence, and abuse and enjoy all that life offers. I'm so happy I made up with Kathy and that I'm still in touch with Amy. As for the rest, we may never be close, but they will always be in my heart. And my empathy for the kids in the Home has broken through years of suppressing it. I'm glad I took my time to tell my story. I'm glad I stopped judging myself for not being able to be completely honest about my past. I understand now that I wasn't ready and that's okay. This understanding really started when I saw Olga Lopez and Mita fifteen-plus years ago. Olga expressed how it took her years to even tell her kids about the Home. We were able to share and cry and laugh, knowing we went through something very extraordinary. But not for nothing, I could have done without the Home and Sister Renata beating the crap out of me—you know what I'm saying? But I must admit the Home gave and taught me so much. Yes, it would have been better if I was left with Tia, but Saint Joseph's Catholic Home for Children was most definitely a better choice than being raised by Mom—gosh, that's so sad, but true.

Yes, it's very hard to go there. But when you do, you will find yourself along the way . . . and I hope your hair looks fabulous while doing it—holla!

ACKNOWLEDGMENTS

My sincere and many thanks to David Kuhn, Suzanne O'Neill, and to the staffs at Kuhn Projects and Crown Archetype. Now, I know I was a walk in the park, but let's be honest here for a moment, there were times when things got . . . just a little bit heavy, but all is forgiven—ha! Seriously, David and Suzanne, your help, wisdom, and most important, patience were deeply appreciated. Thanks for enduring and supporting a new writer.

I want to thank the following people for being there for me. If I have left out anyone—my apologies. You all played a part in helping me write this book, whether you knew it or not . . . even you, Sixto.

Family: Ana Dominga "Minguita" Serrando-Roque Otero, Ismael "Daddy/Pops/Papi" Serrano-Roque, Lydia Fontanez-Perez, Eric Haze, Sixto Ramos, Carmen Serrano, Angela Sorrentine, Tito "Fat" Serrano-Roque, Erica "Miss America" Rosenfeld, Millie Otero, Lorraine Cruz, Lourdes Otero, Eddie Sostre, Margie Ramos, Cousin Charles, Cousin Brian, Cousin Jonathan, Cousin Silvia, Cousin Freddie, Titi Santi, Tio Monseratte, Tia Blanca, all the rest of my cousins, aunts, and uncles (too many to list), Madga Perez (God bless your soul—miss you terribly), Sally Pabon, Lydia Pabon, and Sonia Perez.

Very special thanks to my Lil' Guys/Babies/Best Friends/doggies—may your souls rest in peace. Thank you for everything: Freckles, Citizen, Sammy Samowitz, and Rainy—Raindrops Girl—my dearest loves/cats, Dukie-Ma, Fleabag.

Friends: Julie Shannon, Ramon Rodriguez, Eric Johnson, George C. Wolfe, Chris Franko, Valerie Joyner, Marian Wade, Chuckie Doss (RIP), Rhonda Cowan, Ileana Angelo, David Angelo, Lisa Leone, April Walker, Tracey Waples, Marc Balet, Seth Rosenfeld, Anna Strout, Ramier Sellers, Arthur Rainier, Roger Cabello, Hilton Als, Sandra Guzman, Rosanna Rosario, Liz Manne and Fred Burner, Joe Montello, Michael Ealy, Peter "Bass" Tulloch, Laurie Fabiano, Liani Graves, Neil Meyers, Carol Bodie, Tom Burke, Don "With a D" Wongprapang, Jon Rubenstein, Mark Maynard, Ammie Graham, Rebecca James, Jane Berliner, Johnny Lavoy, and John Hullen.

Special thanks: Sister Margaret-Francis, Eileen and Gene, Lydia Plunkett, Amelia Rayford, Bruni Torres, Carmen Velez, Beth, Janis, Ed Yano, Nigel Johnson and Michelle Johnson, Joanne Hernandez, Jeanette Hernandez (RIP), Louis Padilla, Anthony Torres, Mr. Mackie, Sue Grand, Ph.D., aka Dr. Sue, and Dr. Catherine Buttinger-Fedeli, M.D., Ph.D., Urban Arts Partnership.

. . . And last but not least, Angela. Wherever you are, know that you are not and never will be forgotten. xo